An R Companion to Political Analysis

Second Edition

Sara Miller McCune founded SAGE Publishing in 1965 to support the dissemination of usable knowledge and educate a global community. SAGE publishes more than 1000 journals and over 800 new books each year, spanning a wide range of subject areas. Our growing selection of library products includes archives, data, case studies and video. SAGE remains majority owned by our founder and after her lifetime will become owned by a charitable trust that secures the company's continued independence.

Los Angeles | London | New Delhi | Singapore | Washington DC | Melbourne

An R Companion to Political Analysis

Second Edition

Philip H. Pollock III

University of Central Florida

Barry C. Edwards

University of Central Florida

FOR INFORMATION:

CQ Press
An imprint of SAGE Publications, Inc.
2455 Teller Road
Thousand Oaks, California 91320
E-mail: order@sagepub.com

SAGE Publications Ltd.
1 Oliver's Yard
55 City Road
London EC1Y 1SP
United Kingdom

SAGE Publications India Pvt. Ltd.
B 1/I 1 Mohan Cooperative Industrial Area
Mathura Road, New Delhi 110 044
India

SAGE Publications Asia-Pacific Pte. Ltd.
3 Church Street
#10-04 Samsung Hub
Singapore 049483

Acquisitions Editor: Carrie Brandon
Development Editor: Anna Villarruel
Editorial Assistant: Duncan Marchbank
eLearning Editor: John Scappini
Production Editor: Kelly DeRosa
Copy Editor: Christina West
Typesetter: C&M Digitals (P) Ltd.
Proofreader: Sarah J. Duffy
Cover Designer: Anupama Krishnan
Marketing Manager: Amy Whitaker

Printed in the United States of America

Library of Congress Cataloging-in-Publication Data

Names: Pollock, Philip H., III., author. | Edwards, Barry C., author.

Title: An R companion to political analysis / Philip H. Pollock III, University of Central Florida, Barry C. Edwards, University of Central Florida.

Description: Second edition. | Thousand Oaks, California : CQ Press, [2018] | Includes bibliographical references and index.

Identifiers: LCCN 2017003186 | ISBN 9781506368849 (pbk. : alk. paper)

Subjects: LCSH: Political statistics—Computer programs—Handbooks, manuals, etc. | Analysis of variance—Computer programs—Handbooks, manuals, etc. | R (Computer program language)—Handbooks, manuals, etc.

Classification: LCC JA86 .P639 2017 | DDC 320.0285/5133—dc23
LC record available at https://lccn.loc.gov/2017003186

This book is printed on acid-free paper.

19 20 21 10 9 8 7 6 5 4 3

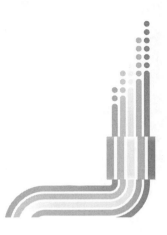

Contents

List of Boxes and Figures

Boxes

Figures

Preface

In many ways, the second edition of *An R Companion to Political Analysis* follows the template of the book that preceded it. Thus, this volume guides students in the use of R for constructing meaningful descriptions of variables and performing substantive analysis of political relationships, from bivariate cross-tabulation analysis to logistic regression. As before, all of the examples and exercises use research-quality data—including two survey datasets (the 2012 American National Election Study and the 2012 General Social Survey) and two aggregate-level datasets (one based on the 50 U.S. states and one based on countries of the world). And, as in the first edition, each chapter is written as a tutorial, taking students through a series of guided examples that they then use to perform the analysis.

The second edition improves upon the first in three ways. First, we have added an "Introduction to R" to familiarize students with the R environment and help them understand the logic of objects and functions. Second, we have repurposed Chapter 9 to emphasize how R's plotting functions can be used to show the results of regression analysis.

The third and most important change from the first edition is the development and release of an R package called "poliscidata" that bundles the functions and datasets used in this book. Students can now simply install this book's R package, load it in R, and then jump right into executing commands and analyzing results. The book's R package is freely available on the Comprehensive R Archive Network (CRAN). The installation process is detailed in Chapter 1.

Each chapter has been revised to reflect the updated datasets that accompany this book. Where possible, we've revised our examples and model solutions to offer students simpler, more intuitive approaches. Throughout the text, we emphasize simple solutions that accommodate missing data and allow the research to apply sampling weights. We've also made a special effort to show how to use R to create publication-level tables and figures. Data visualization is an especially exciting field and a relative strength of R. Because most students are visual learners, giving them the opportunity to see relationships in data and statistical concepts in action is also a great teaching tool.

We have updated the end-of-chapter exercises for the second edition of this book. In our exercises, we attempt to test students' understanding of the methods demonstrated in each chapter.

Students can log on to **edge.sagepub.com/pollock** to access datasets used in *An R Companion to Political Analysis* as well as tables and figures from the book to strengthen understanding of key terms and concepts.

ADVICE FOR INSTRUCTORS

This book is intended to help college students learn to apply political science research methods using the R program. We emphasize developing good writing habits, proper interpretation of statistics, and clear presentation of results. This book isn't a comprehensive reference to R's data analysis functions. This book is intended to serve as a companion to textbooks that emphasize the general concepts of political science research. We hope this book helps your students use the R program to apply textbook and lecture concepts to solve problems and conduct research.

Those of us who teach political science research methods understand there are pros and cons to using different statistics programs. We think instructors should be aware of the advantages and disadvantages of using R and, if they choose R, work to maximize its advantage and minimize its potential problems.

The primary benefit of using R for teaching students to use political science research methods is that R is a free program that works well on both Windows and Mac OS platforms. Students don't have to work on certain computers on campus or under an expiring software license. In our experience teaching this class, students really like the convenience of being able to work on their own laptops, even though we have computer labs on campus. Working with R gives students the option of working on or off campus, at times that fit in their schedules. Although R is sometimes seen as a program reserved for hardcore quants, it may be more appropriate to view R as a program made for everybody. We think it's great that students can build a toolkit of R scripts over the course of a term and take it with them into other classes or the workplace. The only real limitation to using R is the willingness to learn how.

In this book, we try to identify the fundamental research methods used by political scientists and demonstrate the simplest ways of applying these methods using R. In a number of instances, we've written very simple functions to execute certain tasks with minimal coding. Of course, we recognize that there are many different ways to implement research methods in R. We think it makes sense to teach students how R functions are called, demonstrate the simplest possible solution to a problem, and encourage students to demonstrate their creativity and initiative by refining the basic solution or trying other solutions to the problem. If you've mastered different solutions to some of the problems we discuss in this book, we'd encourage you to teach R strategies that are familiar to you in place of, or as alternatives to, the strategies we demonstrate here.

As noted in the preface to the first edition, teaching students to use R presents a number of challenges. Students are used to using computer software for everyday tasks and entertainment. Chances are, they've never had to use an instruction manual to operate a computer or electronic device, so using a manual to operate a statistics program is an unfamiliar task. Our suggestion is to be frank with students about the pros and cons of R and explain why you're using it to teach research methods. We've found that many students (although often reluctant to admit it) actually enjoy the challenge of learning a new skill that demands precision and attention to detail. When students learn that R is widely used in the private sector and familiarity with R is a desirable skill to potential employers, they are likely to prefer using R to working with other statistics programs.

One specific suggestion we'd like to offer instructors who plan on using R to teach political science research methods is to consider devoting at least part of one class session to helping students get R and the R package that bundles the functions and datasets used in this book installed and operational. Encourage students to bring their personal laptops to this session to get them set up to work independently. If you've worked with R for a while, it's easy to forget how confusing the R environment appears to a new user. Help students get to the point where they can execute commands and observe R's response. Make sure your students are prepared to start making mistakes and learning from them; trial and error is essential, so you don't want students to get caught up on one-time, set-up issues.

If you think that learning how to use R is a learning objective in and of itself and not merely a means to other ends, consider incorporating some computer lab sessions into your course if time and facilities allow you to do so. One of us (Edwards) teaches research methods with equal parts lecture and lab sessions. In the lab sessions, students work on solving problem sets using R for statistical analysis. When students have questions, they raise their hands and receive one-on-one instruction. Edwards has been fortunate to work with some excellent graduate teaching assistants who join the class lab sessions to work one-on-one with students. He has also recruited top students to return to lab sessions in subsequent terms to help other students learn to use the R program. It's a lot of fun and the hands-on experience with R reinforces the general concepts from lectures and the textbook.

ACCOMPANYING CORE TEXT

Instructors will find that this book makes an effective supplement to any of a variety of methods textbooks. However, it is a particularly suitable companion to Pollock's own core text, *The Essentials of Political Analysis*, now in its fifth edition. The textbook's substantive chapters cover basic and intermediate methodological issues and ideas: measurement, explanations and hypotheses, univariate statistics and bivariate analysis, controlled relationships, sampling and inference, statistical significance, correlation and linear regression, and logistic regression. Each chapter also includes end-of-chapter exercises. Students can read the textbook chapters, do the exercises, and then work through the guided examples and exercises in *An R Companion to Political Analysis*. The idea is to get students to experience political research firsthand, early in the academic term. An instructor's solutions manual, free to adopters, provides solutions for all the textbook and workbook exercises.

ACKNOWLEDGMENTS

We would like to thank the wonderful editorial team at SAGE Publications for their continued support and encouragement. It's a real pleasure to work with such a talented and professional group. We would also like to thank the R Development Core Team and the authors whose functions we use throughout this book.

Pollock would like to thank his co-author, Barry Edwards, who took on the lion's share of the revisions and who is responsible for making this edition much better than the last. Pollock would also like to extend a special thanks to Charisse Kiino, who saw to it that the first edition of this project got off the ground.

Edwards would like to thank, first and foremost, his co-author, Philip Pollock, for inviting him to help revise the first edition of this book. Pollock is a terrific co-author and has a great sense of humor. Edwards would also like to thank the graduate and undergraduate teaching assistants he's had the pleasure of teaching POS 3703 with: Christine Regnier-Bachand, David Shabat-Love, Jason Christensen, Preeti Prakash, Sydney Dotson, Ryan Allen, Marissa Hall, Bobby Sells, and Jessica Lago. He also thanks all of the University of Central Florida students who have endured all his corny jokes in Howard Phillips Hall and inspired him to strive for better and better ways to teach this material.

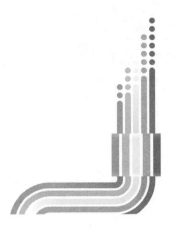

A Quick Reference Guide to R Companion Functions

FUNCTION ARGUMENTS

Symbol	What It Means
x	Variable; independent variable
y	Dependent variable
z	Control variable
w	Optional weight variable
dataset	Dataset (gss, nes, states, or world)
design.dataset	Dataset created with svydesign (gssD, nesD, statesD, or worldD)

FUNCTION USAGE

AdjR2*(tdf=total.df, null.dev=null.deviance, resid.dev=residual.deviane, k=#indepvars)*
CI95*(m=mean, se=standard.error)*; CI99 *(m=mean, se=standard.error)*
Colors()
compmeans*(x=y, f=x, w=w, plot=T/F ...)*
CramersV*(chi=chi2.statistic, r=#rows, c=#columns, n=sample.size)*
crosstab*(dep=x, indep=y, weight=w)*
csv.get*("csv.dataset.csv")* [import data in .csv format)
cut2*(x=variable, cuts=cutpoints, m=min.obs, g=num.groups ...)* [use cuts or g]
ddply*(.data, .variables, .function ...)* [see help(ddply) for special input format]
describe*(x=variable, weights=w ...)*
fit.svyglm*(svyglm=svyglm.model)*

(Continued)

(Continued)

freq(*x=variable, w=w, plot=T/F ...*); freqC (*x=variable, w=w*)
imeansC(*function1=~y, function2=~x + z, data=design.dataset*)
lineType()
logregR2(*model=logit.model ...*)
orci(*model= logit.model ...*)
pchisqC(*reduced=reduced.logit.model, full=full.logit.model ...*)
plotChar()
plotmeans(*formula=y ~ x, data=dataset ...*)
plotmeansC(*data=dataset, formula2=~y, formula3=~x, formula4=y~x, w=~w ...*)
printC(*objx=table.output*)
prop.testC(*y=y, x=x, w=w*)
scatterplot(*formula=y~x, data=dataset ...*)
somersD(*formula~x+y=, data=design.dataset*)
sortC(*data=dataset, id=identifier/name, by=sort.criteria, descending=T/F*)
spss.get(*"SPSS.dataset.sav"*) [import SPSS dataset]
stata.get(*"Stata.dataset.dta'*) [import Stata dataset]
svyboxplot(*formula=y~x, design=design.dataset ...*)
svyby (*formula=~y, by=~x, design=design.dataset, FUN=function.applied ...*)
svychisq (*formula=y~x, design=design.dataset ...*)
svychisqC (*formula=y~x, design=design.dataset*)
svydesign(id=~1, data=*data*, weights=~*w ...*) [create *design.dataset*]
svyglm(*formula=binary.y ~ x l... xn, design=design.dataset*, family=quasibinomial)
svyglm(*formula=y ~ xl ... xn, design=desig n.dataset ...*)
svytable(*formula=y~x, design=design.dataset*)
welcome()
wtd.boxplot(*formula=y ~ x, weights=w ...*)
wtd.chi.sq(*var1=x, var2=y, weight=w ...*)
wtd.cor(*x=variable.matrix, weight=w ...*)
wtd.hist(*x=variable, weight=w ...*)
wtd.mean(*x=variable, weights=w ...*)
wtd.median(*x=variable, weights=w*)
wtd.mode(*x=variable, weights=w*)

wtd.quantile*(x=variable, weights=w ...)*
wtd.sd*(x=variable, weights=w)*
wtd.t.test*(x=variable, y=test.value, weight=w ...)* [One sample t-test]
wtd.t.test*(x=var1, y=var2, weight=w1, weighty=w2 ...)* [Two sample t-test]
wtd.ttestC*(f1=~y, f2=~x, data=design.dataset)*
wtd.var*(x=variable, weights=w)*
xtabC*(function1=y~x, data=dataset)*
xtp*(data=dataset, y=y, x=x , w=w ...)*
xtp.chi2*(data=dataset, y=y, x=x , w=w ...)*

For more detailed help files on these functions, enter ? followed by the function's name or help(function_name) in R. Functions from base installation packages are not listed.

Introduction:
Getting Acquainted with R

Objective	Functions Introduced	Author or Source
Demonstrating R capabilities	c {base} data.frame {base} seq {base} sqrt {base} mean {base} help {utils}	All functions by R Development Core Team[1]

As you have learned about political research and explored techniques of political analysis, you have studied many examples of other people's work. You may have read textbook chapters that present frequency distributions, or you may have pondered research articles that use cross-tabulation, correlation, or regression analysis to investigate interesting relationships between variables. As valuable as these learning experiences are, they can be enhanced greatly by performing political analysis firsthand—handling and modifying social science datasets, learning to use data analysis software, learning to describe variables, setting up the appropriate analysis for interesting relationships, and running the analysis and interpreting your results.

This book will guide you as you learn these practical and creative skills. Using R, powerful data analysis software, to analyze research-ready datasets, you will learn to obtain and interpret descriptive statistics (Chapter 2), to collapse and combine variables (Chapter 3), to perform cross-tabulation and mean analysis (Chapter 4), and to control for other factors that might be affecting your results (Chapter 5). Techniques of statistical inference (Chapters 6 and 7) are covered too. On the somewhat more advanced side, this book introduces correlation and linear regression (Chapter 8). You will learn how to create graphics that show relationships among variables and the results of regression analysis (Chapter 9). Chapter 10 provides an introduction to logistic regression, an analytic technique that has gained wide currency in recent years. Chapter 11 shows you how to code your own data, and it provides guidance on writing up your results. Virtually every chapter in this book places special emphasis on the graphic display of data, an area of increasing interest to the scholarly community.

---

[1] R Development Core Team. (2011). *R: A language and environment for statistical computing.* Vienna, Austria: Author. Available at http://www.R-project.org/

To get started with this book, you will need access to a computer with an Internet connection. After you set up your computer with the right software and add-ons, you'll be able to work offline. All of the necessary files are freely accessible on the Internet.

ABOUT R

What is R? R is free software developed in the public domain to analyze data. You can run R on a variety of operating systems. The base version of R performs many of the statistical procedures you will learn in this book. In addition, hundreds of users have written a large number of specialized programs for R, all of which are available from the Comprehensive R Archive Network (CRAN), a clearinghouse for R resources of all kinds.[2]

In the world of multi-faceted computer software, R is something of a youthful upstart—version 1.0.0 was released in early 2000—but its user base has steadily expanded.[3] Indeed, by 2014, R had an estimated 2 million regular users. Large corporations, such as Google and Facebook, use R for special applications, such as data visualization.

Powerful, flexible, richly supported, increasingly popular—and free. What's the downside? This: R is hard. The learning curve is steep. The R interface can be described as either retro or primitive, depending on how charitable you wish to be. Although a handful of promising graphical user interfaces (GUIs) for R exist, R's core power is unlocked by the keyboard, not the mouse. (Yes, R is command line.) Because different programmers have contributed to R's development, not all commands adhere to the same syntactical rules. Until you get the hang of it, you will find yourself frequently referring to the reference card provided with this book. Above all—and subsuming all these challenges—R's approach to computing, its *idea* of computing, is almost certainly different from the approach you have grown accustomed to. The R statistical environment takes some getting used to. However, when you get comfortable working with objects and using functions, you'll appreciate the program's flexibility and the wealth of tools available for data analysis.

INSTALLING R

There is no substitute for practical experience with R. Let's install R so we can begin seeing how R thinks and behaves.

To install R, follow these steps, illustrated in Figures I.1–I.5:

1. Open http://cran.r-project.org/, the home page of the R Project for Statistical Computing.

2. Under the "Download" heading on the left side of the home page, click the link for "CRAN" (the Comprehensive R Archive Network).

3. Select a repository near you from the list. The 0-Cloud options at the top of the list offer automatic redirection to servers worldwide, so they make a good default choice.

4. Under the heading "Download and Install R", select the link that corresponds to your computer's operating system.

   - *For Windows*: Click "base" or "install R for the first time" to install the basic version of the most recent version of R. *Note to Windows users*: The Windows installer should determine whether to install the 32-bit or the 64-bit version of R. However, if you need to determine your machine's bit count, find help here: http://support.microsoft.com/kb/827218.
   - *For Mac*: Select the most recent version of the R program your operating system can support. As of the time of this writing, the most recent version of R (3.3.1) requires Mac OS X 10.9 or higher. If your Mac OS is older than that, select the R version appropriate for your system.
   - *For Linux*: Follow instructions specific to your Linux distributor.

5. Follow normal installation procedures. Click through the installation dialogues. Accept the default settings.

---

[2] See http://cran.r-project.org/
[3] Ashlee Vance, "Data Analysts Captivated by R's Power," *New York Times*, January 6, 2009.

Figures I.1–I.5   R Project for Statistical Computing Home Page, Location of Repositories, Windows Download Options, Mac OS Download Options, Linux Download Options

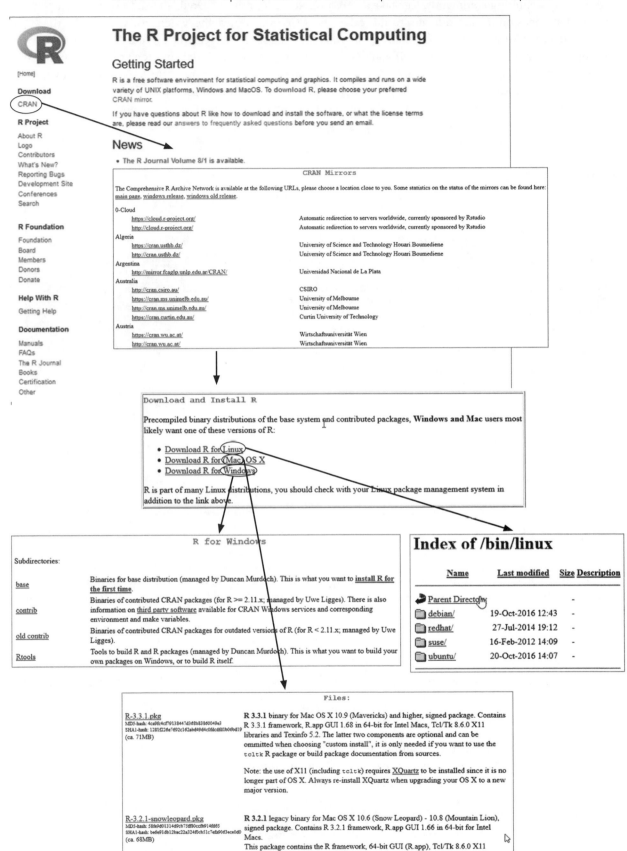

A QUICK TOUR OF THE R ENVIRONMENT

Before we start entering commands, let's take a look around the R program. Double-click the R icon. The window that opens on the left side of screen is called the R Console. Above the R Console, at the top of the screen, you'll see a row of drop-down menus. You can edit some settings to customize your R environment, but the drop-down menus are pretty spare. If you're running R on Mac OS or Linux, your R environment may look different than how it's depicted in Figure 1.6. (You have some options to customize the look and feel of your R environment with the "GUI preferences . . . " option under the Edit menu tab.)

Notice the > sign on the last line of the R Console in Figure 1.6? R is awaiting your commands.

Figure I.6   R Console

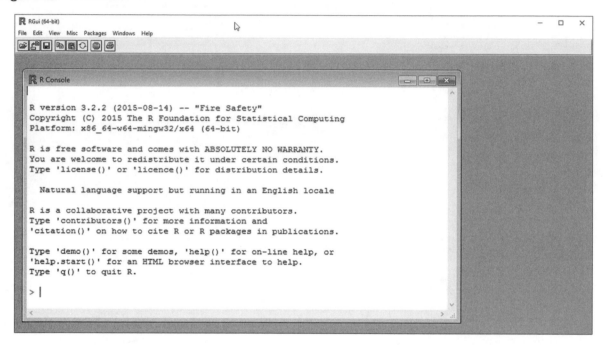

Now that you've got R running and know where you can enter commands, let's see what R can do. It can be helpful to think of R as an overgrown programmable calculator. Like a calculator, if you ask R to calculate a number like "2 + 2", it will return the answer, 4, to you.

```
2 + 2                            # Enter "2+2" and R returns "4"
```

```
[1] 4
```

Notice that R's response to the command "2 + 2" starts with the [1]. Rather than clear your command, R *indexes* its answer, "[1]", and returns it on the next line. In this case, the answer is just one number, but we'll soon see that R can work with long series of numbers, in which case indexing helps us make sense of results.

In our simple 2 + 2 example, we see an example of an *operator* used by the R program. The + sign is a mathematical operator that adds numbers together. As you might guess, R also uses the familiar mathematical operators: – (dash, to subtract), / (forward slash, to divide), * (asterisk, to multiply), and ^ (caret, to raise to a power). The equal sign (=) is particularly important in the R environment and we will focus on it in the next section.

Comparing R to a calculator helps us get started, but it only scratches the surface of what R can do. To start unlocking R's potential, we need to learn about *objects* and *functions*.

To understand computations in R, two slogans are helpful:

- Everything that exists is an object.
- Everything that happens is a function call.

— John Chambers (a co-creator of R)

OBJECTS

Objects are used to store information in an accessible manner. Just as all things are nouns in the English language, all things are objects in R. Some objects encapsulate just one value; other objects store vast arrays of data. Objects in R store different things, but they all are equally accessible in the workspace, ready to be put to use—no opening, entering, creating, saving, or exiting required. You can think of objects as all-purpose containers for information, much like the contacts list in your phone. You could key in a friend's number every time you want to call them, but it's easier to retrieve their phone number by associating it with their name. The contact object may have several attributes, such as an e-mail address, mailing address, and photo. Similarly, in R you can create objects and assign numbers and text—even other objects—to the object. We use the *assignment operator* to assign values to objects. The equal sign (=) is the intuitive choice, although R traditionalists prefer the classic assignment operator (<-), which does provide some advantages when it comes to writing functions.[4]

```
phoneNumber = 4078232608            # Assigns number to "phoneNumber"
phoneNumber <- 4078232608           # Alternate assignment operator
```

Object names must be one word, no spaces. If you were to insert a space in the middle of an object name, R would think you are referring to two different objects. There are a few limits on the names you can give objects. Names cannot begin with a digit or with a period followed by a digit. Some objects are already defined by the system, so you should avoid using them: T, F, and pi are examples. (For a complete list, type "?Reserved" at the R prompt.) As a general rule, avoid using single-character object names because they are not clear, descriptive names for the values of their contents. There is no character limit on object names, so you don't need to sacrifice clarity to save computer memory.

Just as you assigned a number to the object phoneNumber, you may also want the value of an object to be a word or phrase. Use quotation marks to assign text as a value to an object, otherwise R thinks you are referring to an object or doing math. (If we wanted to store the phone number in the above example with formatting, that is, as 407-823-2608, we would need to put the value in quotation marks.)

```
name = "UCF Poli Sci Dept"      # Assigns text in quotes to "name"
```

Successful object assignments work quietly in R. If you make an error, such as forgetting the closing quotation mark, R will let you know. If you type in the name of the object, R will return its assigned value.

Objects are the building blocks of the R environment. Two or more objects can be combined to produce a more complex and information-rich object. Suppose we wanted to create a new object, "directory", that combines the two objects created previously, "name" and "phoneNumber". The following assignment would do the trick. (This assignment statement uses a function, data.frame. We will take a closer look at functions in the next section.)

```
directory = data.frame(name, phoneNumber)   # Object from objects
```

Now enter "directory" to retrieve the contents of the combined object:

```
> directory
              name phoneNumber
1 UCF Poli Sci Dept  4078232608
```

---

[4] See http://www.r-bloggers.com/assignment-operators-in-r-%E2%80%98%E2%80%99-vs-%E2%80%98-%E2%80%99/

The new object is a *data frame*, which stores data in two dimensions: rows and columns. To be sure, our "directory" object is pretty sparse; it is a dataset with only one row and two columns. (In the next section, we will look at how to add names and phone numbers.) Even so, our tiny directory can illustrate how to use *brackets* to access values stored in objects. To access parts of the directory, you specify the row, column, or both the row and column, or you use the "$" sign to specify a variable in a dataset.

```
directory[1, ]              # returns first row
directory[, 1]              # returns first column
directory[, 2]              # returns second column
directory[1, 1]             # returns value of first row, first column
directory[1, 2]             # returns value of first row, second column
directory$name              # returns value of "name" variable
directory$phoneNumber       # returns value of "phoneNumber" variable
```

Note especially the role played by the dollar sign symbol, "$". This symbol tells R exactly where to locate an attribute stored in an object. Thus, the statement "directory$name" means, "Look in the object named 'directory' and output the attribute 'name'." The "$" symbol is important syntax, as we will see in Chapter 2, when we start working with variables.

R recognizes six types of objects. For the purposes of this book, the most important are data frames (such as "directory") and *vectors*, which are strings of numbers (1, 2, 7, -4), words ("one", "two", "seven", "negative four"), or logical operators (TRUE, TRUE, TRUE, FALSE).

FUNCTIONS

Functions perform a defined sequence of actions. If objects are the equivalent of nouns, then functions are the equivalent of verbs. Functions are *generic*, meant to be used in a wide range of similar, but not identical, tasks. Functions are called by name, followed by a set of parentheses. A name without parentheses is an object. Good developers give their functions descriptive names. Function names must be one word, no spaces. If you insert a space in the middle of a function name, R will think you're referring to an object and a function and this will cause an error.

Some functions create objects, others don't. Some functions take input from the user. When you call a function, you may specify the values of the function's arguments, separating each argument with a comma, inside the parentheses that follow the function name. The argument values you specify in your function call are passed to the function and affect what the function does. As an R user, you should think about functions in terms of what you can input and what functions will output when you call them. To illustrate how you interact with functions, consider a hypothetical R function, makeWidget. The function allows you to specify the shape, color, and size of the widget you want made. Someday you may want to discover exactly how widgets are made but, for now, ignore the processes inside the box we put around the makeWidget function. What's important is the function's output, a widget made to your specifications, and to which we assign the name "myWidget".

Figure I.7 Hypothetical "makeWidget" Function

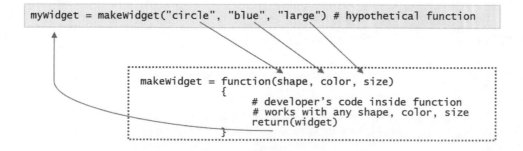

The author of a function defines how it is to be used and how any user-supplied information is processed within the function. The pieces of information that the user supplies the function, like the shape, color, and size of the widget to make, are called *arguments*. Some arguments are required, others are optional. You could imagine, for example, additional options to customize your widget beyond the standard features. A good developer would write a function that easily creates simple widgets with sensible default options, but also gives users access to advanced settings to customize their widgets. For the purposes of this book, you need not be too concerned about the code that is inside the R functions included in the base installation of the program or in the packages you install to expand R's functionality. Instead, you should focus on the flow of information between the function call and the function.

In the preceding section, we used the data.frame() function to create a data frame object, "directory", from two other objects, "phoneNumber" and "name", each of which contain only one value. Now we will take a look at another useful function, concatenate. It has a simple name: c. Suppose you wanted to create an object with several phone numbers. You could use the concatenate function to create a vector, which is an object with multiple values. The following example uses concatenate to produce two vectors, "name" and "phoneNumber". The two vectors are then combined to update the "directory" data frame.[5]

```
name         = c("UCF Poli Sci", "HPH lab", "Orlando") #name has three values
phoneNumber  = c(4078232608, 3215555252, 2025678901)   #phoneNumber's 3 values
directory    = data.frame(name, phoneNumber)           #updates data frame
directory                                               #outputs data frame
```

```
          name phoneNumber
1 UCF Poli Sci  4078232608
2      HPH lab  3215555252
3      Orlando  2025678901
```

Another function, seq(), provides an opportunity to learn about function arguments. This is a very useful function, but we must supply it with a few vital pieces of information. Take a look at this function's usage statement:

$$seq(from, to, by)$$

The seq function creates a sequence of numbers, provided that you supply it with the start-from number, the go-to number, and the count-by increment. Supply that information inside the parentheses that follow the name of the function. Notice that, because it allows the user to set the parameters, the seq function becomes more versatile. That is, we don't need one function to count up, another to count down, another to count by twos, and so on. The seq function will perform any of those actions. The following code creates a vector object, "vec1", that ranges from 1 to 49 in increments of 3:

```
vec1 = seq(from = 1, to = 49, by = 3)    # using function arguments by name
vec1 = seq(1, 49, 3)                     # using function arguments by position
vec1
```

```
[1]  1  4  7 10 13 16 19 22 25 28 31 34 37 40 43 46 49
```

---

[5] If we had more phone numbers than names (or vice versa), we could not store these vectors together in a data frame; instead, we would need to use another function, such as list (), that works with vectors of different lengths. If you want to create large data frames or lists with many values, you don't want to create these objects and assign them values in an R script; instead, you'd want to create a spreadsheet-like file for your data and read that file as an object (loading external data files is discussed in Chapter 11).

Notice that the first two statements above produce the same result. If we do not specify the names of function arguments, R will use positional matching and assume that the first value in parentheses corresponds to the first argument in the definition of the function, the second value in parentheses to the second argument in the defined usage of the function, and so on. (Consult the help page for a function to see how the function is defined and what its required and optional arguments are.) Now study these next lines of code and try to predict what they'll do when you enter them.

```
seq(3, 50, 1)              # what sequence will this generate?
seq(by=3, to=50, from=1)   # will this generate same output?
seq(10, 2, from=1)         # what's wrong with this command?
```

It is important to understand how functions are defined because one of the most common mistakes is to not supply function inputs in the right order or with the correct syntax. Remember, R is open source software with many contributors; there is no single, centralized authority to enforce uniform practices, so you will see different expressions of the same idea across packages and functions. Because R is open source, many people write functions for the program, which helps explain its rapid growth and incredible versatility. However, R's radically decentralized development also means that authors are not required to adhere to consistent function definitions.

When you are working with simple functions—functions with only a few essential arguments—positional matching is usually fine. For more complex functions, you might want to use keyword matching. Our first use of the seq() function used keyword matching because we used the arguments named in the definition of the function. Throughout this book, when we discuss a particular function, we'll show you how to call the function correctly.

Sometimes the output of one function is the input to another function. When you nest one function inside another, pay particular attention to your use of parentheses. In the first example below, we use R's sqrt() function to compute the square roots of a sequence of numbers created by the seq() function. The second example uses the mean() function to calculate the mean of the same sequence.

```
sqrt(seq(1, 50, 3))    # nested function outputs a vector
mean(seq(1, 50, 3))    # nested function outputs a single number
```

Notice what happens when you input these commands. One returns a new series of numbers, the other just one number. Why? R is calculating the square root of each number in the sequence. The mean() function, by definition, calculates one number from a set of numbers. If we wanted to calculate the square root of the sum, or square root of the mean, we'd use parentheses to establish the order of operations.

Don't think of functions as formulas you should memorize. There are far more functions written for R than you could possibly memorize. (At the time of this writing, there are nearly 10,000 packages written for R containing approximately 200,000 different functions.) It's much more important to understand the general logic of functions. While functions do many different things, you use them the same way. You execute a function by its name followed by a set of parentheses. Inside the parentheses, you may specify the values of arguments used by the function. The information you specify in parentheses is supplied to the function and processed within the function, and the result of the operation is returned to you. When you're working with a new function, try executing it in the simplest manner possible before fine-tuning your function usage by setting optional arguments.

GETTING HELP

To obtain information on a function from a package that is installed and loaded, type '?*function.name*' or help(function.name) at the prompt.[6] For example, if you want to know more about the seq function, type: '?seq' or 'help(seq)'. Because the base package is loaded, R will show us the R documentation for the seq function:

---

[6] For an alphabetical list of R packages, see https://cran.r-project.org/web/packages/available_packages_by_name.html

Figure I.8   Function Help File

Double question marks, '??*function. name*', extend the scope of the inquiry to R documentation that includes your search term. Below, we show the results of entering "??scatterplot" to learn more about R's impressive graphics capabilities.

Figure I.9   Extended Search Results

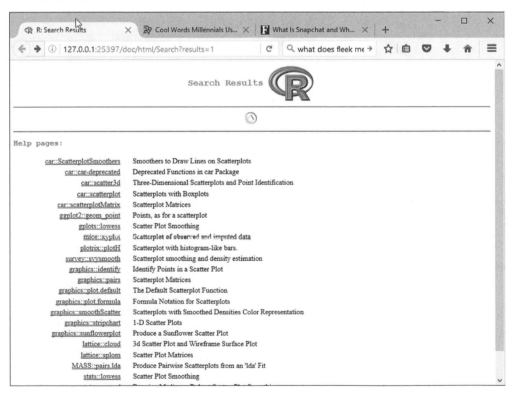

R documentation is highly technical and, truth be told, is not always helpful for beginners. Even so, if you are working with a new function, the usage section of the help file will show you the arguments you can include inside the parentheses. It may seem like a long list, but many of a function's arguments are optional. If you are relying on positional matching, make sure you put the arguments in the expected order. If you're using keyword matching, make sure you have the correct argument names. The arguments section of a function help file can tell you whether you have argument values in the right format; for example, you might need to set the value of an argument to a number rather than quoted text.

One of the best things about R is its enthusiastic online community. There are excellent resources available to help you learn about R. A particularly accessible source is Quick-R, http://www.statmethods.net/, created by Robert I. Kabacoff. With Quick-R, you can learn about the methods introduced in this book in greater detail as well as methods beyond the scope of this book. There are also some excellent video tutorials available. On YouTube.com, you can find concise, well-produced R tutorial videos from Phil Chan, Mike Marin (Marin Stats Lectures), and Lynda.com. For an in-depth treatment, the entire series of lectures from Emory University Professor Courtney Brown's "Statistics With R" course is available online. When you encounter problems, there's a great chance that someone has encountered the same problem and has published a helpful solution already.

EXERCISES

1. Which of the following are advantages of using the R statistical program? (Check all that apply.)

   ❑ Free to use

   ❑ Produces high-quality graphics

   ❑ Thousands of user-contributed packages extend functionality

   ❑ Live tech support available from the R Corporation

2. Create another object called "myName" and use an assignment operator to assign your name to this object. Be sure to use quotation marks around your name. Create an object called "myAge" and assign it your age in years. Next, apply the data.frame function to these objects to start a data frame object called "quickBio". Have R display the contents of your quickBio by entering "quickBio" in the R Console and copy the output here:

   _____

   _____

3. Consider the following R Commands:

```
                    thisNumber = 8
       anotherNumber = thisNumber / 4 ∧ 3 * 2
            nextNumber = sqrt(anotherNumber)
             theAnswer = nextNumber + thisNumber
```

   A. What is the value of "theAnswer"? (Circle one.)

16	8.5
8.25	12

   B. Which of the following objects has the largest value? (Circle one.)

thisNumber	anotherNumber
nextNumber	theAnswer

    C. Which of the following objects has the smallest value? (Circle one.)

       thisNumber   anotherNumber

       nextNumber   theAnswer

4. Consider the following R Commands:

```
seq1 = seq(from=1, to=10, by=1)

theSolution = max(seq1) - length(seq1[1:5])
```

What is the value of "theSolution"? (Circle one.)

1   5

10   0

5. Everything that exists in the R environment is an object. Everything that happens is a function call. (Circle one.)

True   False

1

The R Companion Package

Objective	Functions Introduced	Author or Source
Installing and loading the poliscidata package	install.packages {utils} library {base} welcome {poliscidata}	R Development Core Team R Development Core Team Philip Pollock and Barry Edwards
Exploring package contents	ls {base}	R Development Core Team
Demonstrating R capabilities	freq {descr} printC {poliscidata} getwd {base}	Jakson Aquino[1] Philip Pollock and Barry Edwards R Development Core Team

In the preceding Introduction, you became acquainted with some R basics: objects, functions, vectors, and data frames. For this book, we have developed a more specialized collection of additional objects and functions that will permit you to analyze, present, and interpret data. A specialized collection of R elements is called a *package*. The package we have created for this book, "poliscidata", contains the functions and datasets we use in this book and is available through an online repository. In this section, you will (1) run the install.packages function to install the poliscidata package, (2) run the library function to load the poliscidata package contents, and (3) run the poliscidata package's welcome function to produce some basic information about your working environment.

To install the poliscidata package, enter the following command:

```
install.packages("poliscidata")      # install bundled datasets and
                                      # functions for R companion
```

This command will prompt you to select a repository from which to download the poliscidata package. The repositories mirror one another, but you may want to select a repository close to you to save download time. See Figure 1.1.

You can also download an R package by selecting the "Install package(s) . . . " option under the Packages menu. This method will also prompt you to select a nearby repository to download the package from, and then select the "poliscidata" package from the long alphabetical list of R packages.

You will need to install the poliscidata package on each computer you use. When you install the poliscidata package, R will automatically install the functions and datasets you'll be using as well as the packages that the poliscidata package requires. The installation process may take a couple of minutes.

---

[1] Aquino, J. (2012). *descr: Descriptive statistics* (R package version 0.9.8). Includes R source code and/or documentation written by Dirk Enzmann, Marc Schwartz, and Nitin Jain. Available at http://CRAN.R-project.org/package=descr

Figure 1.1   Installing R Companion's Package

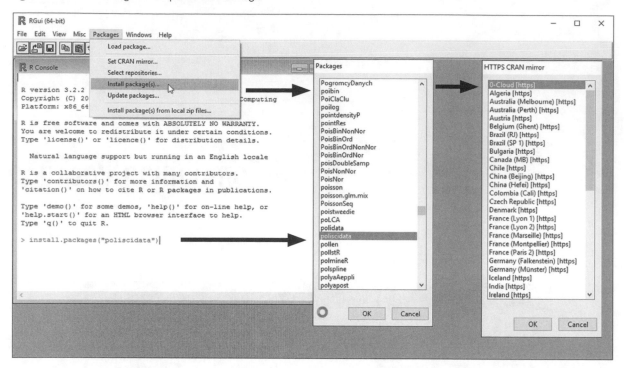

You might wonder why the R program does not come with all the packages you need. There are thousands of different packages available to extend R's capabilities. Chances are, you will use only a fraction of them (even if you become a lifetime R user). So the R Project keeps the base version of the program relatively light and allows users to add on functionality based on their individual preferences.

Box 1.1   Missing Packages

When you install the poliscidata package, R should automatically install all the packages that our package depends on. We've found, however, that R sometimes fails to install all the required dependencies. If this happens, you will see an error message that you are missing a required package. Don't panic. You can fix this problem pretty easily. You just need to install the missing packages manually. You can either select the "Install package(s) . . . " option from the Packages drop-down menu, select a repository near you, and select the missing package from the very long list of available packages, or you can type:

```
install.packages("name_of_missing_package")
```

on the Console command line, substituting the name of the missing package where indicated. If R reports that it is missing another package, keep installing missing packages until the missing package error messages go away. You will not have to do all this each time you use R. It is simply a set-up issue.

Now that you've downloaded the poliscidata package, you need to load the package in your current R session using the library command. When you download R packages, they aren't automatically available every time you use R. The program allows you to selectively load installed packages so you can make efficient use of your computer's memory. It might be helpful to think about R packages likes apps you download to your phone; your phone doesn't come with all available apps pre-installed: It lets you pick and choose which ones you want. After you've downloaded an app, you have to open it to use it; you don't want all your phone apps to open and run automatically.

After you've installed the poliscidata package, you load it with the library command. You can also load the poliscidata package by selecting the "Load package . . . " option under the Packages menu. See Figure 1.2.

```
library(poliscidata)            # Loads R companion package in session
```

Figure 1.2   Loading R Companion's Package

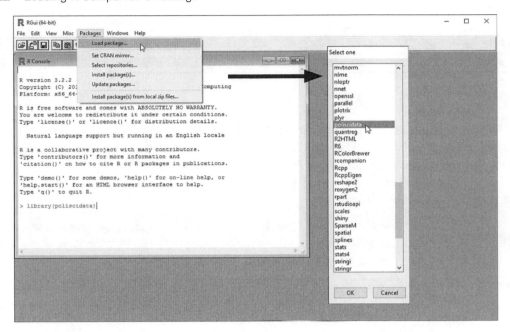

When you execute the library(poliscidata) command, it may look like R didn't do anything. Actually, there is a lot going on behind the scenes, but R won't output any messages to the console unless there is a problem. We created the poliscidata package to make getting started with R as simple and as straightforward as possible. At this point, you should be ready to go.

To acquaint you with the R working environment and the contents of the poliscidata package, we've written a special function called welcome. This command will generate a welcome message, output some basic information about your R session, and list the objects and functions in the poliscidata package.

```
welcome()                       # introduction to the companion environment
```

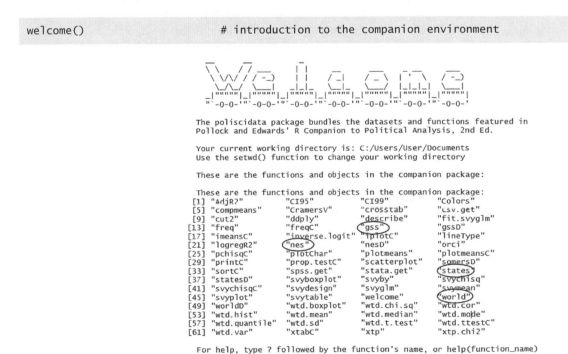

The circled objects on the list above are the four datasets that you will analyze: gss, nes, states, and world. (For a detailed description of the datasets, see Box 1.2.) You'll also notice that the package contains four objects with similar names as our four datasets: gssD, nesD, statesD, and worldD. These are special design datasets that are used by a useful suite of functions that analyze weighted data.

The list of objects and functions in the poliscidata package may look pretty long at first, but we'll introduce them gradually and, with some practice, you'll learn how to use all sorts of R functions to analyze politics.

Box 1.2   The *Companion* Datasets

The poliscidata package has four datasets.

1. **gss**. This dataset has selected variables from the 2012 General Social Survey, a random sample of 1,974 adults aged 18 years or older, conducted by the National Opinion Research Center and made available through the Inter-university Consortium for Political and Social Research (ICPSR) at the University of Michigan. Some of the scales in gss were constructed by the authors. The variables in the gss dataset are described in the Appendix (Table A.1).

2. **nes**. This dataset includes selected variables from the 2012 National Election Study, a random sample of 5,916 citizens of voting age, conducted by the University of Michigan's Institute for Social Research and made available through ICPSR. See the Appendix (Table A.2).

3. **states**. This dataset includes variables on each of the 50 states. Most of these variables were compiled by the authors from various sources. A complete description of variables in the states dataset is found in the Appendix (Table A.3).

4. **world**. This dataset includes variables on 167 countries of the world. These variables are based on data compiled by Pippa Norris, John F. Kennedy School of Government, Harvard University, and made available to the scholarly community through her Internet site. See the Appendix (Table A.4) for a complete description of variables in the world dataset.

The four datasets included in the R package that accompanies this book contain a wealth of information about political behavior and institutions. We'll use these datasets to demonstrate a variety of research methods, but we hope your curiosity will be sparked to explore variables and relationships that we don't address here. To see the names of variables contained in the datasets, you can use the names function. For example, the following command will return the names of all the variables in the world dataset.

```
names(world)              # list names of variables in dataset
```

```
[1]    "country"             "gini10"                 "dem_level4"
[4]    "dem_rank14"          "dem_score14"            "lifeex_f"
[7]    "lifeex_m"            "literacy"               "oil"
[10]   "pop_0_14"            "pop_15_64"              "pop_65_older"
[13]   "fertility"           "govregrel"              "regionun"
[16]   "religoin"            "spendeduc"              "spendhealth"
[19]   "spendmil"            "hdi"                    "pop_age"
[22]   "sexratio"            "pop_total"              "pop_urban"
[25]   "gender_unequal"      "gender_unequal_rank"    "arda"
[28]   "lifeex_total"        "debt"                   "colony"
[31]   "confidence"          "decent08"               "dem_other"
[34]   "dem_other5"          "democ"                  "democ11"
```

```
[37]  "democ_regime"       "democ_regime08"     "district_size3"
[40]  "durable"            "effectiveness"      "enpp3_democ"
[43]  "enpp3_democ08"      "dnpp_3"             "eu"
[46]  "fhrate04_rev"       "fhrate08_rev"       "frac_eth"
[49]  "frac_eth2"          "frac_eth3"          "free_business"
[52]  "free_corrupt"       "free_finance"       "free_fiscal"
[55]  "free_govspend"      "free_invest"        "free_labor"
[58]  "free_monetary"      "free_property"      "free_trade"
[61]  "free_overall"       "free_overall_4"     "gdp08"
[64]  "gdp_10_thou"        "gdp_cap2"           "gdp_cap3"
[67]  "gdpcap2_08"         "gdpcap3_08"         "gdpcap08_2"
[70]  "gdppcap08"          "gdppcap08_3"        "gender_equal3"
[73]  "gini04"             "gini08"             "hi_gdp"
[76]  "indy"               "muslim"             "natcode"
[79]  "oecd"               "pmat12_3"           "polity"
[82]  "pr_sys"             "protact3"           "regime_type3"
[85]  "rich_democ"         "unions"             "unnetgro"
[88]  "unnetuse"           "unpovnpl"           "unremitp"
[91]  "unremitt"           "vi_rel3"            "votevap00s"
[94]  "votevap90s"         "women05"            "women09"
[97]  "women13"            "ipu_wom13_all"      "womyear"
[100] "womyear2"           "dem_economist"      "democ.yes"
[103] "country1"
```

An important note to commit to long-term memory: Each time that you open a new session to work with the poliscidata package, you will need to execute the following command:

library(poliscidata)

As we noted above, you can also load the poliscidata package using the "Load package" option under the Packages menu tab. We encourage you to use R commands when possible because you can save a series of commands in a script file (more on using scripts below).

We've designed this material so you can start analyzing real political science data with R quickly and easily. You may still encounter some problems or receive some unexpected warnings from the R program. You might also see a warning message that one or more packages were built under an earlier version of R than the one you are running. This issue does not seem to pose any serious problem.

RUNNING SCRIPTS

In this book, you will create, run, and save R scripts. R scripts (called R documents on Mac OS) are documents that contain the lines of code you want R to execute (as well as comments that make your scripts easier to read and understand). You can think of an R script as a set of step-by-step instructions for the R program.

By this point, you probably have already executed some R commands successfully from the console's command line prompt, so why bother opening another window in the program and creating a script file? Sometimes getting R to do what you want it to do is tricky, so when you figure out what works, it is a good idea to save your work so you won't make the same mistakes again. If you are going to execute the same commands repeatedly, like the lines of code you need to execute each time you work with the *R Companion*, save those commands in a script file, making it easy to repeat them. Just like you save someone's phone number so you can call or text them at the touch of a button, rather than manually entering each digit of their number every time you want to contact them, saving your work in well-written script files saves time and prevents mistakes.

To create an R script, select the "New script" option under the File menu tab (or press Ctrl-N). If you're running R on a Mac OS, your version of R will say "New document" rather than "New script".

Figure 1.3 R Script Editor

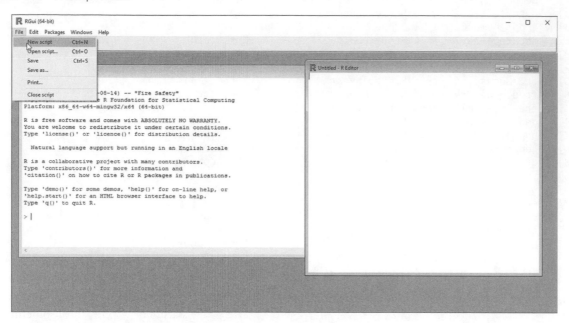

The unassuming R script editor should now appear. Click in the script editor and type a couple of lines (refer to the Introduction for sample lines of R code). When you finish typing a line of code and start a new line, the line you've completed isn't automatically executed. You can run lines one at a time by clicking on the line and pressing Ctrl-R. (If you are running Mac OS, you'll *execute* a line of code by pressing Command-Enter.) You can also select the "Run line or selection" option from the Edit menu tab or right-click the line and select "Run line or selection" from the pop-up menu, but you'll find the keyboard shortcut a time-saving practice. R will execute the line of code the cursor is on and get ready to run the next line.

When you execute a line of code from the script editor, R reacts just like you entered that line of code at the command prompt in the console widow. In fact, if you look closely at the Console output, you'll see that when you execute a line of code from your script, the line you ran appears in the Console window.

To run multiple lines of code at once, select (highlight) the lines of code you want to run and press Ctrl-R (or the "Run line or selection" options discussed above). You can run an entire script at once by pressing Ctrl-A and then Ctrl-R (or the "Run all" option from the Edit menu).

Sometimes it's very helpful to run just a fragment of a line of code. We often do this to debug a line of code that's not working the way we expected. You can run part of a line of code by highlighting part of the line and pressing Ctrl-R (or the alternatives discussed above).

After you've had the chance to write and run a couple lines of test code from the script editor, let's learn how scripts are saved and re-opened. This is the big advantage of writing a script, rather than entering command line statements: You can save your work and pick up from where you left off later. To save your test script, press Ctrl-S, the ubiquitous keyboard shorthand for save. Give the script a descriptive filename, such as "testScript.R". Make sure to type the entire filename, including the .R extension. You might want to create a folder for your R scripts; you'll hopefully be developing a nice, well-organized collection soon. Feel free to close your script and even quit the R program.

To re-open a script and continue working with it, you'll need to start the R program first and select "Open script . . . " under the File menu. The R program doesn't automatically launch when you double-click an .R file the way double-clicking a word document launches a word processor. The .R extension helps the R program recognize a script file, so it is a good script-naming practice to follow. Your test script may not be especially useful moving forward, but getting in the habit of writing good R script files will pay dividends.

TEN TIPS FOR WRITING GOOD R SCRIPTS

Just as you can learn to write good essays, you can learn to write good code for a computer program. In fact, many of the principles you've learned for composing effective prose apply just as well to writing good R code. Following these suggestions will save you time and aggravation.

1. Good scripts are user-friendly. We write R code for our benefit, not the computer's. (To the computer, it all becomes a stream of 0s and 1s.) So you should write scripts that are clear and comprehensible to you.

2. When you create objects or generate new variables, give your creations clear, descriptive names. You aren't limited to names with a limited number of characters, like some old computer programming languages. Avoid the temptation to give objects fanciful, humorous, or arbitrary names (they won't be very amusing when they give you problems).

3. Understand how R treats white space and line breaks. R will interpret the space between words as the separation between objects. If you want to give an object a multi-word name, use underscores or periods to connect the words, or use camelCase (capitalizing the first letter of each subsequent word). If you enclose words in parentheses, R will interpret the quoted expression as a value to be assigned to an object or passed to an argument in a function. If you want to include a quotation mark, or some other special characters, as part of a quoted expression, you need to use special escape sequences. (Enter ?Quotes for more information.) R will interpret line breaks as the start of new commands. Sometimes, you'll want to execute long lines of code that are more easily read and edited if broken into several lines. You can enclose multiple lines of code in parentheses and R will then interpret everything enclosed in parentheses as belonging to the same command. We'll take advantage of this feature to demonstrate how to use functions with multiple arguments.

4. Lines of code that work together to complete a particular task should appear like single-space text in a script. A block of code is a set of instructions that complete a single task, are run together, and look like a block in a script file. Lines of code that complete another task should be separated into another block. For example, your script should keep a block of statements that transform a dataset variable together, a block of statements that create a graphic together, and a block of statements that estimate a statistical model together. It's the same logic you follow when you use paragraphs to organize an essay. You use several sentences to express some idea in a single paragraph and when you're ready to move on to a new idea, you start a new paragraph.

5. Easy on the eyes, easy on the brain. Use comments, white space, and line breaks to write subheadings and create visual separation in long scripts. Comments are statements intended for human readers that R does not attempt to execute. Anything you write on a line to the right of a # sign is strictly commentary (including more # signs).

```
# ------------- Create Plot of Multiple Regression Results ---------------
```

Format longer scripts using comments, spaces between lines, and indentations, just as you would use subheadings, paragraphs, and punctuation to organize words in an essay. You want to be able to quickly skim a script to understand its basic design and purpose. This will help you locate particular lines that you want to copy or revise.

6. Use comments like "sticky note" reminders to yourself. For example, one of the early lessons in this book is how to generate descriptive statistics for different types of variables. When you learn how to produce a frequency table for an ordinal-level variable, insert a comment in your script like:

```
# Create frequency table for ordinal-level variable
# The w and plot arguments are optional
freq(x=nes$budget_deficit_x, w=nes$wt, plot=FALSE)
```

There's a good chance you'll be asking yourself at the end of the term how you created the frequency tables you made early in the term. If you follow these suggestions, you'll find a script called something like "describingVariables.R" on your computer and when you open it, you'll see your comment telling you which line(s) of code create the descriptive statistics you need. (Feel free to pat yourself on the back at this point.) What may seem like a few minutes of extra, unnecessary work in the moment will save you hours of time in the long run.

7. Save your scripts with names that clearly describe what the script does. For example, when you write an R script that makes comparisons between groups, save that script with a name like "makingComparisons.r". Don't save it with a name like "homeworkForClass.r" or "assignment4.r" because those names aren't going to help you find the code you want to use to solve a problem in the future. Write separate scripts for separate projects, just like you have different work documents for different papers.

8. Set a working directory to keep your files organized. Use a separate working directory for each project. If you're using this book as part of a class, create a directory for your class. If, subsequent to taking this class, you want to apply some of the research methods you've practiced to analyze data in a paper or for a project, you'll have a well-organized toolkit at your disposal.

9. Type the name of objects and variables as seldom as possible. Each time you type the name of an object or variable, there's a chance you type it incorrectly. Instead, to use an object declared earlier in your script, highlight the object's name, copy it, and paste the copied name where you need to reference it. If you are executing a statement that's similar to one you've already written, copy and paste what you've already written and then edit only those parts of the copied code that needed to be changed to complete the task at hand. If you're working on a project that's similar to one you've worked on before, re-use your earlier work as much as possible.

10. Save your scripts frequently in case R stops responding. It's a stable program, but it will occasionally seize up. Even better, save your work on some kind of Cloud storage so it's convenient for you to work on multiple machines.

MANAGING R OUTPUT: GRAPHICS AND TEXT

For practically all of the examples and exercises in this book, you will produce and interpret text output—frequency distributions, cross-tabulations, tables of regression coefficients, and so on. Quite often, you will want to create an accompanying graph or chart, such as a mosaic plot or scatterplot. R graphics are remarkably easy to work with: Create them, print them, or copy/paste them into a document, such as a Word document. By contrast, nicely formatted text requires a bit more work.

To illustrate, we will use the freq command (from the descr package) to obtain a frequency distribution (text) and bar chart (graphic) of nes$pid_x, a measure of party identification.[2] The nes dataset needs to be weighted, so we will include the weight variable, nes$wt, in the freq command. (Be sure to read Box 1.3, A Special Note on Weights). At the prompt or in the script file, type and run the following function call:

```
freq(nes$pid_x, nes$wt)          # Example: graphics and text output
```

```
nes$pid_x
          Frequency  Percent  Valid Percent
StrDem     1156.02  19.5405          19.61
WkDem       890.31  15.0492          15.10
IndDem      690.86  11.6778          11.72
Ind         839.33  14.1875          14.23
IndRep      720.81  12.1841          12.22
WkRep       731.41  12.3632          12.40
StrRep      867.52  14.6640          14.71
NA's         19.74   0.3337
Total      5916.00 100.0000         100.00
```

---

[2] Chapter 2 covers the freq command in detail.

Box 1.3 A Special Note on Weights

The states and world datasets are unweighted. In analyzing unweighted data, you do not need to adjust for sampling bias, because each state or country is equally and adequately represented in the dataset. For example, to calculate the average percentage of women in parliaments of the world (recorded in the variable world$women09), you would ask R to sum the percentages for each country and divide by the number of countries.

By contrast, the gss and nes datasets must be weighted. Why is this? In unweighted form, these datasets contain sampling bias—that is, some groups are over- or under-represented when compared with the overall population of adults. So, for example, if you wanted to calculate the average age of respondents in the nes dataset, the unweighted average would be distorted, because not all age groups are equally and adequately represented in the dataset. To correct for this bias, survey designers provide sampling weights. Therefore, in order to obtain accurate results from the two survey datasets, gss and nes, you will need to weight your analyses by the appropriate sampling weight. For nes, the weight variable is nes$wt; for gss, it is gss$wtss.

Most of the base R functions do not permit sampling weights. Fortunately, the extra packages you installed in this chapter contain procedures that can be used with weighted data (such as gss and nes) or unweighted data (such as states and world). On rare occasion, however, you will learn separate procedures, one for weighted data and one for unweighted data.

Figure 1.4 Sample R Graphics Output

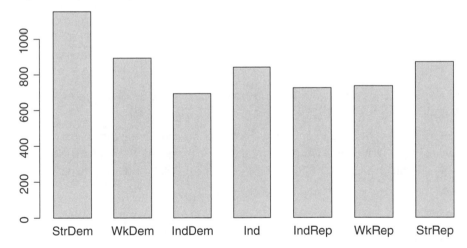

Consider the results. As you can see, R creates a graphic, a bar chart of nes$pid_x, and displays it in a separate window. If you're using Windows, you can right-click on the graphic to copy or save the figure in a desired format, or you can print it directly. Not too much to it. An editable version of the console's frequency distribution table, on the other hand, requires a few additional steps. There are a couple of ways to manage R Console output. You'll frequently want to incorporate the results of your analysis into documents.

To incorporate R Console output into informal documents, like rough drafts of papers or class assignments (check with your instructor though), you can copy text from the R Console and paste it into a word processor. The result typically looks disorganized and confusing because the pasted text appears in your word processor's default font, which is typically a proportional font (such as Times New Roman). If you change the font used to display R Console out in a Word document to a monospace font (such as Courier New or Lucida Console), you can replicate the basic formatting of tabular results you see in the R Console.

Figure 1.5 Simple Table Formatting

Default Word Format

nes$pid_x

Frequency Percent Valid Percent

StrDem 1156.02 19.5405 19.61

WkDem 890.31 15.0492 15.10

IndDem 690.86 11.6778 11.72

Ind 839.33 14.1875 14.23

IndRep 720.81 12.1841 12.22

WkRep 731.41 12.3632 12.40

StrRep 867.52 14.6640 14.71

NA's 19.74 0.3337

Total 5916.00 100.0000 100.00

Monospace Font, Single Spaced

```
nes$pid_x
          Frequency   Percent Valid Percent
StrDem     1156.02   19.5405          19.61
WkDem       890.31   15.0492          15.10
IndDem      690.86   11.6778          11.72
Ind         839.33   14.1875          14.23
IndRep      720.81   12.1841          12.22
WkRep       731.41   12.3632          12.40
StrRep      867.52   14.6640          14.71
NA's         19.74    0.3337
Total      5916.00  100.0000         100.00
```

For more formal presentations, like final drafts of papers or any analysis you plan on sharing with an audience, you should edit and format Console output. The printC function will export R tabular output as an .html file to your working directory. These files can subsequently be opened in a web browser, copied/pasted into a document file such as Word, and then edited for appearance and readability. The printC function will create an .html file, named "Table.Output.html", that will be the repository for all the tables you wish to export, edit, and print. To create an editable table using the printC function, insert the desired command within printC's parentheses.[3] For example, to print the frequency distribution table for nes$pid_x using the printC function, enter the following:

```
printC(freq(nes$pid_x, nes$wt))      # Print table output to html file
```

This statement quietly exports the frequency distribution to Table.Output.html in the working directory. If you don't know where to find the Table.Output.html file, enter the getwd() command. (See the section "Creating Tables of Regression Results" in Chapter 8 for more instruction on the printC command and formatting tables for formal works.)

ADDITIONAL SOFTWARE FOR WORKING WITH R

In this section, we discuss some options to making the R environment easier to use. As we've discussed, the R environment is relatively spare and efficient. Its graphical user interface is limited and little analysis can be conducted using its pull-down menus. Fortunately, some software developers are working to address this void and make R more intuitive and user-friendly. We'll take a look at two of these developments, R Studio and R Commander.

R Studio is an interface for R that is available for Windows, Mac OS, and Linux. It's a free program (commercial enterprises may pay more for technical support). You can download R Studio and learn more about it from its website: https://www.rstudio.com/. For new R users, R Studio has some excellent features. We particularly like R Studio's ability to suggest and auto-complete code. If you look closely at the screenshot in Figure 1.6, you'll see that when we type "nes$" we get a pull-down menu of variables in the nes dataset, a very helpful feature. Other nice features include an enhanced Editor with line numbers and smart text coloring, a command history pane, a help file pane, and some nice options for saving graphics.

---

[3] If you get an error message that says "function not found", that means you either haven't loaded the companion packages or didn't type the name of the function correctly.

Figure 1.6 R Studio Screenshot

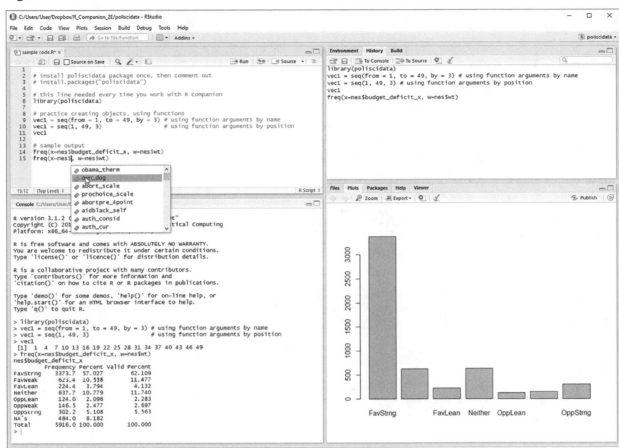

R Commander is an R package that allows users to execute a suite of commands using drop-down menus and a graphical user interface. If you have used statistics programs like Stata or SPSS before, you might like the look and feel of R Commander. Once you have R up and running, it's easy to install and load R Commander:

```
# Install and load the R Commander package
install.packages("Rcmdr")
library(Rcmdr)
```

Figure 1.7 R Commander Screenshot

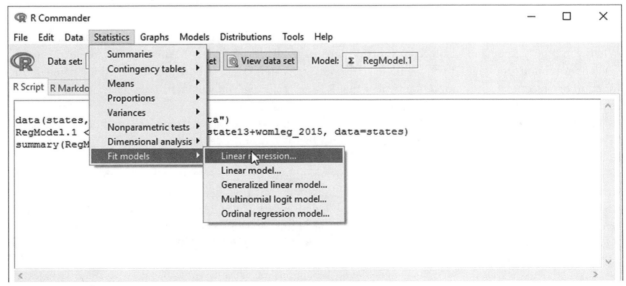

(Continued)

Figure 1.7 (Continued)

```
Output                                                         [Submit]

> RegModel.1 <- lm(abortlaw10~demstate13+womleg_2015, data=states)

> summary(RegModel.1)

Call:
lm(formula = abortlaw10 ~ demstate13 + womleg_2015, data = states)

Residuals:
    Min      1Q  Median      3Q     Max
-4.8602 -1.0406  0.3041  1.2472  3.6356

Coefficients:
             Estimate Std. Error t value Pr(>|t|)
(Intercept) 12.59982    0.99335  12.684  < 2e-16 ***
demstate13  -0.06160    0.01621  -3.800 0.000415 ***
womleg_2015 -0.14423    0.04351  -3.315 0.001773 **
---
Signif. codes:  0 '***' 0.001 '**' 0.01 '*' 0.05 '.' 0.1 ' ' 1

Residual standard error: 1.878 on 47 degrees of freedom
Multiple R-squared:  0.5069, Adjusted R-squared:  0.4859
F-statistic: 24.15 on 2 and 47 DF,  p-value: 6.091e-08


Messages

with the single-document interface (SDI); see ?Commander.
[3] NOTE: The dataset states has 50 rows and 135 columns.
```

Of course, not all R packages and functions are integrated into R Commander, but the package makes some of the most commonly used statistical methods easy to use.

DEBUGGING R CODE

When you execute a statement in R, you might get an error message telling you that an action you performed did not achieve the desired result. In fact, this happens all the time. Learning how to identify and correct mistakes is how you practice and develop your skills as an R user. Error messages are different from—and worse than—warning messages, in which R simply makes note of something it encountered while executing a command, such as missing data.

In our experience working with students, most errors are caused by typos and minor syntactical mistakes. When you type the name of an object or function incorrectly, you typically get a "Function not found" or "Object not found" message. If you see these error messages, carefully check how you've spelled the name of the function or object that's not found. Remember that R is case sensitive and will interpret a space between words as the beginning of a new object or function.

Test lines of code as you write them. Don't wait until you've written all the commands you think necessary to complete a task before running the code. Remember that R can run code one line at a time, just part of a line, or all lines at once.

If you are working with a function that has many arguments, start by executing the function in its most basic form and add arguments incrementally. Most R users start by finding a working example that's similar to what they want to do and adapting the example to suit their needs. It's an iterative process with a lot of trial and error. Functions that create graphics are a good example of this. The best way to create beautiful graphics in R is to start with a basic working figure and then refine that figure by defining values for optional arguments and adding layers of information.

If your function call isn't working, test each executable component of a function call. For example, if you're applying a function to a variable, highlight the name of the variable and run it to see its contents. Are you applying the function to a variable that isn't there or is not in the form you expected? One of the most common errors that a user makes when working with a variable is not specifying the dataset in which it resides.

What if you run a function and you see a plus sign (+), rather than the > prompt? The plus sign is the continuation prompt, meaning that R is waiting for more user input. The most common cause for this error is having more open parentheses signs than closed parentheses signs in a statement, which tells R you hasn't finished calling a function yet. Either execute the right number of closing parentheses signs or click the "STOP" button on the console window. (To wake up the STOP button, click in the Console window.) Parentheses, brackets, and quotation marks come in pairs. Make sure each opening parenthesis "(" and opening bracket "[" has a corresponding closing parenthesis ")" and closing bracket "]". This can get a little confusing when you write complex statements with nested functions. Develop the habit of typing a set of parentheses, quotations marks, brackets, or braces anytime you use them, then move the cursor back inside the set to fill in values, arguments, and so forth. Some script editors will do this automatically and that can be helpful.

If you copy and paste sample code from a Word document or web page, beware of curly quotation marks. When you use single or double quotation marks in a word processor, the program uses "curly" quotation marks for style. In contrast, your R script editor uses "straight" quotation marks. This can be a difficult bug to spot in code.

If you run a number of statements at once and get a lot of error messages, locate the first line in your script that prompted an error message—that's probably where you need to start debugging. A small typo early in a script can set off a chain reaction of errors. Don't be alarmed by a cascade of errors and warnings: Just locate the start of the error messages, read the message for any helpful information, and address one problem at a time.

In the following chapter of this book, we are going to show you how to conduct some fundamental analysis using R. For particular methods, we will feature one function or set of functions. As mentioned above, there are thousands of R packages and hundreds of thousands of functions. It should be no surprise, then, that there is a lot of overlap among functions and there is often more than one way to solve a particular problem. In this book, we emphasize functions with sensible default values, including handling of missing data, that allow researchers to use sampling weights. We have only scratched the surface of R's capabilities, but we believe the best way to learn how to use R is hands-on experience solving problems with the program.

EXERCISES

1. This chapter described R's names function. Use the names function to find out which variables are contained in the states dataset. Which of the following variables are in the states dataset? (Check all that apply.)

    ❑ cigarettes

    ❑ denom

    ❑ gunlaw_scale

    ❑ rep_therm

    ❑ partyid3

    ❑ attend_pct

2. Which of the following uses correct form in telling R where to locate the variable named gini10 in the world dataset? (Check one.)

    ❑ gini10

    ❑ gini10$world

    ❑ world$gini10

3. The states dataset contains abortlaw10, the number of restrictions that each state puts on access to an abortion. Values range from 0 (no restrictions) to 10 (ten restrictions). Use the freq command to obtain a

frequency distribution and bar chart. (*Hint*: The states dataset does not require weighting, so you do not need to include a weight variable in the freq expression.)

A. Print the graph.

B. Following this chapter's printC example, create a nicely formatted table of the abortlaw frequency distribution in a word-processing file, such as Word. When you edit the table in your word processor, give it this title: "Number of Abortion Restrictions." Print the formatted table.

4. Each time you start an R session using the R package that bundles the functions and dataset used in this book, you must type and run which one of the following expressions? (Check one.)

❑ 'library(poliscidata)'

❑ 'welcome()'

❑ 'help( )'

2

Descriptive Statistics

Objective	Functions Introduced	Author or Source
Measuring central tendency	freq {descr}	Jakson Aquino[1]
	freqC {rcompanion}	Philip Pollock and Barry Edwards[2]
	wtd.mode {rcompanion}	Philip Pollock and Barry Edwards
	wtd.median {rcompanion}	Philip Pollock and Barry Edwards
	wtd.mean {Hmisc}	Frank E. Harrell, Jr.[3]
	describe {Hmisc}	Frank E. Harrell, Jr.
Measuring dispersion	wtd.hist {weights}	Josh Pasek[4]
	wtd.var {Hmisc}	Frank E. Harrell, Jr.
	wtd.sd {rcompanion}	Philip Pollock and Barry Edwards
Getting case-level information	sortC {rcompanion}	Quan Li[5]

Analyzing descriptive statistics is the most basic—and sometimes the most informative—form of analysis you will do. Descriptive statistics reveal two attributes of a variable:

- Central tendency (the variable's typical value)
- Dispersion (how spread out or varied the variable's values are)

---

[1] Aquino, J. (2012). *descr: Descriptive statistics* (R package version 0.9.8). Includes R source code and/or documentation written by Dirk Enzmann, Marc Schwartz, and Nitin Jain. Available at http://CRAN.R-project.org/package=descr

[2] The companion function, freqC, is a slightly modified version of freq.

[3] Harrell, F. E., Jr. (2012). *Hmisc: Harrell miscellaneous* (R package version 3.9-3). Contributions from many other users. Available at http://CRAN.R-project.org/package=Hmisc

[4] Pasek, J. (2012). *weights: Weighting and weighted statistics* (R package version 0.75). With some assistance from Alex Tahk and some code modified from R-core. Available at http://CRAN.R-project.org/package=weights

[5] Pollock, P. H. (2013). *An R companion to political analysis.* Thousand Oaks, CA: SAGE/CQ Press. Based on order {base}, R Development Core Team. (2011). *R: A language and environment for statistical computing.* Vienna, Austria: Author. Available at http://www.R-project.org/

The precision with which we can describe central tendency for any given variable depends on the variable's level of measurement. Nominal-level variables—for example, gender, race, or religious denomination—have values that simply differentiate categories: Women are in one category, men in a different category. R refers to nominal variables as *unordered factors*. For unordered factors, we can identify the *mode*, the most common value of the variable. Ordinal-level variables—a survey question gauging strength of partisanship, for example, or measuring level of support for or opposition to public policy—are *ordered factors*. Because ordinal variables, or ordered factors, have values that convey the relative amount of a characteristic—an individual who "strongly" supports a policy has a greater amount of support than does an individual who "somewhat" supports it—we can find the mode and the *median*, the value of the variable that divides the cases into two equal-size groups. For interval-level or *numeric* variables, we can obtain the mode, median, and arithmetic *mean*, the sum of all values divided by the number of cases.

Finding a variable's central tendency is ordinarily a straightforward exercise. Simply read the output and report the numbers. Describing a variable's degree of dispersion or variation, however, often requires informed judgment.[6] Here is a general rule that applies to any variable at any level of measurement: A variable has no dispersion if all the cases—states, countries, people, or whatever—fall into the same value of the variable. A variable has maximum dispersion if the cases are spread evenly across all possible values of the variable such that the number of cases in one category equals the number of cases in every other category. For example, if observations take on one of two values of a variable, dispersion is greatest when half of the observations have one value and half, the other value. This general rule is particularly useful for variables measured at the nominal or ordinal level. When a variable is measured at the interval level, we can calculate statistical measures of dispersion, such as variance and standard deviation.

INTERPRETING MEASURES OF CENTRAL TENDENCY AND VARIATION

Central tendency and variation work together in providing a complete description of any variable. Some variables have an easily identified typical value and show little dispersion. For example, suppose you were to ask a large number of U.S. citizens what sort of economic system they believe to be the best: capitalism, communism, or socialism. What would be the modal response, the economic system preferred by most people? Capitalism. Would there be a great deal of dispersion, with large numbers of people choosing the alternatives, communism or socialism? Probably not. In other instances, however, you may find that one value of a variable has a more tenuous grasp on the label "typical." And the variable may exhibit more dispersion, with the cases more evenly spread out across the variable's other values. For example, suppose a large sample of voting-age adults were asked, in the weeks preceding a presidential election, how interested they are in the campaign: very interested, somewhat interested, or not very interested. Among your own acquaintances, you probably know a number of people who fit into each category. So even if one category, such as "somewhat interested," is the median, there are likely to be many people at either extreme: "very interested" and "not very interested." This would be an instance in which the amount of dispersion in a variable—its degree of spread—is essential to understanding and describing it.[7]

These and other points are best understood by working through some guided examples using the GSS dataset. In the examples that follow, you will become better acquainted with the freq function, introduced in Chapter 1. The freq command produces frequency distributions and bar charts for nominal, ordinal, or interval variables. In this chapter, you also will use the describe function to obtain descriptive statistics for interval-level variables. You will learn to use wtd.hist (from the weights package) to create histograms, graphic displays that enhance the description of interval variables. Finally, you will learn to sort a dataset to obtain case-specific information about interesting variables using the sortC function.

---

[6] In this chapter, we will use the terms *dispersion*, *variation*, and *spread* interchangeably.

[7] For elaboration on these points with additional examples, see Pollock, P. H. (2016). *The essentials of political analysis*, 5th ed. Thousand Oaks, CA: SAGE/CQ Press, Chapter 2.

DESCRIBING NOMINAL VARIABLES

Nominal-level variables simply differentiate the unit of analysis into different groups or categories. One value of a nominal-level variable is no more or less than another value, they are just different values. In the R environment, nominal-level variables are classified as unordered factors.

In this section, you will obtain a frequency distribution for a nominal-level variable, zodiac, which records GSS respondents' astrological signs. The variable, zodiac, is in the GSS dataset, which requires a weight variable, wtss. Recall R's rule: To R, zodiac is gss$zodiac, and wtss is gss$wtss. To obtain a frequency distribution table and bar chart of zodiac, enter:

```
freq(gss$zodiac, gss$wtss)        # Describing a Nominal-Level Variable
```

	Frequency	Percent	Valid Percent
ARIES	145.78	7.381	7.649
TAURUS	171.59	8.688	9.003
GEMINI	161.40	8.172	8.469
CANCER	147.73	7.480	7.751
LEO	190.35	9.638	9.988
VIRGO	158.58	8.029	8.321
LIBRA	183.37	9.285	9.621
SCORPIO	145.12	7.348	7.614
SAGITTARIUS	145.36	7.360	7.627
CAPRICORN	140.29	7.104	7.361
AQUARIUS	173.52	8.786	9.104
PISCES	142.78	7.229	7.492
NA's	69.14	3.501	
Total	1975.00	100.000	100.000

Figure 2.1 Distribution of Zodiac Signs in the GSS Dataset

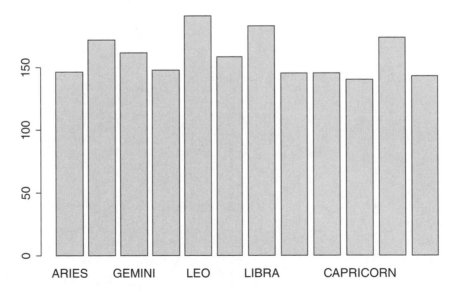

R produces a frequency distribution table in the console window and a bar chart in the graphics window. If you want to generate descriptive statistics for a nominal-level variable without weighting observations (for instance, if you are analyzing a variable in the states or world datasets), simply omit the second argument in the function above.

The value labels for each astrological sign appear in the left-most column of the frequency distribution table, with Aries occupying the top row of numbers and Pisces the bottom row. There are three columns of numbers: Frequency, Percent, and Valid Percent. The Frequency column tells us the number of respondents—more accurately, the number of respondents weighted by the sampling weight—having each zodiac sign. Percent is the percentage of respondents in each category of the variable, counting missing cases (NA's). Valid Percent is the column to focus on. So, for example, ignoring NA's, about 172 respondents (171.59), or 9.003 percent of the sample, have Taurus as their astrological sign.

Consider the Valid Percent column of the frequency distribution table with the central tendency of this variable in mind. What is the mode, the most common astrological sign? For nominal variables, the answer to this question is (almost) always an easy call: Simply find the value with the highest percentage of responses. Leo is the modal sign. To simply identify a variable's mode, without consulting a frequency distribution table, try the wtd.mode function:

```
wtd.mode(gss$zodiac, gss$wtss)        # Finding the Modal Value
```

[1] "LEO"

Do zodiac signs have little dispersion or a lot of dispersion? Take a close look at the Valid Percent column of the frequency distribution table and consider the height of the bars in the bar chart. Recall that a variable has no dispersion if the cases are concentrated in one value of the variable; there would be only one bar containing 100 percent of the cases. A variable has maximum dispersion if the cases are spread evenly across all values of the variable; all the bars would be the same height. Are most of the cases concentrated in Leo, with only one or two heavily populated bars? Or are there many cases in each value of zodiac, with many bars of roughly equal height? Since respondents are widely dispersed across the values of zodiac, we would conclude that zodiac has a high level of dispersion.

When you visually represent data, your plot or chart may need refinement. This is especially true for factor variables having a large number of categories (zodiac has 12) with long value labels. For example, notice that freq labeled only 5 of the 12 zodiac signs in the chart (you may see fewer or more labels depending on the size of your graphics window; Figure 2.1). Later in this chapter, and throughout the remainder of the book, you will learn how to fine-tune R's graphics, adding axis labels, titles, legends, line types, and so on. For present purposes, however, a slight variation on the freq function, freqC, comes in handy for factors with many possible values and long value labels. Try this:

```
freqC(gss$zodiac, gss$wtss)        # Describing a Nominal-Level Variable
                                   # Uses Modified Plot Settings
```

(*Hint*: In the script editor, copy your original freq command, paste it onto a new line, and edit 'freq' to read 'freqC'. Minimize typing to avoid introducing typos in your R code.) The frequency distribution reappears, accompanied by a bar chart in which all the values of zodiac are labeled (Figure 2.2). Also, the vertical axis records valid percentages instead of frequencies.[8]

Figure 2.2 Distribution of Zodiac Signs in the GSS Dataset

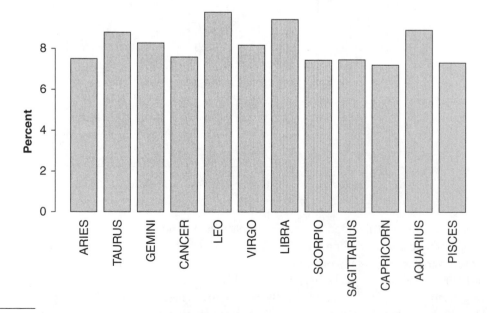

---

[8] If the x-axis labels are still cropped by the graphics window, try re-sizing your graphics window to a narrower shape and re-running the freqC command with the graphics window open. If this doesn't resolve the problem, you may need to add a line of code to specify the width of the outer margin around the bar chart. To do this, try executing this line of code *before* the freqC command: par(omi=c(.2, 0, 0, 0)). This code sets a graphics parameter for the outside margin size clockwise around the figure (below, left, above, right).

Bar charts can be a useful interpretive tool. Even so, you may not always want freq to produce one. You can suppress the chart by including the additional argument, 'plot=FALSE', which may be abbreviated, 'plot=F'. For example:

```
freq(gss$zodiac, gss$wtss, plot=F)   # Describing a Nominal-Level Variable
                                     # Suppresses Plot of Results
```

DESCRIBING ORDINAL VARIABLES

Next, you will analyze and describe ordinal-level variables, two of which have relatively little variation and a third which is more spread out. These variables appear in the NES dataset, which contains a wealth of survey data gauging individuals' opinions on a variety of public policies.

The NES variable, budget_deficit_x, asks whether respondents favor reducing the federal budget deficit. Similarly, the variable congress_job_x asks whether respondents approve of the way Congress does its job. On both questions, respondents could favor strongly, favor moderately, favor slightly, take a middle position, oppose slightly, oppose moderately, or oppose strongly. For seven-category ordered factors like these, we will run freqC. To obtain representative results, we should use the survey weights variable, nes$wt.

To create descriptive summaries of nes$budget_deficit_x and nes$congress_job_x, we execute the following lines of R code:

```
freqC(nes$budget_deficit_x, nes$wt)       # Describing Ordinal Variable

freqC(nes$congapp_job_x, nes$wt)          # Additional Example
                                          # Describing Ordinal variable
```

Figure 2.3 Public Support for Reducing the Federal Deficit

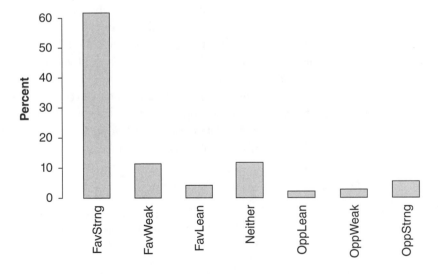

	Frequency	Percent	Valid Percent
FavStrng	3373.7	57.027	62.109
FavWeak	623.4	10.538	11.477
FavLean	224.4	3.794	4.132
Neither	637.7	10.779	11.740
OppLean	124.0	2.096	2.283
OppWeak	146.5	2.477	2.697
OppStrng	302.2	5.108	5.563
NA's	484.0	8.182	
Total	5916.0	100.000	100.000

Figure 2.4 Public Opinion of Congress

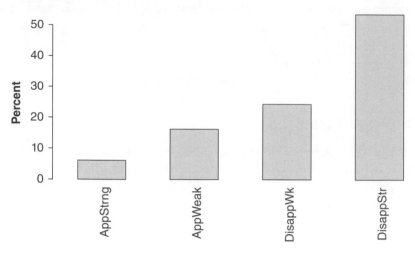

	Frequency	Percent	Valid Percent
AppStrng	342.3	5.786	6.177
AppWeak	899.8	15.209	16.236
DisappWk	1343.9	22.717	24.250
DisappStr	2955.9	49.964	53.337
NA's	374.1	6.323	
Total	5916.0	100.000	100.000

The results of these lines of code are similar to descriptive statistics we generated for the nominal variable zodiac above. In both cases, R produces a frequency distribution table in the console and a bar chart in the graphics window.

How would you describe the central tendency and dispersion of NES respondents' opinions about reducing the federal budget deficit or how Congress is doing its job? Because budget_deficit_x and congress_job_x are ordinal variables, we can report both their modes and their medians. The modal mode opinion regarding budget deficit reduction, clearly enough, is "FavStrng" (favor strongly), the option chosen by 62.11% of NES respondents (Figure 2.3). Fully 53.34% of respondents "DisappStr" (disapprove strongly) of the job being done by Congress (Figure 2.4). (As before, make sure to focus on the Valid Percent column.)[9]

What about the median values of these variables? For ordered factors, freq and freqC return a cumulative percent column ("Cum Percent").[10] This column reports the percentage of cases falling in *or below* each value of the variable. *The median for any ordinal or interval variable is the 50th percentile, the category below which 50 percent of the cases lie.* Is the first category, "favor strongly," the median public opinions about budget deficit reduction? Yes, it is. The 50th percentile must lie within this heavily populated response category. To simply identify a variable's median value, without consulting a frequency distribution table, try the wtd.median function, illustrated below:

```
wtd.median(nes$budget_deficit_x, nes$wt)        # Finding Median Value

wtd.median(nes$congapp_job_x, nes$wt)           # Additional Example
                                                # Finding Median Value
```

[1] "FavStrng"

[1] "DisappStr"

---

[9] The encoded values for these variables are abbreviated in the dataset. While the abbreviated labels are useful, one might want to modify the value labels to produce a table and/or figure for an audience. In Chapter 3, we discuss methods for transforming and relabeling variable values.

[10] If the frequency distribution table that the freq or freqC functions generate in the R console, omit cumulative percentages and use the class function to determine whether the variable you are analyzing is classified as an ordered factor. If not, you can use the as.ordered function to reclassify the variable as an ordered factor; either nest the as.ordered command as the first argument to freq or freqC or create a new variable and use your new variable as the first argument to freq or freqC. See Chapter 3 for additional information on reclassifying variables.

The output from these commands should coincide with what you learned from studying the cumulative percentages in the frequency distribution table: The median NES respondent strongly favors reducing the budget deficit and strongly disapproves of the job being done by Congress.

Does budget_deficit_x have a high or low degree of dispersion? If budget_deficit_x had a high level of variation, then the percentages of respondents holding each position would be about equal, much like the zodiac variable that you analyzed earlier. So roughly one-seventh, or 14 percent, would fall into each of the seven response categories. If budget_deficit_x had no dispersion, then all the cases would fall into one value. That is, one value would have 100 percent of the cases, and each of the other categories would have 0 percent. Which of these two scenarios comes closest to describing the actual distribution of respondents across the values of budget_deficit_x? It seems clear that budget_deficit_x is a variable with a relatively *low* degree of dispersion. Indeed, over three-quarters of all respondents fall on the "favor" side of this policy issue (cumulative percentage, 77.72), differing only in the strength of that opinion.

Now let's take a look at another NES variable, nes$presapp_war_x, an ordinal-level variable that encodes how NES respondents feel about President Barack Obama's handling of the war in Afghanistan. Execute the following code to generate a frequency distribution table and a bar graph that describe public opinion. Consider the distribution of public opinion presented here. Examine the Valid Percent column and the bar graph.

```
freqC(nes$presapp_war_x, nes$wt)          # Example, Descriptive Statistics
                                          # Describing Ordinal Variables
```

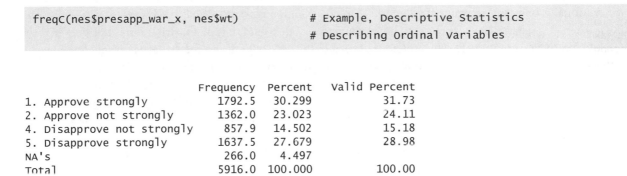

	Frequency	Percent	Valid Percent
1. Approve strongly	1792.5	30.299	31.73
2. Approve not strongly	1362.0	23.023	24.11
4. Disapprove not strongly	857.9	14.502	15.18
5. Disapprove strongly	1637.5	27.679	28.98
NA's	266.0	4.497	
Total	5916.0	100.000	100.00

Figure 2.5 Public Support for President's Handling of War in Afghanistan

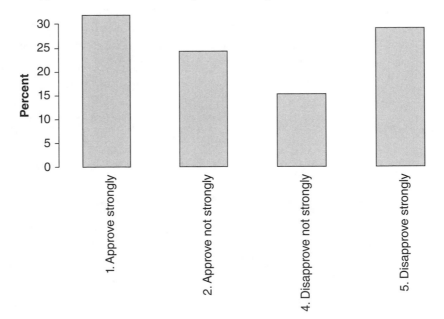

Do common measures of central tendency such as the mode and the median accurately convey public sentiment about the president's handling of the war in Afghanistan? The two measures provide inconsistent impressions of public opinion. What is the mode? Technically, "approve strongly" (31.73 percent) is the mode, although "disapprove strongly" (at 28.98 percent) is a close rival for that designation (Figure 2.5). The median sentiment is "approve not strongly." Split results like this tell us that high variation, not central tendency, is the character trait to emphasize. One could say that public opinion is deeply divided on this controversial issue, with slightly more than half of the electorate on the "approve" side of the scale and slightly less than half on the disapprove side.

If you try to apply mathematical functions like mean, wtd.var, or wtd.sd to ordinal or nominal variables, you may see the "not meaningful for factors" error message. This error indicates you are attempting to use a function that is not intended for ordered factors. In some cases, changing the class of the variable to numeric solves the problem (assuming the variable can be treated as numeric data). In Chapter 3, we discuss methods for converting ordinal values to numeric values.

DESCRIBING THE CENTRAL TENDENCY OF INTERVAL VARIABLES

We now turn to the descriptive analysis of interval-level variables (classified as numeric data in R). An interval-level variable represents the most precise level of measurement. Unlike nominal variables, whose values stand for categories, and ordinal variables, whose values can be ranked, the values of an interval variable *tell us the exact quantity of the characteristic being measured.*

Because interval variables have the most precision, they can be described more completely than can nominal or ordinal variables. For any interval-level variable, we can report its mode, median, and arithmetic average, or *mean.* In addition to these measures of central tendency, we can make more sophisticated judgments about variation. The most common measures of the dispersion of interval variables are variance and standard deviation.

Additionally, one can determine if an interval-level distribution is *skewed.* What is skewness and how do you know it when you see it? Skewness refers to how symmetrical a distribution is. If a distribution is not skewed, the cases tend to cluster symmetrically around the mean of the distribution, and they taper off evenly for values above and below the mean. If a distribution is skewed, by contrast, one tail of the distribution is longer and skinnier than the other tail. Distributions in which a small number of cases occupy extremely high values of an interval variable—distributions with a longer, skinnier right-hand tail—have a *positive skew.* If the distribution has a few cases at the extreme lower end—the distribution has a longer, skinnier left-hand tail—then the distribution has a *negative skew.*

When a distribution is highly skewed, it is a good practice to use the median instead of the mean in describing central tendency. Skewness has a predictable effect on the mean. A positive skew tends to pull the mean upward; a negative skew pulls it downward. However, skewness has less effect on the median. Since the median reports the middle-most value of a distribution, it is not tugged upward or downward by extreme values.

To illustrate how we can use R to describe the central tendency and dispersion of an interval-level variable, we will analyze gss$age, a numeric variable. Age qualifies as an interval-level variable since its values impart each respondent's age in years. To obtain a frequency distribution table and bar chart, run freqC on gss$age, weighted by gss$wtss. (Notice that the R functions we used to generate descriptive statistics for nominal and ordinal-level variables also work for interval-level variables.)

```
freqC(gss$age, gss$wtss)        # Describing Interval Variables
```

	Frequency	Percent	Valid Percent
18	18.113	0.9171	0.9195
19	27.737	1.4044	1.4081
20	27.165	1.3754	1.3790
21	40.968	2.0743	2.0798
22	44.855	2.2711	2.2770
23	38.798	1.9645	1.9696
24	32.007	1.6206	1.6248
25	34.618	1.7528	1.7574
26	30.872	1.5631	1.5672
		. . .	
87	8.077	0.4090	0.4100
88	4.581	0.2320	0.2326
89	8.439	0.4273	0.4284
NA's	5.144	0.2604	
Total	1975.001	100.0000	100.0000

```
Note: Table output edited to save space.
```

Figure 2.6 Ages of GSS Respondents

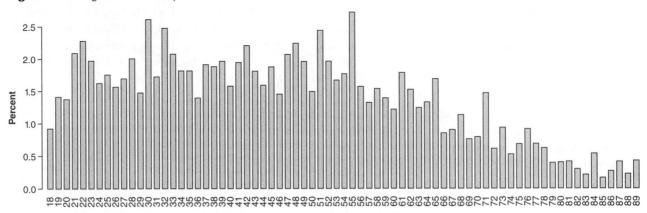

You can use the frequency distribution table and bar graph to identify the mode and median ages of GSS respondents, or use the wtd.mode and wtd.median functions introduced above.[11] (The modal age is 55 and median age is 45.)

Before we make further observations about the central tendency and dispersion of this variable, we will apply a different function, describe, to generate a bumper crop of information about this numeric variable. The generic syntax for the describe function is as follows:

```
describe(x, weights=optional.weight)
```

If you wish to include a weight variable, the argument, 'weights=', needs to be typed out.[12] To describe the age of GSS respondents, we would type:

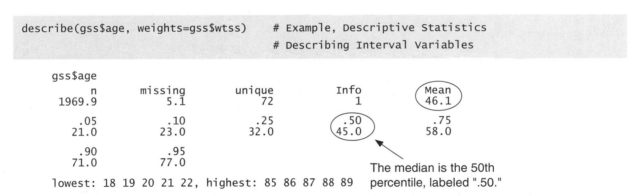

```
describe(gss$age, weights=gss$wtss)    # Example, Descriptive Statistics
                                       # Describing Interval Variables

     gss$age
           n      missing       unique          Info          Mean
      1969.9          5.1           72             1          46.1

         .05          .10          .25           .50           .75
        21.0         23.0         32.0          45.0          58.0

         .90          .95
        71.0         77.0                    The median is the 50th
   lowest: 18 19 20 21 22, highest: 85 86 87 88 89    percentile, labeled ".50."
```

The top row of describe's output tells us the weighted numbers of valid cases and missing cases (1969.9 and 5.1, respectively), the number of unique values (72), and the mean age (46.1 years). Next, describe reports a series of percentiles. For example, the label, ".05," and its associated value of age, "21.0," tells us that 5 percent (.05) of the individuals in the survey are 21 years old or younger. The 50th percentile, labeled ".50", is the median age, 45.00. Half of the GSS respondents are younger than 45 and half are older than 45. Finally, the output of the describe function reports the five lowest and highest ages found in the GSS dataset.

To simply calculate an interval variable's mean value, without consulting all the summary information produced by the describe function, you can use the wtd.mean function. This function will yield the same mean value, but it is sometimes useful for a function to generate a result rather than extracting it from console output.

```
wtd.mean(gss$age, weights=gss$wtss)    # Describing Interval Variables
```

```
[1] 46.10235
```

---

[11] The frequency distribution table and bar graph produced from this sample code may represent the distribution in too much detail. It may be more useful to describe the relative distribution of different age groups in the GSS survey rather than break down each individual age. In Chapter 3, we'll discuss some techniques to create age groupings.

[12] To supply weights to the describe function, we need to use keyword matching. We cannot rely on positional matching because "weights" is not the second argument to this function as defined by the Hmisc package.

Describe is so meticulous in providing percentiles, the numbers permit us to determine the *interquartile range*, the values of a variable that bracket the "middle half" of a distribution, between the top of the lowest quartile (".25") and bottom of the highest quartile (".75"). For age, we can see that the middle half falls between 32 and 58 years of age. The interquartile range has limited analytic value for describing a single variable; however, interquartile ranges are quite useful when comparing two or more distributions. (This is illustrated in Chapter 4.)

We have discovered that the mean age, at 46.1, is higher than the median age of 45. What does this comparison tell us about the skewness of the distribution? When a distribution is perfectly symmetrical—no skew—its mean will be equal to its median. If the mean is lower than the median—that is, if a few extremely low values pull the mean down, away from the center of the distribution—the distribution has a negative skew.[13] If the mean is higher than the median, as is the case with our current analysis, the distribution has a positive skew.[14] The bar chart from the freq analysis (Figure 2.6) lends visual clarity. The skinnier right-hand tail is a tell-tale sign of positive skewness. Even so, the mean (46.1) and the median (45) are just over one year apart. In this case, it would not be a distortion of reality to use the mean instead of the median to describe the central tendency of the distribution.

DESCRIBING THE DISPERSION OF INTERVAL VARIABLES

Sometimes the mean value of an interval variable provides a misleading impression of a variable's typical value. To illustrate this point—and to introduce another useful graphic form—we will obtain descriptive statistics for a variable in the states dataset, hispanic10, the Hispanic percentage of each state's population (as of 2010). This time we will bypass freq and go directly to describe. (For unweighted data, like states or world, you might prefer R's summary function.)

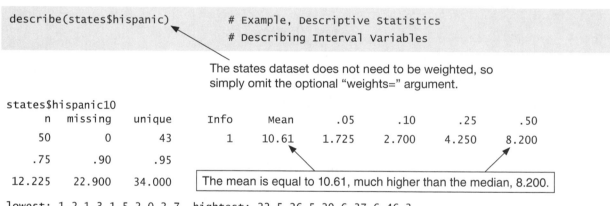

```
describe(states$hispanic)          # Example, Descriptive Statistics
                                   # Describing Interval Variables
```

The states dataset does not need to be weighted, so simply omit the optional "weights=" argument.

states$hispanic10

n	missing	unique	Info	Mean	.05	.10	.25	.50
50	0	43	1	10.61	1.725	2.700	4.250	8.200

.75	.90	.95
12.225	22.900	34.000

The mean is equal to 10.61, much higher than the median, 8.200.

lowest: 1.2 1.3 1.5 2.0 2.7, highest: 22.5 26.5 29.6 37.6 46.3

The mean percentage Hispanic, 10.61, is more than two units of measure higher than the median percentage Hispanic, 8.20, indicating a strong positive skew. The bottom row of describe's output provides a clue to the skew: The percentage of Hispanics in the five lowest-percentage states tops out at 2.7. The percentages of the five highest-percentage states range from 22.5 to 46.3. These high values pull the mean upward, off the median. In this case, the median, 8.20, is the more accurate measure of central tendency.[15]

What about graphic accompaniment for describe's numbers? We could ask freq (or freqC) for a bar chart, but because states$hispanic10 has so many unique values relative to the number of cases—according to describe,

---

[13] For a precise method of measuring the skew of a distribution, see the skewness function in the "moments" package.

[14] We don't observe a left-side tail of the age distribution because the GSS does not survey children.

[15] Many demographic variables are skewed, so their median values rather than their means are often used to give a clearer picture of central tendency. One hears or reads reports, for example, of median family income or the median price of homes in an area.

44 of the 50 states have unique values on hispanic10—a bar chart would not be informative.[16] An alternative form, a *histogram*, is preferred. A histogram is similar to a bar chart, but instead of displaying each discrete value, it collapses categories into ranges (called "bins"), resulting in a compact display. The wtd.hist function, which can be used for weighted or unweighted data, will give us the graph we want. The general syntax:

$$wtd.hist(x, optional.weight)$$

To create a histogram of states$hispanic10, we can call the following function:

```
wtd.hist(states$hispanic10)        # Histogram of Interval Level Variable
```

Figure 2.7 Histogram of Hispanic Population in U.S. States

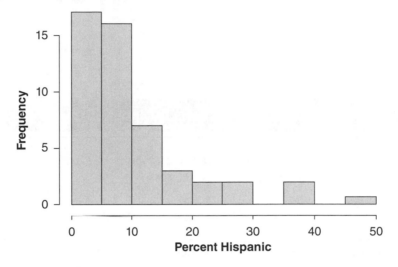

As shown in Figure 2.7, the wtd.hist function collapses the values of states$hispanic10 into 5-percentage-point intervals, thus condensing and simplifying the display without obscuring the essential features of the distribution.

R offers users fine-tuned control over data visualizations. You are not limited to "canned" methods of displaying information and should take advantage of R's graphics capabilities. In our preceding example of the Hispanic percentages in U.S. states, the default horizontal axis title and main chart title are not as clear and descriptive. Like virtually all of R's graphic commands, wtd.hist permits the user to add optional parameters to modify the graphical output. Let's re-create our histogram and supply the wtd.hist function with some additional arguments: one to modify the horizontal axis (x-axis) label, another to color the bars gray, and a third optional argument to give our histogram a nice chart title. When you add axis labels, enclose the desired text labels in quotation marks and put the commas separating function arguments outside the quotation marks.

```
# Histogram of Interval Level Variable with Some Formatting
wtd.hist(states$hispanic10, xlab="Percent Hispanic", col="gray",
        main="Hispanic Population in U.S. States")
```

In this case, the argument names are fairly descriptive: "xlab" adds a label to the x-axis label, "col" colors the vertical bars, and "main" sets the main title of the histogram. Notice that we put the x-axis label and main title in quotation marks in the function call. A modified histogram appears in the graphics window. What other optional parameters are available to further refine this histogram? Enter ?wtd.hist or help(wtd.hist) to see the help file for this function (the arguments section will enumerate all the options). You don't need to set

---

[16] For the same reason, the mode value of states$hispanic10 is not a good measure of its central tendency. Although we can calculate the modes of interval-level variables, the modal values of finely grained variables are rarely informative.

all the optional arguments; default settings often work well, but it's great to be able to customize graphics to communicate the essential aspects of data most effectively.[17]

With variables measured at the interval level, we can measure dispersion more precisely than we can with nominal- or ordinal-level variables. The two most common measures of the dispersion of interval variables are *variance* and *standard deviation*. Both of these measures of dispersion express the typical amount of variation one observes in the values of a variable. The R functions used to calculate variance and standard deviation are fairly straightforward, as their names suggest, and both functions allow the user to define sampling weights.

```
wtd.var(gss$age, gss$wtss)              # Measuring Variance

wtd.sd(nes$polknow_combined, nes$wt)    # Measuring Standard Deviation
```

[1] 298.5129

[1] 1.770014

Box 2.1 Additional Math Functions for Interval-Level Variables

In addition to the wtd.var() and wtd.sd() functions, you can use the following R functions to help describe the dispersion of interval variables:

Function	Description
summary()	returns basic descriptive statistics
range()	identifies the minimum and maximum values (technically, the range is the difference between these extremes)
min()	returns the minimum value of a variable
max()	returns the maximum value of a variable
IQR()	calculates the difference between first and third quartiles (the 25% and 75% values)
boxplot()	can generate a box and whiskers plot of values of one variable

---

A couple suggestions may help you avoid the feeling of information overload. First, when you generate descriptive statistics, you should focus on the most interesting, pertinent aspects of the variable. You don't need to subject every variable to the complete battery of R functions. Second, when you develop an understanding of how to use functions, you won't need to memorize many functions; you'll be able to use any function you encounter by following examples and reading function documentation.

---

[17] In reality, we've only scratched the surface of R's capacity for graphically representing the distribution of variables. The wtd.hist function works well in many situations, but students are encouraged to try other plotting functions as they gain experience with R. The base function hist() is highly adaptable; the histogram() function in the lattice package quickly creates a pleasant-looking figure. Some methods of visualizing the distribution of interval-level data, like the densityplot() function in the lattice package, use smooth lines, rather than vertical bars, to represent relative frequencies. To find still more options, enter ??histogram and/or ??density in your R console.

OBTAINING CASE-LEVEL INFORMATION

When we analyze a large survey dataset, such as the NES or GSS, we generally are not interested in how a particular individual answered a specific question. Rather, we want to know how the entire sample of respondents distributed themselves across the response categories of a variable. Sometimes, however, we gather data on particular cases because the cases are themselves inherently important. The states dataset (50 cases) and world dataset (191 cases) are good examples. When we are analyzing states or countries, we may want to push the descriptions beyond the relative anonymity of the freq() or describe() functions and rank states or countries based on a variable of interest.

Suppose that we are interested in studying state laws that regulate abortion. The states dataset contains the variable abortlaw10, which records the number of restrictions on abortion imposed by each state in 2010. The values of this variable range from no restrictions (a value of 0 on abortlaw10) to 10 restrictions (abortlaw10 value of 10). But which states impose the fewest restrictions on abortion? Which impose the most restrictions?

By enlisting the sortC() function, we can sort states on the basis of abortlaw10, from most restrictive to least restrictive (or from least restrictive to most restrictive, if we use an optional argument). The sortC syntax:

$$sortC(data,\ id,\ by,\ descending=T/F)$$

In this example, the variable "state" in the states dataset identifies the states by name, so our id is state (the name of each state), and we want to sort the cases by abortlaw10. Therefore, we would type:

```
sortC(states, state, abortlaw10)          # Case level information

sortC(states, state, abortlaw10, FALSE)   # Sort in ascending order
```

	state	abortlaw10		state	abortlaw10
15	Indiana	10	46	Vermont	0
36	Oklahoma	10	30	New Hampshire	1
40	South Carolina	10	37	Oregon	1
3	Arkansas	9	11	Hawaii	2
10	Georgia	9	47	Washington	2
13	Idaho	9	20	Maryland	3
18	Louisiana	9	32	New Mexico	3
24	Missouri	9	34	New York	3
28	North Dakota	9	5	California	4
41	South Dakota	9	6	Colorado	4
44	Utah	9	7	Connecticut	4
45	Virginia	9	21	Maine	4
48	Wisconsin	9	49	West Virginia	4
2	Alabama	8	1	Alaska	5
16	Kansas	8	8	Delaware	5
22	Michigan	8	31	New Jersey	5
23	Minnesota	8	50	Wyoming	5
29	Nebraska	8	4	Arizona	6
35	Ohio	8	12	Iowa	6
38	Pennsylvania	8	14	Illinois	6
9	Florida	7	19	Massachusetts	6
17	Kentucky	7	26	Montana	6
25	Mississippi	7	27	North Carolina	6
42	Tennessee	7	33	Nevada	6
43	Texas	7	39	Rhode Island	6
4	Arizona	6	9	Florida	7
12	Iowa	6	17	Kentucky	7
14	Illinois	6	25	Mississippi	7
19	Massachusetts	6	42	Tennessee	7
26	Montana	6	43	Texas	7
27	North Carolina	6	2	Alabama	8

33	Nevada	6	16	Kansas	8
39	Rhode Island	6	22	Michigan	8
1	Alaska	5	23	Minnesota	8
8	Delaware	5	29	Nebraska	8
31	New Jersey	5	35	Ohio	8
50	Wyoming	5	38	Pennsylvania	8
5	California	4	3	Arkansas	9
6	Colorado	4	10	Georgia	9
7	Connecticut	4	13	Idaho	9
21	Maine	4	18	Louisiana	9
49	West Virginia	4	24	Missouri	9
20	Maryland	3	28	North Dakota	9
32	New Mexico	3	41	South Dakota	9
34	New York	3	44	Utah	9
11	Hawaii	2	45	Virginia	9
47	Washington	2	48	Wisconsin	9
30	New Hampshire	1	15	Indiana	10
37	Oregon	1	36	Oklahoma	10
46	Vermont	0	40	South Carolina	10

The number along the left edge of the output is each case's observation number, which you can ignore. (For example, because the states dataset is organized alphabetically, Vermont is the 46th observation.) Focus on the number beneath the variable of interest. We can see that Vermont has no restrictions; New Hampshire and Oregon have one restriction. At the other end of the scale, a large contingent of 10 states have nine restrictions each, and three (Indiana, Oklahoma, and South Carolina) have 10.

You can also use the sortC function to obtain case-level information sorted by ordinal-level variables. If you sort cases by nominal-level variables, R will output a list of cases grouped together, but the ordering is essentially arbitrary because nominal variables can't be compared in terms of higher or lower values.

EXERCISES

1. (Dataset: world. Variables: women13, country.) What percentage of members of the U.S. House of Representatives are women? In 2013 the number was 17.8 percent, according to the Inter-Parliamentary Union, an international organization of parliaments.[18] How does the United States compare to other democratic countries? Is 17.8 percent comparatively low, comparatively high, or average for a typical national legislature?

    A. The world dataset contains women13, the percentage of women in the lower house of the legislature in each of 90 democracies. (i) Use describe to obtain descriptive statistics for world$women13. (ii) Use wtd.hist to produce a histogram. Fill in the blanks: The mean of women13 is equal to _____. The median is equal to _____.

    B. Analysts generally prefer to use the mean to summarize a variable's central tendency, except in cases where the mean gives a misleading indication of the true center of the distribution. Make a considered judgment. For women13, can the mean be used, or should the median be used instead? (Circle your answer.)

    Mean   Median

    Explain your answer:

    _____

    _____

---

[18] See the Inter-Parliamentary Union web site at http://www.ipu.org/english/home.htm

C. Recall that 17.8 percent of U.S. House members are women. Suppose a women's advocacy organization vows to support female congressional candidates so that the U.S. House might someday "be ranked among the top one-fourth of democracies in the percentage of female members." According to the output from the describe analysis, women would need to constitute what percentage of the House to meet this goal? (Circle one.)

About 21 percent   About 25 percent   About 28 percent

D. Run sortC, using country as the id variable and women13 as the by variable.

Which five countries have the lowest percentages of women in their legislatures?

_____

_____

_____

Which five countries have the highest percentages of women in their legislatures?

_____

_____

_____

E. Create a nicely labeled version of the histogram you produced in part A. Give the horizontal (x-axis) the following label: "Percentage of Women in Legislature". Give the chart this main title: "Percentage Women Legislators 90 Democracies". Print the histogram.

2. (Dataset: gss. Variables: science_quiz, wordsum, wtss.) The late Carl Sagan once lamented: "We live in a society exquisitely dependent on science and technology, in which hardly anyone knows anything about science and technology." Do the data support Sagan's pessimistic assessment? How does the public's grasp of scientific facts compare with other skills, such as word recognition and vocabulary?

The gss dataset contains science_quiz, which was created from 10 questions testing respondents' knowledge of basic scientific facts. Values on science_quiz range from 0 (the respondent did not answer any of the questions correctly) to 10 (the respondent correctly answered all 10).[19] GSS2012 also contains wordsum, which measures respondents' knowledge of the meanings of 10 words. Like science_quiz, wordsum ranged from 0 (the respondent did not know any of the words) to 10 (the respondent knew all 10 words).

---

[19] Science_quiz was created by summing the number of correct responses to the following questions (all are in true-false format, except for earthsun): The center of the Earth is very hot (GSS variable, hotcore); It is the father's gene that decides whether the baby is a boy or a girl (boyorgrl); Electrons are smaller than atoms (electron); The universe began with a huge explosion (bigbang); The continents on which we live have been moving their locations for millions of years and will continue to move in the future (condrift); Human beings, as we know them today, developed from earlier species of animals (evolved); Does the Earth go around the Sun, or does the Sun go around the Earth? (earthsun); All radioactivity is man-made (radioact); Lasers work by focusing sound waves (lasers); Antibiotics kill viruses as well as bacteria (viruses).

A. Run describe, freqC, and wtd.sd on science_quiz and wordsum. Fill in the following table:

	science_quiz	*wordsum*
Mean	?	?
Median	?	?
Mode	?	?
Standard deviation		

B. Consider the following Sagan-esque statement: "The public knows more about words than about science." Based on your results in part A, is this statement correct or incorrect? (Circle one.)

Correct   Incorrect

Explain your reasoning, making specific reference to the statistics you reported in A.

_____

_____

_____

C. Examine the frequency distributions for science_quiz and wordsum. According to conventional academic standards, scores of 9 or 10 on a 10-point quiz would be A's. What percentage of respondents would receive a grade of A on science_quiz? (Fill in the blank.) _____. What percentage of respondents would receive a grade of A on wordsum? (Fill in the blank.) _____.

D. Consider this statement: "Science_quiz has a greater degree of dispersion than wordsum." Is this statement correct or incorrect? (Circle one.)

Correct   Incorrect

Briefly explain your answer:

_____

_____

_____

3. (Dataset: gss. Variable: attend, wtss) The General Social Survey (GSS) provides a rich array of variables that permit scholars to study religiosity among the adult population. The gss dataset contains attend, a 9-point ordered factor that measures how often respondents attend religious services. Values can range from "Never attend" to "Attend more than once a week".

   A. The shell of a bar chart is given below. The categories of attend appear along the horizontal axis. What would a bar chart of attend look like if this variable had maximum dispersion? Sketch inside the axes a bar chart that would depict maximum dispersion.

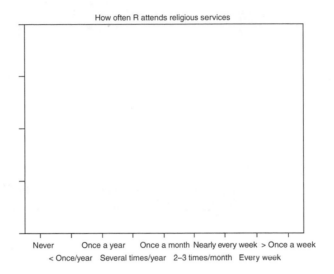

   B. What would a bar chart of attend look like if this variable had no dispersion? Inside the axes, sketch a bar chart that would depict no dispersion.

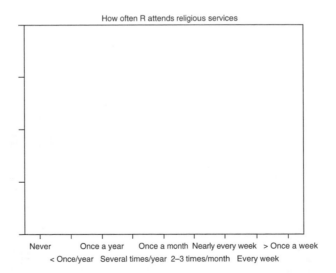

C. Run freqC on attend. (The freqC function will accommodate attend's long value labels.)

    The mode of attend is _____.   The median of attend is _____.

D. Based on your examination of the frequency distribution and bar chart, you would conclude that attend has (Circle one.)

low dispersion.   high dispersion.

Explain your reasoning, making specific reference to the frequency distribution and bar chart.

_____

_____

_____

_____

E. Print the bar chart you created in part C.

F. Exercise a skill you learned in Chapter 1. Use printC to produce a nicely edited table of the frequency distribution you created in part C. Edit the table in word-processing software (e.g., Word). Print the edited table.

3

Transforming Variables

Objective	Functions Introduced	Author or Source
Creating indicator variables	as.numeric {base}	R Development Core Team[1]
Changing variable classes	as.factor {base}	R Development Core Team
	as.ordered {base}	R Development Core Team
	class {base}	R Development Core Team
Adding or modifying labels	levels {base}	R Development Core Team
Collapsing values for simplicity	cut2 {Hmisc}	Frank E. Harrell, Jr.[2]
Centering or standardizing variables	scale {base}	R Development Core Team

When researchers create datasets, they don't know all the ways that other researchers will use their data in the future. We often work with datasets that contain the information we want, just not in the ideal format for our analysis.

There are several situations in which variable transformations become desirable or necessary. The researcher may transform a factor (unordered or ordered) into a numeric indicator variable, coded 1 for all cases having a certain attribute and 0 for all cases not having that attribute. Imagine starting with marital status—an unordered factor with codes that distinguish individuals who are married, divorced, separated, widowed, never married, or partnered—and creating a numeric indicator, coded 1 for all married respondents and 0 for all unmarried respondents. Indicators are essential for graphing relationships between categorical variables (covered in Chapter 4).

In another common circumstance, a researcher may want to collapse a numeric variable, combining its values or codes into a smaller number of theoretically meaningful categories—for example, using respondents' ages to classify them into different political generations. Income is often collapsed into four or five roughly equal-size groups, from lowest income to highest income.

In a somewhat different situation, a dataset may contain several variables that provide similar measures of the same concept. For example, a survey might include a series of questions gauging respondent attitudes toward international affairs. The researcher may combine the codes of these different variables into an additive scale, creating a new and more precise measure.

---

[1] R Development Core Team. (2011). *R: A language and environment for statistical computing*. Vienna, Austria: Author. Available at http://www.R-project.org/

[2] Harrell, F. E., Jr. (2012). *Hmisc: Harrell miscellaneous* (R package version 3.9-3). Contributions from many other users. Available at http://CRAN.R-project.org/package=Hmisc

In this chapter, we explore these functions, plus several others that you will want to add to your R toolkit. The main goal of these variable transformation techniques is to analyze data in the most clear and meaningful terms possible. You can use these methods to present the results of data analysis to an audience in tables and figures with the appropriate level of detail. Sometimes, effective analysis requires greater detail; other times, simplifying variables helps us focus on key relationships and avoid cluttered presentations. The utility of these methods may not be immediately apparent because they are commonly intermediate steps, but we use them often and will refer back to these techniques in later chapters so they're worth learning early on. These methods can help you use datasets for creative, original research.

APPLYING MATHEMATICAL AND LOGICAL OPERATORS TO VARIABLES

Some of the simplest and most useful variable transformations use mathematical operators. As we work through some examples, keep in mind that the variables we're working with are not single-number solutions to algebra problems, but rather long series of values that vary from one observation to the next in a dataset.

In the states dataset, we find the variable prcapinc, which encodes the average income (in dollars) per person in each U.S. state. This is a very precise measure of average individual income in each state, but it may make more sense to analyze the effect of a thousand dollars of additional income rather than the effect of one more dollar. We can modify the units of income, without distorting the data, by creating a new variable from the existing one.

```
# Applying mathematical operator to transform variable
# The new variable should have a different name than the original
states$prcapinc.k = states$prcapinc / 1000
```

A common use of mathematical operators is converting a variable encoded as a percentage to one encoded as a proportion by dividing by 100 (or converting proportions to percentages by multiplying by 100).

Another useful application of math operators is inverting variable values so that higher values correspond to more of the characteristic being measured. Numeric rankings, in particular, can be confusing because the natural interpretation of a "higher" ranking is actually a lower number (i.e. #1 ranking). Strictly speaking, Southern states are ranked more positively by the Brady Campaign to Prevent Gun Violence, a group in favor of gun control laws, than non-Southern states. To avoid the mental gymnastics of "more actually means less," you can invert the rankings so higher values correspond to more gun control laws (the characteristic the Brady Center is really measuring). Since this is already done for you in the states dataset (see states$gun_rank_rev), let's practice using math operators to create a clearer measure of support for a federal program.

Box 3.1	Mathematical Operators in R

Operator	Description
+	Addition
−	Subtraction
*	Multiplication
/	Division
^	Exponents
%%	Modulus (remainder after division)
%/%	Integer Division (drops remainder)

The NES asked respondents whether the federal government should make a concerted effort to improve the social and economic conditions of African Americans. The responses are coded as nes$aidblack_self, with 1 representing a great deal of support for these types of programs and 7 representing the view that the federal government should make no special effort. If you wanted to analyze the average responses for different subpopulations, this coding is potentially confusing because more support for federal aid corresponds to lower numbers. If you found that some condition was positively correlated with this measure of support for federal aid, you'd have to remind yourself (and others) that this actually means less support for aid programs. To facilitate more straightforward analysis, you could apply a simple mathematical operator to invert the scale (so higher scores represent more support for the program being analyzed):

```
# Invert scale for ease of interpretation, 1's become 7's
nes$aidblack_self.rev = 8 - nes$aidblack_self
```

Notice that we're creating a new variable in the NES dataset from this operation, rather than rewriting the original variable. Whenever you transform variables, keep the original variable intact for future reference.[3]

Logical operators apply a statement that is either true or false to each value in a variable. Keeping with our average state income example, we could test whether the per capita income in a state is greater or less than some specific dollar amount. Because our variable states$prcapinc.k is not one number, but rather a series of 50 numbers, R will apply the logical statement to each entry, rendering a series of TRUE and FALSE results. For example, we could use a logical operator to identify states where the average income is more than the mean state income.

```
states$prcapinc.k > wtd.mean(states$prcapinc.k)  # Applying Logical Operator
```

As was the case with mathematical operators, there is a set of logical operators available in R. You can apply more than one logical operator using the "&" operator (when you want to test if several logical operators are true at once). Similarly, you can use the "|" operator to test if any logical operator is true. If you write statements using "&" and/or "|", use parentheses to make your code clearer and less confusing.

Box 3.2 Logical Operators in R

Operator	Description
>	Greater than
<	Less than
>=	Greater than or equal to
<=	Less than or equal to
==	Exactly equal to
!=	Not equal to
|	Or
&	And

The logical operator == (double equals) should not be confused with the assignment operator = (single equal sign). For example, nes$gender == "Female" is rendered as a logical statement, testing whether the value of the variable gender in the NES data is equal to the value "Female". By contrast, nes$gender = "Female" (don't enter this!) is an assignment statement that will set the value of the variable gender to "Female" for every entry in the NES dataset (reassigning the gender of thousands of males from a simple typo!).

Another word of caution when working with logical operators: R's case sensitivity frequently comes into play when working with logical operators, particularly when variable values are encoded as text. If you enter any of the following statements: nes$gender == "female", nes$gender == "F", nes$gender == "Woman", or

---

[3] The R function to reverse a vector, rev(), should not be used to reverse the numeric values of a scale. The rev() function changes the order, but not the values of a variable. In other words, rev() will make the first observation last and the last observation first but will not change their values.

nes$gender == "FEMALE", the result will be FALSE for every observation in the NES dataset because the value in quotation marks doesn't exactly match the value used to identify women in the NES dataset, "Female".[4]

When you work with observational data, you are certain to encounter missing data, which appear as NA in R. What happens when you apply a mathematical or logical operator to missing data? Because missing values are unknown, the results of mathematical or logical operations are indeterminate and remain NA.

CREATING INDICATOR VARIABLES

In the preceding section, we looked at logical operators that apply a statement and report whether the statement is TRUE or FALSE for each observation. Indicator variables are numeric interpretations of logic statements. An indicator is a numeric variable that can take on only two values: 1 for any case having a measured attribute, and 0 for any case not having that attribute. Indicator variables, also known as dummy variables or binary variables, are essential for many of R's graphing functions (and other R functions that work with numbers rather than text). Indicator variables are frequently used to analyze the difference that belonging to a group makes on some outcome of interest.

We can create indicators using logical operators. (It's helpful to see a logical operator produce a series of TRUE and FALSE values to understand how logical operators work, but you should store the result as an object to make it easy to use the results of the operator.) Imagine, for example, we wanted to analyze whether military veterans have different political opinions than those who never served in the military. The GSS dataset records how many years respondents served in the military (gss$vetyears), but we simply want to distinguish people with no military experience from those with any number of service years. We can apply a logical operator and the as.numeric() function to the existing ordinal variable to create a nominal indicator.

```
# Creating a numeric indicator variable
gss$veteran = gss$vetyears != "NONE"     # Any years of service yields TRUE
gss$veteran = as.numeric(gss$veteran)    # TRUE and FALSE values now 1s and 0s
```

In this example, the as.numeric function translates TRUE and FALSE values into a series of 1's and 0's (TRUE becomes 1 and FALSE becomes 0). We can accomplish the same result in one line of code by nesting the logical operator inside the as.numeric function, but it might be easier to understand creating indicator variables as a two-step process initially.

The most error-prone part of this process occurs in typing the level name accurately. Remember, we are comparing values recorded as text (not numbers) and some human researcher had to decide whether no years of military service should be recorded as "NONE", "none", "None", "NO", "Nil", or some other equivalent expression. You need to know how the responses were actually recorded so the logical operation is applied properly. To ensure the error-free creation of an indicator from a factor, follow these steps:
(1) Run the levels command on the original variable to check the existing values of the variable.
(2) Select/copy the level name in the console, including the quotation marks. (3) Paste the value into the logical expression.

When you generate an indicator variable, it's a good idea to verify that your efforts have yielded the desired results. Sticking with our veterans indicator, we could compare the frequency distribution of the original variable to our new variable using the following lines of code:

```
freq(gss$vetyears)          # Make sure indicator variable correct
freq(gss$veteran)           # by comparing frequencies
```

---

[4] It helps to remember that these data are recorded by real people. There's no universal rule of political science research that requires researchers record a survey respondent's gender as "female", "Female", or "FEMALE", so it's helpful to get to know how variables you work with are actually encoded.

```
gss$vetyears
                    Frequency   Percent Valid Percent
NONE                     1745    88.399        88.534
LESS THAN 2 YRS            49     2.482         2.486
2 TO 4 YEARS             107     5.420         5.429
MORE THAN 4 YRS           70     3.546         3.551
SOME,DK HOW LONG           0     0.000         0.000
NA's                       3     0.152
Total                   1974   100.000       100.000


gss$veteran
        Frequency   Percent Valid Percent
0            1745    88.399        88.53
1             226    11.449        11.47
NA's            3     0.152
Total        1974   100.000       100.00
```

Does the percentage of GSS respondents in the "NONE" category match the percentage of respondents with 0's as the value of our new gss$veteran variable? If so, we've successfully created our indicator variable; if not, we'll troubleshoot our R code piece by piece to find the error.

CHANGING VARIABLE CLASSES

You will often encounter variables with different levels of measurement. Political scientists generally use three levels of measurement to classify variables: nominal, ordinal, and interval. Levels of measurement are important because we use different methods depending on the levels of measurement involved. The terminology used in R to describe levels of measurement takes a little getting used to, but you may sometimes need to change the level, or class, of a variable for an R function to work correctly. In the R environment, nominal variables are known as unordered factors; ordinal variables are considered ordered factors, and interval variables are classified as numerics.

Unlike other data analysis software, R is quite rigid in its definition of variable classes. Functions that run fine for numeric variables will not run for factors, and vice versa. For example, when you use the freq() function, you need to work with an ordered factor to see a column of cumulative frequencies in your frequency distribution table; however, you must apply the function to a numeric variable to obtain information on numbers of cases, missing cases, means, and percentiles. Fortunately, in some situations, you can reclassify a numeric as a factor, or a factor as a numeric.

For example, consider gss$authoritarianism, a numeric variable that summarizes GSS respondents' support for order and conformity. The values of this variable range from 0 to 7, with higher numbers corresponding to more support for authoritarianism. The following two expressions create two new variables from authoritarianism, an unordered factor (gss$authoritarianism.nom) and an ordered factor (gss$authoritarianism.ord):

```
# Changing variable classes
# The as.factor function creates an unordered factor
gss$authoritarianism.nom = as.factor(gss$authoritarianism)


# The as.ordered function creates an unordered factor
gss$authoritarianism.ord = as.ordered(gss$authoritarianism)
```

The class() function is used to check how a variable is classified in the R environment. This function can help diagnose the cause of errors that arise when we attempt to apply a function to the wrong class of variable. We can also use the class() function to verify that we have created a factor and an ordered factor from the numeric variable gss$authoritarianism.

```
class(gss$authoritarianism.nom)      # Should be a factor
class(gss$authoritarianism.ord)      # Should be an ordered factor
class(gss$authoritarianism)          # original version is a numeric
```

Suppose you want to go the other way and define a factor as a numeric. This transformation may be necessary to summarize the mean value of a variable for different groups (for example, if we wanted to compare the average party identification for veterans and non-veterans). It is also useful if we want to incorporate an ordinal-level measure as a control variable in a regression model without creating a large number of dummy variables. The as.numeric function will usually permit you to do this. The following expression creates a numeric, gss$partyid.n, from a factor, gss$partyid:

```
gss$partyid.n = as.numeric(gss$partyid)      # creates a numeric variable
class(gss$partyid.n)                          # confirm new variable class
```

After you create a numeric version of gss$partyid, it's a good idea to check your work. For example, you might use the freq() command to compare the distribution of the original factor variable, gss$partyid, with the newly created numeric, gss$partyid.n. These variables should have the same distributions, but different labels. You couldn't calculate the mean of the original variable but should be able to find the mean of gss$partyid.n.

ADDING OR MODIFYING VARIABLE LABELS

Although an indicator variable should be encoded as a numeric for some types of analysis, you may want a nicely labeled factor version of an indicator, to be used in cross-tabulation or mean comparison analysis. (R does not permit text value labels for numerics.) This is easily accomplished with the as.factor and levels functions. We introduced the as.factor function in the preceding section. The generic syntax for the levels function is:

```
levels(varname) = c("label1", "label2", "label3", … , "labeln")
```

As you saw earlier, you can also use the levels function to check a variable's level names. Simply type "levels(*varname*)".

Let's add labels to the indicator variable we created earlier, gss$veteran, which encoded GSS respondents with any years of military service as 1's and those with no years of service as 0's. This works well for some purposes, but it isn't very clear and descriptive on a table or plot. To accomplish this, we'll create a factor version of our indicator variable and then label its levels "No" and "Yes".

```
gss$veteran.f = as.factor(gss$veteran)       # creates a factor variable
levels(gss$veteran.f) = c("No", "Yes")       # label levels of the factor
freq(gss$veteran.f)                          # confirm variable labels
```

```
gss$veteran.f
          Frequency  Percent  Valid Percent
No             1745   88.399          88.53
Yes             226   11.449          11.47
NA's              3    0.152
Total          1974  100.000         100.00
```

When you look at the output of the last command in the box above, make sure you've labelled the larger category of respondents "No" and the smaller group "Yes". (Approximately 10% of GSS respondents served any time in the military.)

If we are working with a variable that's already a factor, modifying the levels is a straightforward operation and can make our results clearer. In Chapter 2, we looked at NES respondents' opinions on the job being done by Congress. The levels of the variable nes$congapp_job_x are abbreviated in the dataset. If we wanted to share the results of our analysis with an audience, we might write out the abbreviations to make the response categories clearer.

```
levels(nes$congapp_job_x)                    # check level order first
levels(nes$congapp_job_x) = c("Strong Approval",  "Weak Approval",
                    "Weak Disapproval", "Strong Disapproval")
freq(nes$congapp_job_x)                       # Create table with clear labels
```

```
nes$congapp_job_x
                    Frequency  Percent  Valid Percent
Strong Approval        342.3   5.786           6.177
Weak Approval          899.8  15.209          16.236
Weak Disapproval      1343.9  22.717          24.250
Strong Disapproval    2955.9  49.964          53.337
NA's                   374.1   6.323
Total                 5916.0 100.000         100.000
```

COLLAPSING VARIABLES INTO SIMPLIFIED CATEGORIES

For collapsing numeric variables into specifically defined categories, or into equal-size groups, the cut2 function from the Hmisc package is the function of choice. In this guided example, you will collapse the numeric variable, gss$age (respondents' ages in years), into five defined categories: youngest-30, 31-40, 41-50, 51-60, and 61-oldest. First, use the describe function to obtain basic information about the range of gss$age values:

```
describe(gss$age)                    # check variable info before collapsing
```

```
gss$age
            n   missing  unique  Info   Mean   .05  .10  .25  .50
         1969         5      72     1  48.19    22   25   33   47
          .75       .90     .95
           61        73      79
lowest: 18 19 20 21 22, highest: 85 86 87 88 89
```

The age of GSS respondents ranges from 18 to 89 years.[5]

The cut2 function will collapse a numeric into specified intervals. Let's look at the usage statement for this function:

$$newvar = cut2(x, \ cuts \ ... \ )$$

So we supply the cut2 function a numeric variable, referred to generically as "x" in the usage statement, and a numeric vector that specifies the cut points for the categories of a new variable. (We'll look at some of the additional, optional arguments that can be supplied to the cut2 function after we illustrate its basic usage with the gss$age variable.)

To collapse gss$age into a five-category factor, gss$age5, we could first define the cut points we want to use and then apply them to the numeric variable using the cut2 function.

```
cutpoints = c(31, 41, 51, 61, 90)   # define upper limit of each category
gss$age5 = cut2(gss$age, cutpoints) # apply cutpoints to numeric variable
                                    # don't overwrite original variable
                                    # give new variable a different name
```

By and large, the cut2 function has a familiar look. We could supply the vector of cut points as the second argument to cut2, but it helps to take things one step at a time at first. Take a close look at the line that creates the "cutpoints" object. For each category, you must specify a cut point that is one unit higher than the desired category's upper boundary. For example, because 30 is the desired upper boundary of the first category (18-30), the cut point is "31". Follow the plus-1 rule. It will always work, without fail.[6]

---

[5] To obtain accurate descriptive statistics, we would want to incorporate weights in our describe function call. Here, we're simply looking for a basic understanding of the range of gss$age values.

[6] The highest category allows an exception to the plus-1 rule: If the user specifies the highest observed value, cut2 will work fine. So, 'c(31, 41, 51, 61, 90)', would return the same categories of nes$age5 as would, 'c(31, 41, 51, 61)'.

If we now apply the freq() function to gss$age5, R will generate a frequency distribution table as well as a bar plot, but with rather odd value labels. What does the label "[18, 31)" mean? In R esoterica, the square left-hand bracket means "interval includes the next value," and the right parenthesis means "interval excludes the preceding value." While technically precise, these labels may be more confusing than enlightening.

Now is a perfect time to use the levels function to supply useful labels for factor values and the as.ordered function to appropriately classify our new ordinal variable. When cut2 collapses a numeric, it produces an unordered factor, the lowest factor class. We can use the as.ordered function to upgrade the status of a true ordinal variable. This bit of fine-tuning allows us to generate clear and informative results.

```
# label the new variable's level and set class to ordered factor
levels(gss$age5) = c("18-30", "31-40", "41-50", "51-60", "61-")
gss$age5 = as.ordered(gss$age5)

freq(gss$age5, gss$wtss)          # clearer labels, cumulative percent column
```

gss$age5

	Frequency	Percent	Valid Percent	Cum Percent
18-30	448.476	22.7077	22.77	22.77
31-40	367.215	18.5932	18.64	41.41
41-50	367.279	18.5964	18.64	60.05
51-60	347.087	17.5740	17.62	77.67
61-	439.799	22.2683	22.33	100.00
NA's	5.144	0.2604		
Total	1975.001	100.0000	100.00	

In the next example, we'll use the cut2 function to divide a numeric variable into equal-sized groups. Rather than specifying the cut points, as we did with the gss$age5 example, we'll specify the number of equal-sized categories we want to create. To do this, we'll set the optional groups argument, "g", to the number of equal-sized groups we want to create from a numeric variable. For example, if we wanted to compare countries of the world based on varying urban densities, we could divide observations in the world dataset into five categories.

```
# Collapse variable into equal sized categories
# "g" argument is number of categories to create
world$pop_urban.5cat = cut2(world$pop_urban, g=5)
```

Figure 3.1 Ages of GSS Respondents, Five Categories

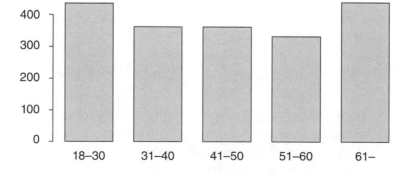

In the preceding examples, we collapsed numeric variables into ordinal categories. What if the original variable is already an ordered factor but has more levels than we want? In other words, we want to collapse some of the categories of an ordinal variable. There are at least a couple of ways to do this.

If the number of categories of the original variable isn't very large, you can simply redefine the levels, using the same label for the categories you want to join together. You want to create a new variable when you do this and keep the original variable intact. Recall the NES variable that asked respondents their opinion about the job being done by Congress. Let's simply separate the responses into "Approve" and "Disapprove" categories.

```
levels(nes$congapp_job_x)                    # Levels of original variable

nes$congapp_2cat = nes$congapp_job_x         # Copy original as new variable
levels(nes$congapp_2cat) = c("Approve", "Approve", "Disapprove","Disapprove")

levels(nes$congapp_2cat)                      # Levels of the new variable
```

```
[1] "AppStrng"    "AppWeak"    "DisappWk"   "DisappStr"
[1] "Approve"     "Disapprove"
```

If the number of categories of the original ordered factor is large, manually overwriting the levels as we did with nes$congapp_2cat can be a bit tedious and prone to typing errors. Instead, you can apply the as.numeric function to the original variable and then use the cut2 function's "cuts" or "g" arguments to create new categories. To illustrate, consider the variable measuring GSS respondents' family income, gss$income06. Rather than specify a dollar amount, respondents are categoried into 25 family income ranges. We may prefer to work with less detail and broader categories.

```
gss$income06.n = as.numeric(gss$income06)    # Create numeric version of var.
cutpoints = c(11, 21, 26)                    # Group numbers, not $ income
gss$income06.3cat = cut2(gss$income06.n, cutpoints)

# alternative method, split into 4 equal sized groups
gss$income06.4groups = cut2(gss$income06.n, g=4)

# Add labels to levels and classify as ordinal variable
levels(gss$income06.3cat) = c("Under $15k", "$15k - $74.9k", "$75k and Over")
gss$income06.3cat = as.ordered(gss$income06.3cat)
levels(gss$income06.4groups) = c("First Quartile", "Second Quartile",
                                 "Third Quartile", "Fourth Quartile")
gss$income06.4groups = as.ordered(gss$income06.4groups)
```

The challenge of specifying cut points in this case is keeping track of the numeric equivalent of the income brackets of the gss$income06 variable (i.e., that the 11th level is family incomes "$15000 TO $17499"). The numeric version of gss$income06 yields the number of the group, not the income in thousands of dollars. Specifying the cut points gives us more control over the resulting categories than simply setting the number of groups we want to create. Whether we collapsed categories by specifying cut points or the desired number of groups, both approaches collapsed the 25-category family income variable gss$income06 into a smaller number of categories.

CENTERING OR STANDARDIZING A NUMERIC VARIABLE

In some situations, it is helpful to transform an interval-level variable by centering or standardizing its value. Centering a variable means subtracting the variable's mean value from each observation. Standardizing takes this a bit further by dividing the result by the standard deviation of the variable. These transformations are useful when we are not particularly interested in the units of measurement but are interested in the difference that a standard deviation of the variable makes. The scale() function in the base installation of R can be used to center or standardize variables. The generic usage statement of this function is:

```
scale(x, center = TRUE, scale = T)
```

The "x" here is a numeric variable you want to transform; "center" and "scale" are arguments that can be set to TRUE or FALSE (they are true by default not specified in the function call).

Let's apply the scale function to an interesting variable in the states dataset, gun_dealer, which is equal to the number of gun dealers per 100,000 people in each state. We could center or standardize this variable to focus on whether a state has more or fewer gun dealers than other states.

```
# center variable by subtracting mean
states$gun_dealer.centered = scale(states$gun_dealer, scale=FALSE)

# standardize by subtracting mean, dividing by standard deviation
states$gun_dealer.standard = scale(states$gun_dealer)
```

The values of the two new variables created by the code above, states$gun_dealer.centered and states$gun_dealer.standard, will have the same distribution as the original variable, states$gun_dealer (you can confirm this using the freq or wtd.hist functions), but the scale of measurement will change.[7] By default, the scale function will output results in a matrix format (listing our new values in a column). You can convert the output to a vector in which the values are listed in a row using the as.vector() function.

CREATING AN ADDITIVE INDEX

Creating additive scales is about as straightforward a task as you will encounter in R. Often a dataset will contain several variables that measure the same concept. Researchers will combine these different variables into an *additive index*, creating a more precise measure of the concept. Additive indexes allow researchers to achieve higher levels of measurement of variables they're interested in and to reduce random measurement error.

Consider a simple illustration. Suppose you have three variables, each of which measures whether someone engaged in the following political activities:

- Wrote a letter to a newspaper about a political issue
- Joined a protest march
- Posted a message on Facebook or Twitter about politics

Each variable is identically coded: 0 if the respondent did not engage in the activity and 1 if he or she did. Now, each of these variables is interesting in its own right, but you might want to add them together to create an overall measure of political engagement. People who did not engage in any of these activities would end up with a value of 0 on the new variable; those who engaged in one activity, a code of 1; two activities, a code of 2; and all three activities, a code of 3.[8]

Here are a couple of rules to follow when creating a simple additive index. First, make sure that each of the variables is identically coded. In the above illustration, if the "letter to newspaper" variable were coded 1 for no and 2 for yes, and the other variables were coded 0 and 1, the resulting additive index would be incorrect. Second, make sure that the variables are all coded in the same *direction*. If the "protest march" variable were coded 0 for yes and 1 for no, and the other variables were coded 0 for no and 1 for yes, the additive index would again be incorrect.[9]

The GSS dataset includes a good example of an additive index created from a series of related questions about circumstances that justify having an abortion. The survey asked respondents whether they thought abortion was justified in seven different conditions (summarized by Figure 3.2):

---

[7] The remaining possible usage of the scale function in this example, scale(states$gun_dealer, center=F), yields a transformation that is not particularly useful. In this specification, the value of gun_dealer in each state is divided by the root mean square of the variable, a measure of deviation from 0 (as opposed to deviation from the mean, which is the variable's standard deviation).

[8] These three variables are found in the NES dataset along with seven additional variables about respondents' political engagement. See NES variables with stem "dhsinvolv" in the Appendix for more information. These variables present the opportunity to create a finely tuned measure of political engagement.

[9] Survey datasets are notorious for "reverse coding." Survey designers do this so that respondents don't fall into response bias or automatically give the same response to a series of questions. Be on the lookout for reverse coding in your future research.

1. Strong chance of serious birth defect (gss$abdefect)

2. Woman's health seriously endangered (gss$abhlth)

3. Married woman wants no more children (gss$abnomore)

4. Parents can't afford more children (gss$abpoor)

5. Pregnant as result of rape (gss$abrape)

6. Mother not married (gss$absingle)

7. If woman wants for any reason (gss$abany)

For each of these variables, respondents replied either "YES" or "NO". The yeses all express more permissive attitudes about abortion. To create the additive index, gss$abortion, that's already included in the GSS dataset, each "YES" response is converted to a 1 (using the process for creating indicator variables outlined above) and the 1's are added together. Here is sample code that reproduces the abortion scale gss$abortion.

```
# indicator variable created for each abortion variable
gss$abdefect.n = as.numeric(gss$abdefect=="YES")
gss$abhlth.n   = as.numeric(gss$abhlth  =="YES")
gss$abnomore.n = as.numeric(gss$abnomore=="YES")
gss$abpoor.n   = as.numeric(gss$abpoor  =="YES")
gss$abrape.n   = as.numeric(gss$abrape  =="YES")
gss$absingle.n = as.numeric(gss$absingle=="YES")
gss$abany.n    = as.numeric(gss$abany   =="YES")

# individual indicators added together to create 0-7 scale
gss$abortion.scale = gss$abdefect.n + gss$abhlth.n + gss$abnomore.n +
                     gss$abpoor.n   + gss$abrape.n + gss$absingle.n +
                     gss$abany.n

# describe the additive index to see results
freqC(gss$abortion.scale, gss$wtss)
```

	Frequency	Percent	Valid Percent
0	122.02	6.178	11.253
1	73.60	3.726	6.787
2	121.20	6.137	11.177
3	172.93	8.756	15.947
4	83.66	4.236	7.715
5	56.04	2.837	5.168
6	46.46	2.353	4.285
7	408.48	20.682	37.669
NA's	890.61	45.094	
Total	1975.00	100.000	100.000

While this may seem like a lot of extra work, upgrading our measurement of individuals' attitudes about abortion allows us to apply simpler statistical methods. Consider, for example, comparing how different subpopulations feel about abortion rights. If we are limited to seven yes/no questions, we may be compelled to compare subpopulation responses to each question. In contrast, when we use an additive index, which is an interval-level measure of the concept being measured in each of the yes/no questions, we can summarize each group's sentiment by calculating the mean of its additive index values and compare groups using a single number.

Figure 3.2 Public Opinion on Number of Acceptable Reasons for Abortion

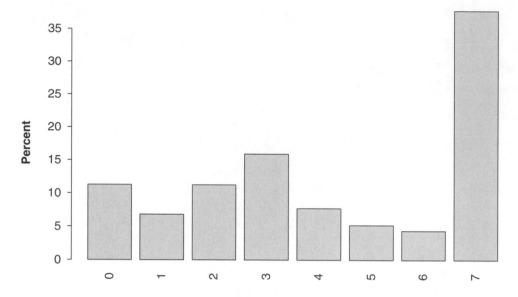

In the preceding examples involving political engagement and abortion attitudes, additive indexes were created by summing a series of nominal-level variables. It's also possible to create an additive index from a series of related ordinal-level variables. The patriotism scale in the NES dataset, nes$patriotism, provides a nice example of an additive index based on ordinal variables. NES respondents were asked on a 1–5 scale the importance they place on being an American (nes$patriot_amident), the emotion they feel seeing the American flag fly (nes$patriot_flag), and their love of the country (nes$patriot_love). It's important to pay attention to how each of these three ordinal variables is coded because they aren't coded in the same direction. To create the additive index, you need to invert the values of two of the ordinal variables before summing them together. Here is sample code to replicate the nes$patriotism additive index.

```
# ordinal variables converted to numerics coded in the same direction
nes$patriot_amident.n = 5 - as.numeric(nes$patriot_amident)
nes$patriot_flag.n    = 5 - as.numeric(nes$patriot_flag)
nes$patriot_love.n    =     as.numeric(nes$patriot_love) - 1

# individual questions added together to create 0-12 scale
nes$patriotism.scale = nes$patriot_amident.n + nes$patriot_flag.n +
                   nes$patriot_love.n

# describe the additive index to see results
freqC(nes$patriotism.scale, nes$wt)
```

	Frequency	Percent	Valid Percent
0	4.00	0.06762	0.07351
1	10.83	0.18299	0.19893
2	30.97	0.52344	0.56906
3	48.70	0.82317	0.89491
4	110.04	1.86003	2.02212
5	101.16	1.70987	1.85888
6	298.94	5.05301	5.49337
7	278.68	4.71063	5.12115
8	393.29	6.64787	7.22722
9	567.82	9.59800	10.43445
10	749.47	12.66857	13.77261
11	987.41	16.69046	18.14500
12	1860.47	31.44815	34.18879
NA's	474.24	8.01620	
Total	5916.00	100.00000	100.00000

Figure 3.3 Scale of Patriotic Feelings in the General Public

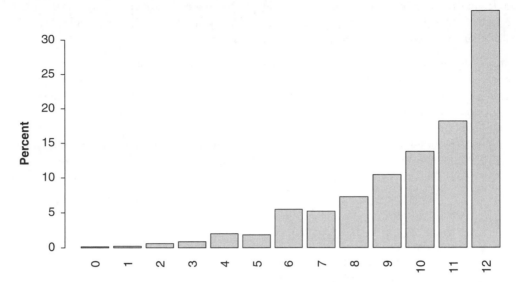

The additive index reveals greater variation in respondents' patriotism. We can now make some fairly subtle distinctions among respondents and compare the patriotism of different subpopulations in the dataset by calculating means. In the next chapter, you'll learn how to make comparisons among groups using R and present the results of these comparisons effectively in tables and figures.

EXERCISES

1. (Dataset: gss. Variables: polviews, wtss.) The gss dataset contains polviews, a seven-category factor that measures political ideology—the extent to which individuals "think of themselves as liberal or conservative."

    A. Run freq on gss$polviews, making sure to weight by gss$wtss. Add up the percentages of all liberals. The percentage of respondents who are either "extremely liberal," "liberal," or "slightly liberal" is (Fill in the blank.)

    _____ percent.

    B. The percentage of "moderates is equal to (Fill in the blank.)

    _____ percent.

    C. Now add up the percentages of all conservatives. The percentage of respondents who are either "slightly conservative," "conservative," or "extremely conservative" is (Fill in the blank.)

    _____ percent.

    D. You are going to use cut2 to create a new variable, gss$polview3, that combines the three liberal categories, keeps moderates in their own category, and combines the three conservative categories. Cut2 will not work on factors, so use the as.numeric function to create a numeric version of gss$polviews. Name the numeric version gss$polviews.n. Run freq on gss$polviews.n (again weighting by gss$wtss).

    On gss$polviews.n, liberals have the following three numeric codes: _____, _____, _____.

    On gss$polviews.n, moderates have the following numeric code: _____.

    On gss$polviews.n, conservatives have the following three numeric codes: _____, _____, _____.

    E. Use cut2 to create a new variable, gss$polview3. Collapse gss$polviews.n's three liberal codes, keep moderates in their own category, and collapse the three conservative codes. Remember to apply cut2's plus-1 rule. Run freq on gss$polview3, weighting by gss$wtss. Record the percentages in each category (Fill in the blanks.):

    [1, 4) _____   4 _____   [5, 8) _____

Before proceeding, make sure that the percentages you just recorded match the percentages (rounded to two decimals) you calculated in parts A, B, and C. If they match, move on to part F. If they do not match, check the cut2 expression that you typed. Make sure that you followed the plus-1 rule. Also, check to ensure that your freq runs in parts A and E included gss$wtss.

F. Supply gss$polview3 with the following level names: "Liberal", "Moderate", and "Conservative". Use as.ordered to define gss$polview3 as an ordered factor. To check your work, run freq on gss$polview3. Run freq on gss$polview3 once more, this time wrapping it inside printC. Copy/paste the frequency distribution from Table.Output.html into your word processor. Print the table.

2. (Dataset: gss. Variables: income06, wtss.) The gss dataset contains income06. In this exercise, you will use cut2 (with the "g=" argument) to collapse gss$income06 into four equal-sized groups. Follow these steps: (i) Create a numeric version of gss$income06. Name the numeric version gss$income06.n. (ii) Collapse gss$income06.n into four equal-size groups. Name the collapsed variable gss$income06.n4. (iii) Give gss$income06.n4 these level names: "Low", "MedLow", "MedHigh", "High". (iv) Redefine gss$income06.n4 as an ordered factor.

A. Run freq on gss$income06.n4. Print the bar chart of gss$income06.n4.

B. Run printC on the frequency distribution of gss$income06.n4. Copy/paste the frequency distribution into a word-processing document. Print the frequency table.

3. (Dataset: gss. Variables: grass, wtss.) The gss dataset contains the factor grass, which taps respondent opinions about the legalization of marijuana, using levels "LEGAL" and "NOT LEGAL". In this exercise, you will use gss$grass to create an indicator, named gss$grass.yes, coded 1 for respondents who favor legalization ("LEGAL") and coded 0 for those who do not favor legalization ("NOT LEGAL").

A. Run freq on gss$grass, making sure to weight by gss$wtss. What percentage favor legalization? (Fill in the blank.)

_____ percent

B. Run levels on gss$grass. Using the level name for pro-legalization, enlist as.numeric to create an indicator, named gss$grass.yes, coded 1 for those who favor legalization and coded 0 for those who do not favor legalization. Run freq on gss$grass.yes. What percentage are coded 1 on gss$grass.yes? (Fill in the blank.)

_____ percent

Before proceeding, make sure that the percentage you just recorded in part B matches the percentage you recorded in part A. If they do not match, review the procedure for creating indicator variables.

4. (Dataset: gss. Variables: mslm_col.n, mslm_lib.n, mslm_spk.n, wtss.) The gss dataset contains three numerics that gauge tolerance toward "anti-American Muslim clergymen"—whether they should be allowed to teach in college (gss$mslm_col.n), whether their books should be removed from the library (gss$mslm_lib.n), and whether they should be allowed to preach hatred of the United States (gss$mslm_spk.n). For each variable, a less tolerant response has a numeric code of 0 and a more tolerant response is coded 1.

A. Imagine creating an additive index from these three variables. The additive index would have scores that range between what two values?

Between a score of _____ and a score of _____

B. Suppose a respondent takes the more tolerant position on two questions and the less tolerant position on the third question. What score would this respondent have?

A score of _____

C. Create an additive index, named gss$muslim_tol, by summing gss$mslm_col.n, gss$mslm_lib.n, and gss$mslm_spk.n. Run freq on gss$muslim_tol, weighting by gss$wtss. Record the scores, frequencies, and valid percentages in the table below.

Score on gss$muslim_tol	Frequency	Valid Percent
?	?	?
?	?	?
?	?	?
?	?	?
	100.0	

D. Use cut2 to recode gss$muslim_tol into three defined categories, as follows: Make the lowest code its own category; combine the middle two codes into one category; make the highest code its own category. Make sure to apply cut2's plus-1 rule. You can give the collapsed variable a new name, or you can continue with the name gss$muslim_tol. (If the cut2 run goes badly, you can easily go back and re-create gss$muslim_tol from the three original variables.) Run freq on the newly collapsed variable. Make sure that your cut2 run correctly collapsed the middle two codes and left the lowest and highest codes unchanged. If the collapsed variable is incorrect, review the cut2 procedure for collapsing a numeric into defined groups.

E. Define gss$muslim_tol as an ordered factor. Supply these level names: "Low", "Middle", "High". To check your work, run freq on gss$muslim_tol. Run printC on the freq command. Copy/paste from Table.Output .html. Print the frequency distribution.

Making Comparisons

Objective	Functions Introduced	Author or Source
Performing cross-tabulations	xtp[1] {poliscidata}	Philip Pollock and Barry Edwards
Conducting mean comparisons	compmeans[2] {descr}	Jakson Aquino[1]
Visualizing comparisons of proportions or means	plotmeansC[3] {poliscidata}	Philip Pollock and Barry Edwards
Generating box plots with weighted data	svyboxplot[4] {survey}	Thomas Lumley[1]
Visualizing mean comparisons	stripchart[5] {graphics}	R Development Core Team[6]

A ll hypothesis testing in political research follows a common logic of comparison. The researcher separates subjects into categories of the independent variable and then compares these groups on the dependent variable. For example, suppose you think that gender (independent variable) affects opinions about gun control (dependent variable) and that women are more likely than men to favor gun control. You would divide individuals into two groups on the basis of gender, women and men, and then compare the percentage of women who favor gun control with the percentage of men who favor gun control. Similarly, if you hypothesize that Republicans have higher incomes than do Democrats, you would divide individuals into partisanship groups

---

[1] Li, Q. (2013). *An R companion to political analysis*. Based on crosstab {descr}, Aquino, J. (2012). *descr: Descriptive statistics* (R package version 0.9.8). Includes R source code and/or documentation written by Dirk Enzmann, Marc Schwartz, and Nitin Jain (2012).

[2] Aquino, J. (2012). *descr: Descriptive statistics* (R package version 0.9.8). Includes R source code and/or documentation written by Dirk Enzmann, Marc Schwartz, and Nitin Jain (2012).

[3] Based on {gplots}, Warnes, G. R. (2012). *gplots: Various R programming tools for plotting data* (R package version 2.11.0). Gplots includes R source code and/or documentation contributed by Ben Bolker, Lodewijk Bonebakker, Robert Gentleman, Wolfgang Huber Andy Liaw, Thomas Lumley, Martin Maechler, Arni Magnusson, Steffen Moeller, Marc Schwartz, and Bill Venables. PlotmeansC calls svydesign and svyby. Based on {survey}, Lumley, T. (2012). *survey: Analysis of complex survey samples* (R package version 3.28-2). Available at http://cran.r-project.org/web/packages/survey/index.html. See also: Lumley, T. (2004). Analysis of complex survey samples. *Journal of Statistical Software*, 9(1), 1–19; Lumley, T. (2010). *Complex surveys: A guide to analysis using R*. Hoboken, NJ: John Wiley & Sons.

[4] T. Lumley, {survey}.

[5] R Development Core Team, {graphics}.

[6] R Development Core Team. (2011). *R: A language and environment for statistical computing*. Vienna, Austria: Author. Available at http://www.R-project.org/

(independent variable), Republicans and Democrats, and compare the average income (dependent variable) of Republicans with that of Democrats.

Although the logic of comparison is always the same, the appropriate method depends on the level of measurement of the independent and dependent variables. In this chapter, you will learn to address two common hypothesis-testing situations: those in which both the independent and the dependent variables are nominal or ordinal (unordered factors or ordered factors), and those in which the independent variable is a factor and the dependent variable is interval level (numeric). Box 4.1 provides a summary guide to the data analysis and graphics techniques covered in this chapter. For situations in which both the independent and dependent variables are factors, you will learn cross-tabulation analysis using the xtp function. When the independent variable is a factor and the dependent variable is numeric (interval level), you will perform mean comparison analysis using the compmeans function. The xtp function automatically produces a mosaic plot, which helps you visualize the cross-tabulation relationship. The plotting function, plotmeansC, designed as an accompaniment for mean comparison analysis, can be adapted to produce line charts for cross-tabulations as well. For numeric dependent variables, two additional graphic forms come into play: box plots (using the svyboxplot function) and strip charts (using the strip chart function).

Box 4.1 Analysis Guide

Independent Variable	Dependent Variable	Analysis {function}	Graphics {function}	Comments
Factor	Factor	Cross-tabulation {xtp}	Line charts of indicator variable {plotmeansC}	Create indicator from one value of the dependent variable. Multiply indicator times 100 to graph percentages.
Factor	Numeric	Mean comparison {compmeans}	Line charts of dependent variable {plotmeansC} Box plots {svyboxplot} Strip charts {stripchart}	Use box plots for weighted or unweighted data. Use strip charts for smaller, unweighted datasets.

CROSS-TABULATIONS AND MOSAIC PLOTS

Cross-tabulations are the workhorse vehicles for testing hypotheses for factor variables. When setting up a cross-tabulation, you must observe the following three rules.

1. Put the independent variable on the columns and the dependent variable on the rows.

2. Always obtain column percentages, not row percentages.

3. Test the hypothesis by comparing the percentages of subjects who fall into the same category of the dependent variable.

Consider this hypothesis, which we will test using the nes dataset: In a comparison of individuals, Democrats will be more likely than Republicans to have pro-environment opinions. The dependent variable, nes$envjob_3, gauges opinions about the trade-off between environmental protection and jobs. Respondents can choose "environment over jobs," take a middle position, or choose "jobs over environment." The independent variable, nes$pid_3, measures party identification: Democrat, Independent, or Republican. The *R Companion* workspace includes the function xtp based on the crosstab function in the descr package. The xtp function will produce a proper cross-tabulation, constructed according to the rules, and a mosaic plot, a classic representation of cross-tabular relationships.[7] Also, xtp automatically exports the cross-tabulation to Table.Output.html. Xtp's syntax:

xtp (*data, depvar, indepvar, optional.weight, plot.options*)

Plainly enough, the user must identify the dataset, the dependent (row) variable, and the independent (column) variable. Optionally, xtp accepts a weight variable (required for nes or gss) and optional labeling information for the mosaic plot. First we'll do a bare-bones xtp run, ignoring the plot embellishments. For the hypothesis at hand, we need the first four arguments. Type 'xtp (nes, envjob_3, pid_3, wt)', as shown here:

```
xtp(nes, envjob_3, pid_3,wt)
```

Turn your attention to the console output:

```
===================================
         x
y        Dem    Ind    Rep   Total
-----------------------------------
Envir   1005    721    212    1938
        59.8   38.2   15.3
-----------------------------------
Mid      508    749    525    1782
        30.2   39.7   37.9
-----------------------------------
Jobs     167    415    649    1231
         9.9   22.0   46.8
-----------------------------------
Total   1680   1885   1386    4951
        33.9   38.1   28.0
===================================
```

The cross-tab is set up according to protocol, with each value of the independent variable, nes$pid_3, occupying its own column: the 1680 Democrats on the left, the 1885 Independents in the middle, and the 1386 Republicans on the right. The column percentages record the distribution of each partisan group across the values of the dependent variable, nes$envjob_3. For example, 212 of the 1386 Republicans (15.3 percent) fall into the "Envir" value of the dependent variable, 525 (37.9 percent) are in the middle category, and 649 (46.8 percent) fall into the "Jobs" category. These three numbers—15.3 percent, 37.9 percent, and 46.8 percent—sum to 100 percent, although the table does not display the sum. Instead, the percentages along the bottom row show the overall distribution of the independent variable: Of the 4951 respondents, 33.9 percent are Democrats, 38.1 percent are Independents, and 28.0 percent are Republicans. And note that the right-most Total column gives us raw counts, but it does not convert the counts into the percentages falling into each value of the dependent variable.

These minor deficiencies aside, this is an attractive, readable table. What do you think? Does the cross-tabulation fit the hypothesis? The third rule of cross-tabulation analysis is easily applied. Focusing on the "Envir" value of the dependent variable, we see a clear pattern in the hypothesized direction. A comparison of Democrats with Independents reveals over a 20-point drop in the "Envir" percentage, from 59.8 percent to 38.2 percent. Moving from Independents to Republicans reveals another 20-point-plus decline, from 38.2 percent to 15.3 percent. Thus, from pole to pole, from Democrat to Republican, the percentage choosing the environment over jobs declines almost 45 percentage points, from 59.8 percent to 15.3 percent. Yes, the analysis supports the hypothesis.

Now consider the mosaic plot (Figure 4.1), an intriguing and informative type of graph. Viewed as separate columns, the tiles communicate the cross-tabulation percentages just discussed. For example, of the three tiles in the Democrat column, the "Envir" tile occupies 59.8 percent of the vertical space, the "Mid" tile 30.2 percent, and the "Jobs" tile 9.9 percent. Viewed horizontally, the widths of the tiles reflect the relative number of cases in each value of the independent variable. Notice, for example, that the tiles in the Independent column are about a third wider than the tiles in the Republican column, visually telling us that the number of Independents is about 1.3 times the number of Republicans. The areas of the tiles, which combine the vertical and horizontal

---

[7] For an excellent discussion of the history and implementation of this graphic form, see Cox, N. J. (2008). Speaking Stata: Spineplots and their kin. *Stata Journal, 8*(1), 105–121.

information, are proportional to the cell frequencies in the cross-tabulation. This provides a quick visual cue to the relative importance of different groups. For example, the Democrat-environment tile clearly is predominant—the product of the large size of this partisan group combined with its consensus on environmental priorities.

Figure 4.1 Mosaic Plot

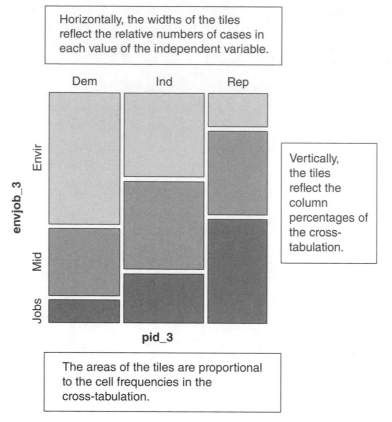

All right, this mosaic plot definitely adds interpretive value. Let's run xtp again, adding labels to the x and y axes of the graph. Also, we'll provide a main title. Return to the script editor and modify the xtp command as follows:

```
xtp(nes, envjob_3, pid_3, wt,ylab="Environ vs. Jobs",
xlab="Party Identification", main="Environmental Opinions, by Party Identification")
```

The "ylab", "xlab", and "main" arguments add must-have graphic features to the finished product (see Figure 4.2). Also, remember that xtp automatically exports the cross-tab to Table.Output.html.

Figure 4.2 Mosaic Plot with Main Title and Axis Labels

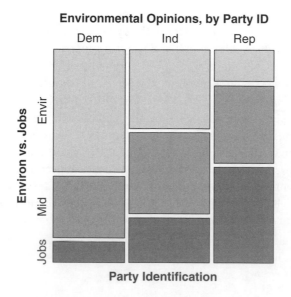

LINE CHARTS

As we have just seen, a mosaic plot paints a nuanced picture of the relationship between two factors. Another plotting function, plotmeansC, provides a straightforward look at the essence of a relationship. Consider Figure 4.3, a line chart that displays the percentage of each partisan group choosing "environment" over "jobs" from the cross-tabulation analysis. Again appreciate the strength and linearity of the relationship: The pro-environment percentages drop from nearly 60 percent to about 15 percent across values of partisanship. How was this graph produced?

Figure 4.3   Line Chart of Indicator Variable

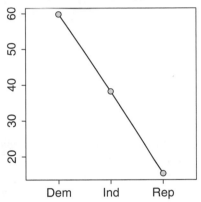

As its name implies, plotmeansC is naturally designed to graph mean values of numeric dependent variables. But plotmeansC will also plot a nominal or ordinal dependent variable—provided that you first transform one category of the dependent variable into an indicator. You learned to create indicator variables in Chapter 3. The following expression uses the level name "Envir" to create an indicator from the factor nes$envjob_3:

```
nes$envir = as.numeric(nes$envjob_3=="Envir")
```

Every respondent in the "Envir" category of nes$envjob_3 will be coded 1 on the indicator, named "nes$envir." Every respondent in "Middle" or "Jobs" will be coded 0 on nes$envir. Create the indicator with the expression above, and then check your work:

```
> freq (nes$envir, nes$wt)
nes$envir
        Frequency   Percent   Valid Percent
0          3022.5     51.09           60.88
1          1942.5     32.83           39.12
NA's        951.1     16.08
Total      5916.0    100.00          100.00


> freq(nes$envjob_3,nes$wt)
nes$envjob_3
        Frequency   Percent   Valid Percent
Envir      1942.5     32.83           39.12
Mid        1787.8     30.22           36.01
Jobs       1234.7     20.87           24.87
NA's        951.1     16.08
Total      5916.0    100.00          100.00
```

The percentage of respondents coded 1 on the indicator, nes$envir, is 39.12 percent, which is identical to the percentage of respondents in the "Envir" category of nes$envjob_3. The indicator checks out. Now, here is a useful fact about indicator variables: The mean of an indicator is equal to the proportion of cases coded 1 on the indicator. Because we want to graph percentages instead of proportions, we first multiply the indicator times 100 and then mobilize plotmeansC to graph it:

```
nes$envir = 100*nes$envir
```

The plotmeansC syntax:

```
plotmeansC (data, ~depvar,~indepvar, depvar~indepvar, w=~weight, plot.options)
```

The following syntax produced the line chart in Figure 4.3:

```
plotmeansC(nes, ~envir, ~pid_3, envir~pid_3, w=~wt,
  xlab="Party Identification",
  ylab="Percent Pro-Environment",
  main="Percentage Favoring Environment over Jobs,\n by Party
      Identification")
#Note for main title: Use "\n" to break long titles into two lines
```

PlotmeansC will run on weighted or unweighted data. When running the function on unweighted data, simply omit the 'w=' argument.

MEAN COMPARISON ANALYSIS

We now turn to another common hypothesis-testing situation: when the independent variable is a factor and the dependent variable is numeric. The logic of comparison still applies—divide cases on the independent variable and compare values of the dependent variable—but the method is different. Instead of comparing percentages, we now compare means.

To illustrate, let's say that you are interested in explaining this dependent variable: attitudes toward Hillary Clinton. Why do some people have positive feelings toward her, whereas others harbor negative feelings? Here is a plausible (if not self-evident) idea: Partisanship (independent variable) will have a strong effect on attitudes toward Hillary Clinton (dependent variable). The hypothesis: In a comparison of individuals, Democrats will have more favorable attitudes toward Clinton than will Republicans.

The nes dataset contains nes$ft_hclinton, a 100-degree feeling thermometer. Each respondent was asked to rate candidate Clinton on this scale, from 0 (cold or negative) to 100 (warm or positive). This is the dependent variable. The nes set also has nes$pid_x, which measures partisanship in seven categories, from Strong Democrat to Strong Republican. The intervening levels of this factor capture gradations between the strong partisans: Weak Democrat, Independent Democrat, Independent, Independent Republican, and Weak Republican. This is the independent variable. If the hypothesis is correct, we should find that Strong Democrats have the highest mean scores on nes$ft_hclinton and that mean scores decrease systematically across categories of nes$pid_x, hitting a low point among respondents who are Strong Republicans. Is this what happens?

To find out, we will run the compmeans function (from the descr package). The compmeans function produces a table of means, numbers of observations, and standard deviations. The syntax:

```
compmean(depvar, indepvar, w=optional.weight, plot=FALSE)
```

Unlike xtp, compmeans does not have a 'data' argument, so we must use the '$' assignment. Also, if a weight variable is specified, it must be preceded by 'w='. Finally, *if you are analyzing weighted data*, make sure to suppress the plot ('plot = FALSE'). The default compmeans graph, a box plot, is incorrect for weighted data. In a later section, you will apply a function, svyboxplot, that produces box plots for weighted or unweighted datasets. Try this:

```
compmeans(nes$ft_hclinton, nes$pid_x, nes$wt, plot=F)
```

```
          Mean    N Std. Dev.
StrDem 82.98116 1154  18.42280
WkDem  69.37778  889  22.65781
IndDem 71.59177  688  21.44760
Ind    55.16249  823  26.97012
IndRep 44.40155  721  25.65332
WkRep  45.98979  730  25.54718
StrRep 31.98259  867  24.99022
Total  58.82567 5871  29.30473
```

The mean comparison table has a precise yet readable layout, a hallmark of the output produced by the descr package. The level names for nes$pid_x appear on the left, beside three columns of numbers: the mean of the dependent variable, nes$ft_hclinton, the number of cases in each value of the independent variable ("N"), and the standard deviation ("Std. Dev."), a measure of variation for numeric variables. Compared with cross-tabulations, mean comparison tables are models of simplicity. There is, after all, only one set of numbers to interpret: the mean value of the dependent variable across values of the independent variable. Clearly, the hypothesis is easily confirmed. Clinton's rating is 82.98 among Strong Democrats and drops to 69.38 among Weak Democrats. Interestingly, Clinton's ratings tick up slightly, to 71.59, among Independent Democrats, and then continue to decline, to 55.16 among Independents and 44.40 for Independent Republicans. Again, notice the anomalous increase among Weak Republicans (45.99), ending with a chilly 31.98 among Strong Republicans. The bottom row of the table records the mean for all 5871 respondents: 58.83.

Do you want to print the cross-tabulation table? Enclose the compmeans expression inside the printC parentheses:

```
printC(compmeans(nes$ft_hclinton, nes$pid_x, nes$wt, plot=F))
#The argument, 'plot=FALSE', can be abbreviated, 'plot=F'
```

The cross-tab will be sent to Table.Output.html in the working directory. For a line chart of the relationship, activate plotmeansC:

```
plotmeansC(nes, ~ft_hclinton, ~pid_x, ft_hclinton~pid_x, w=~wt,
  xlab="Party identification",   ylab="Ratings of Hillary Clinton",
  main="Ratings of Hillary Clinton,\n by Party Identification")
```

A line chart of mean Clinton ratings, across values of partisanship, appears in the graphics window (Figure 4.4).

Figure 4.4   Line Chart of Numeric Variable

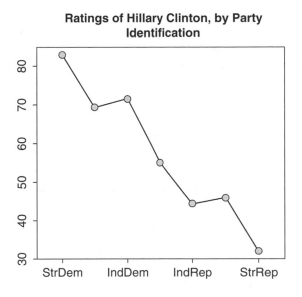

BOX PLOTS
===

A line chart, which plots the mean of a dependent variable across the values of an independent variable, is aimed squarely at visualizing mean comparisons by re-expressing them in graphic form. A box plot favors the display of dispersion over central tendency, providing a valuable complement to mean comparison analysis. Box plots describe a numeric variable by graphing a five-number summary: minimum, lower quartile, median, upper quartile, and maximum. Box plots also reveal outliers.[8]

The svyboxplot function (from the survey package) draws boxplots:

```
svyboxplot (depvar~indepvar, design.dataset, all.outliers=T)
```

```
#Use the design version of the dataset
#To graph outliers, add the argument, 'all.outliers=T'
```

Figure 4.5 Box and Whiskers Plot

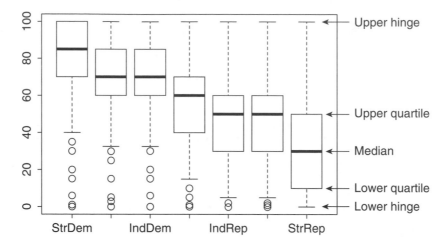

First, we obtain a basic plot of the ft_hclinton-pid_x relationship. We can add options later.

```
svyboxplot (ft_hclinton~pid_x, nesD, all.outliers=T)
```

Consider the graphics window (Figure 4.5). What is depicted by a box plot? The box itself communicates three values: the lower quartile (the value below which 25 percent of the cases fall), the median (the value that splits the cases into two equal-size groups), and the upper quartile (the value below which 75 percent of the cases fall). Thus, the distance between the bottom and top of the box defines the *interquartile range*, the range of a variable that encompasses the "middle half" of a distribution. For example, notice how spread out Strong Republicans are: Their median rating is 30, but half of them rated Clinton in the long interval between 10 (lower quartile) and 50 (upper quartile), an interquartile range of 40 points. Contrast this to the comparative cohesiveness of Strong Democrats, whose median (85) is more closely bounded between 70 and about 100. The lower and upper hinges connect the minimum and maximum values, as long as those values fall within plus or minus 1.5 times the quartile range for the box. Outliers are defined as cases that fall outside those boundaries.

Before moving on, re-run svyboxplot, adding labeling, color, and other enhancements:

```
svyboxplot(ft_hclinton ~ pid_x, nesD, all.outliers=T,
 xlab="Party Identification",
 ylab="Clinton Rating",
 main="Clinton Rating, by Party ID",     col = "lightgray", # Adds color to boxes
 varwidth = T)                                              # Makes box widths proportional
                                                            # to number of cases in groups
```

---

[8] Kabacoff, R. I. (2011). *R in action: Data analysis and graphics with R*. Shelter Island, NY: Manning Publications, p. 133.

Now we have an improved graphic (Figure 4.6). The color adds interest. The widths of the boxes are proportional to the numbers of cases in each group of the independent variable—or, more specifically, they are drawn proportional to the square roots of the numbers of cases in each group. For example, the boxes on the Democratic side are wider than the Republican boxes, reflecting the prevalence of Democrats.

Figure 4.6   Box and Whiskers Plot with Main Title and Axis Labels

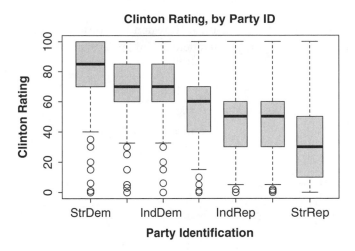

STRIP CHARTS

The graphic types discussed thus far—mosaic plots, line charts, and box plots—excel at displaying summary statistics for large datasets. Strip charts display case-level information, making them particularly appropriate for smaller datasets, such as states or world. Like box plots, strip charts show how the cases are distributed within each value of an independent variable. So the analyst might create a strip chart to complement a mean comparison analysis.

Suppose we are interested in comparing levels of unionization in different regions of the United States. We would run compmeans, obtaining the mean of states$union10 (percentage of the workforce belonging to a union) by states$region (region of the country):

```
compmean(states$union10, states$region, plot=F)
```

	Mean	N	Std. Dev.
Northeast	16.23333	9	4.484975
Midwest	11.63333	12	4.470781
South	6.95625	16	3.441893
West	13.14615	13	6.571227
Total	11.35800	50	5.790671

The Northeast has the highest average level of unionization (16.23 percent), followed by the West (13.15 percent), the Midwest (11.63 percent), and the South (6.96 percent). But examine the corresponding standard deviations, which measure variation. Notice that the standard deviation for the West (6.57) is comparatively large, nearly twice that for the South (3.44). This suggests that the 13 western states are widely dispersed, with some having high levels of unionization and others having lower levels. A strip chart can provide valuable insights on questions of dispersion and skewness. The basic syntax:

```
stripchart(depvar ~ indepvar, data= data, plot.options)
```

The following is a more complete expression, adapted to the example at hand, and shown with familiar options in place (unfamiliar options are annotated):

```
stripchart(union10 ~ region, data=states,
    xlab="Region", ylab="Percent Unionized",
    main="Unionization, by Region",
    vertical=TRUE,                    #Displays strips vertically, not horizontally
    method="jitter",                  #Adds a small amount of random noise to data points
                                      #so data points do not overlap
    font.main=1)
```

The strip chart adds clarity and detail to the union10-region relationship (Figure 4.7). We can see why the mean comparison analysis returned inter-regional differences in the level of unionization. Yet we can also see interesting variation within regions.

Figure 4.7 Strip Chart

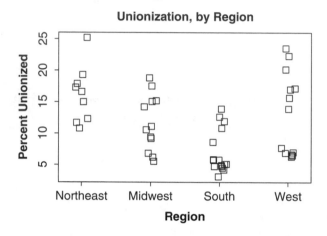

EXERCISES

1. (Datasets: nes, nesD. Variables: fedspend_scale, pid_x, wt.) Here is a widely observed difference between Democrats and Republicans: Democrats are more likely than Republicans to favor government spending. Is this difference borne out by the data? Dataset nes contains the numeric variable fedspend_scale, which measures respondents' spending opinions on a scale that runs from 0 (oppose government spending) to 16 (support government spending). This is the dependent variable. Use the 7-point party identification scale (pid_x) as the independent variable.

    A. If Democrats are more likely than Republicans to favor spending, then Democrats will have (Check one.)

        ❑ a higher mean than do Republicans on fedspend_scale.

        ❑ about the same mean as do Republicans on fedspend_scale.

        ❑ a lower mean than do Republicans on fedspend_scale.

    B. Run compmeans to obtain the mean score on the dependent variable, fedspend_scale, for each category of the independent variable, pid_x. (*Hint*: Remember that compmeans requires "$" in variable names—for example, nes$fedspend_scale. Also, this is nes, so remember to include the weight variable, wt.) Write the results in the table that follows.

Party ID	Mean	N
Strong Democrat	?	?
Weak Democrat	?	?
Independent Democrat	?	?
Independent	?	?

Party ID	Mean	N
Independent Republican	?	?
Weak Republican	?	?
Strong Republican	?	?
Total	?	?

C. Overall, does your analysis support the idea that Democrats are more likely than Republicans to support government spending? (Circle one.)

Yes   No

Briefly explain your answer.

_____

_____

D. The mean comparison results contain two anomalies—two data points that do not fit the overall pattern. Briefly describe the two anomalies.

_____

_____

E. Use svyboxplot to obtain a box plot of the relationship. (*Hint:* Remember that svyboxplot uses the design dataset, nesD.) Apply all the box plot enhancements you learned in this chapter: add an x-axis label ("Party ID"); add a y-axis label ("Pro-spending Scale Score"); provide a main title ("Pro-government Spending Scale, by Party ID"); request light gray boxes (col="lightgray"); and draw the box widths in proportion to the sizes of the party identification groups (varwidth=T). Print the box plot.

F. Examine the box plot you created. Suppose someone made the following statement: "Strong Democrats are more cohesive in their position on government spending than are Strong Republicans."

Based on your examination of the box plot, is this statement correct? (Circle one.)

Yes   No

Briefly explain your answer.

_____

_____

G. Use plotmeansC to produce a line chart of the fedspend_scale-pid_x relationship. Use the same axis labels and main title that you applied to the boxplot. Print the line chart.

2. (Dataset: nes. Variables: gay_marry, libcon3, wt.) Should gay couples be legally permitted to marry? This controversial issue has gained center stage in political debate. One can imagine several characteristics that divide people on this issue. For example, one could hypothesize that self-described liberals are more likely to favor gay marriage than are self-described moderates, who in turn are more likely to favor gay marriage than are self-described conservatives.

Dataset nes contains gay_marry, a two-level factor that gauges approval of same-sex marriage: "No" or "Yes". Nes also has libcon3, a three-category factor that measures respondents' ideological leanings: "Lib", "Mod", or "Cons".

A. Use xtp to test the following hypothesis about the relationship between libcon3 (independent variable) and gay_marry (dependent variable): In a comparison of individuals, liberals will be more likely to favor gay marriage than will moderates, who in turn will be more likely to support gay marriage than will conservatives. In the xtp syntax, add labels to the mosaic plot: a y-axis label ("Opinion on Gay Marriage"), an x-axis label ("Ideology"), and a main title ("Gay Marriage Opinions, by Ideology"). Print the mosaic plot.

B. Fill in the numbers of cases (N) and column percentages (%) next to the question marks (?) in the table that follows. (Two of the values have been entered for you.)

Opinion on Gay Marriage		Lib	Mod	Cons	Total
No	N	611	?	?	?
	%	32.6	?	?	
Yes	N	?	?	?	?
	%	?	?	?	
Total	N	?	?	?	?

C. Consider the mosaic plot and the cross-tabulation. Does the evidence support the hypothesis? (Circle one.)

Yes   No

Explain:

_____

_____

_____

D. Use plotmeansC to create a line chart showing the percentage favoring same-sex marriage (y-axis) by ideology (x-axis). Because gay_marry is a factor variable, getting to plotmeansC requires three steps. (i) Create a numeric indicator for gay marriage supporters, using the "Yes" category of gay_marry. Name the indicator gay.marriage.yes. *Hint:* The following syntax will accomplish this step: nes$gay_marry .yes=as.numeric(nes$gay_marry=="Yes"). (ii) Multiply nes$gay_marry.yes times 100. (iii) Run plotmeansC to obtain the chart of gay_marry.yes (y-axis) and libcon3 (x-axis). Create descriptive labels for xlab, ylab, and main. Print the line chart.

3. (Dataset: gss. Variables: educ_4, mslm_spk, wtss.) Are people who have more education more likely than the less educated to be tolerant of radical Muslim clerics? The hypothesis: In a comparison of individuals, those having higher levels of education are more tolerant of radical Muslims than are those having lower levels of education.

A. The gss dataset contains educ_4, which measures years of educational attainment in four categories: "<HS", "HS", "Some Coll", and "Coll+". The dependent variable, mslm_spk, captures respondents' opinions on whether radical Muslim clerics should be permitted to give a speech: "No" or "Yes". (Remember that gss must be weighted by wtss.) Obtain a cross-tabulation and nicely labeled mosaic plot of the relationship. Print the mosaic plot.

B. Recall that xtp automatically exports the cross-tabulation to Table.Output.html. Copy/paste the table into a word processor and edit it for appearance and readability. Print the edited table.

C. Obtain a line chart showing the relationship between the percentage of respondents saying "Yes" on mslm_spk (y-axis) and level of education (x-axis). Because mslm_spk is a factor, you will need to follow the same three-step procedure you followed in exercise 2, part D. Print the line chart.

D. Consider all the evidence you have gathered: the cross-tabulation, the mosaic plot, and the line chart. Does the evidence support the hypothesis that those having higher levels of education are more tolerant of radical Muslims than are those having lower levels of education? Answer yes or no and explain:

_____

_____

_____

4. (Dataset: world. Variables: regime_type3, durable.) Three comparative politics scholars are trying to figure out what sort of institutional arrangement produces the longest lasting, most stable political system.

Scholar 1: "Presidential democracies, like the United States, are going to be more stable than are any other type of system. In presidential democracies, the executive and the legislature have separate electoral constituencies and separate but overlapping domains of responsibility. The people's political interests are represented both by the president's national constituency and by legislators' or parliament members' more localized constituencies. If one branch does something that's unpopular, it can be blocked by the other branch. The result: political stability."

Scholar 2: "Parliamentary democracies are by far more stable than presidential democracies. In presidential systems, the executive and legislature can be controlled by different political parties, a situation that produces deadlock. Since the leaders of the legislature can't remove the president and install a more compliant or agreeable executive, they are liable to resort to a coup, toppling the whole system. Parliamentary democracies avoid these pitfalls. In parliamentary democracies, all legitimacy and accountability resides with the legislature. The parliament organizes the government and chooses the executive, the prime minister, from among its own leaders. The prime minister and members of parliament have strong incentives to cooperate and keep things running smoothly and efficiently. The result: political stability."

Scholar 3: "You two have made such compelling—if incorrect—arguments that I almost hesitate to point this out: Democracies of any species, presidential or parliamentary, are inherently unstable. Any system that permits the clamor of competing parties or dissident viewpoints is surely bound to fail. If it's stability that you value above all else, then dictatorships will deliver. Strong executives, feckless or nonexistent legislatures, powerful armies, social control. The result: political stability."

The world dataset contains the variable durable, a numeric that measures the number of years since the last regime transition. The more years that have passed since the system last failed (higher values on durable), the more stable a country's political system. The variable regime_type3 captures system type: dictatorship, parliamentary democracy, or presidential democracy.

A. Run compmeans to analyze the relationship between durable and regime_type3. Perform a mean comparison analysis of the relationship between durable and regime_type3. Based on a comparison of means, which is the *apparently correct* ranking of regime types, from most stable to least stable? (Check one.)

❑ parliamentary democracies (most stable), presidential democracies, dictatorships (least stable)

❑ presidential democracies (most stable), parliamentary democracies, dictatorships (least stable)

❑ parliamentary democracies (most stable), dictatorships, presidential democracies (least stable)

B. Run printC to send the mean comparison table to Table.Output.html. Copy/paste the table into a word processor and edit it for appearance and readability. Print the edited table.

C. Run stripchart to obtain a strip chart of the relationship. Run svyboxplot to obtain a box plot. (*Reminder:* svyboxplot uses worldD, the design version of the dataset.) Closely examine the strip chart and box plot. In what way does the graphic evidence support the ranking in part A?

_____

_____

_____

_____

_____

D. In what way does the graphic evidence NOT support the ranking in part A?

_____

_____

_____

_____

E. Print the graphs you created in part C.

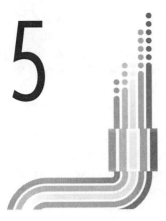

5

Making Controlled Comparisons

Objective	Functions Introduced	Author or Source
Generating controlled cross-tabulations	xtabC {poliscidata}	Philip Pollock and Barry Edwards, uses the colPercents function from John Fox's Rcmdr package[1]
Generating controlled mean comparison tables	imeansC {poliscidata}	Philip Pollock and Barry Edwards, uses the brkdn.plot function from the plotrix package by Lemon et al.[2] and svydesign from Thomas Lumley's survey package[3]
Producing graphs of means or of indicator variables	iplotC {poliscidata}	Philip Pollock and Barry Edwards, uses the brkdn.plot function from the plotrix package by Lemon et al.[2] and svydesign from Thomas Lumley's survey package[3]

Political analysis often begins by making simple comparisons using cross-tabulation analysis or mean comparison analysis. Simple comparisons allow the researcher to examine the relationship between an independent variable, X, and a dependent variable, Y. However, there is always the possibility that alternative causes—rival explanations—are at work, affecting the observed relationship between X and Y. An alternative cause is symbolized by the letter Z. If the researcher does not control for Z, then he or she may misinterpret the relationship between X and Y.

What can happen to the relationship between an independent variable and a dependent variable, controlling for an alternative cause? One possibility is that the relationship between the independent variable and the dependent variable is spurious. In a spurious relationship, once the researcher controls for a rival causal factor, the original relationship becomes very weak, perhaps disappearing altogether. The control variable does all of the explanatory work. In another possibility, the researcher observes an

[1] Fox, J., and Bouchet-Valat, M. (2017). *Rcmdr: R Commander* (version 2.3-2). Contributions from many other users. Available at http://CRAN.R-project.org/package=Rcmdr

[2] Lemon, J., Bolker, B., Oom, S., Klein, E., Rowlingson, B., Wickham, H., Tyagi, A., Eterradossi, O., Grothendieck, G., Toews, M., Kane, J., Turner, R., Witthoft, C., Stander, J., Petzoldt, T., Duursma, R., Biancotto, E., Levy, O., Dutang, C., Solymos, P., Engelmann, R., Hecker, M., Steinbeck, F., Borchers, H., Singmann, H., Toal, T., and Ogle, D. (2016). *plotrix: Various plotting functions* (R package version 3.6-2). Available at http://CRAN.R-project.org/package=plotrix

[3] Lumley, T. (2012). *survey: Analysis of complex survey samples* (R package version 3.28-2). Available at http://cran.r-project.org/web/packages/survey/index.html. See also: Lumley, T. (2004). Analysis of complex survey samples. *Journal of Statistical Software*, 9(1), 1–19; Lumley, T. (2010). *Complex surveys: A guide to analysis using R*. Hoboken, NJ: John Wiley & Sons.

additive relationship between the independent variable, the dependent variable, and the control variable. In an additive relationship, two sets of meaningful relationships exist. The independent variable maintains a relationship with the dependent variable, and the control variable helps to explain the dependent variable. A third possibility, interaction, is somewhat more complex. If interaction is occurring, then the effect of the independent variable on the dependent variable depends on the value of the control variable. The strength or tendency of the relationship is different for one value of the control variable than for another value of the control variable.

In this chapter, you will learn to analyze relationships when all three variables—the independent variable, the dependent variable, and the control variable—are factors. You will also learn to analyze relationships in which the dependent variable is numeric and the independent and control variables are factors. Because graphic displays are especially valuable tools for evaluating complex relationships, we will demonstrate how to obtain multiple line charts. These skills are natural extensions of the procedures you learned in Chapter 4.

Box 5.1 provides a summary guide to the data analysis and graphics techniques covered in this chapter. For situations in which all the variables—the independent variable, the control variable, and the dependent variable—are factors, you will learn controlled cross-tabulation analysis using the xtabC function. When the independent and control variables are factors and the dependent variable is numeric, you will perform mean comparison with the imeansC function. The plotting function, iplotC, designed to produce multiple line charts for controlled mean comparisons, can be adapted (with the creation of an indicator variable) to produce line charts for cross-tabulations as well. The iplotC function does not produce a chart legend, so you will learn to use R's classic legend function. All of the functions introduced in this chapter use the design datasets.

		Box 5.1 Analysis Guide		
Independent Variable and Control Variable	Dependent Variable	Analysis {function}	Graphics {function}	Comments
Factors	Factor	Controlled cross-tabulation {xtabC}	Multiple line charts of indicator variable {iplotC} {legend}	Create indicator in non-design dataset, then run svydesign to update the design dataset. Run iplotC on design dataset.
Factors	Numeric	Controlled mean comparisons{imeansC}	Multiple line charts of numeric variable {iplotC}{legend}	Run iplotC on design dataset.

CROSS-TABULATION ANALYSIS WITH A CONTROL VARIABLE

To demonstrate how to obtain control crosstabulations, we will work through an example with the gss datasets—gss for a preliminary xtp analysis, then gssD for a controlled comparison analysis using a new function, xtabC. We begin with this hypothesis: In a comparison of individuals, those who attend religious services less frequently will be more likely to favor the legalization of marijuana than will those who attend religious services more frequently. In this hypothesis, attend3, which categorizes respondents' church attendance as "Low", "Moderate" , or "High", is the independent variable. The gss dataset contains the variable grass, which records respondents' opinions on the legalization of marijuana: "Legal" and "Not legal". To stay acquainted with cross-tabulation analysis, we will start by using xtp to analyze the uncontrolled relationship between attend3 and grass. In addition to considering whether the hypothesis has merit, we will note the tendency of the relationship, and we will apply a non-statistical measure of the relationship's strength. By determining tendency and gauging strength, you are better able to interpret relationships involving control variables.

Recall xtp's syntax:

```
xtp(data, depvar, indepvar, optional.weight, plot.options)
```

We'll perform a basic xtp analysis:

```
#Cross-tabulation without control variable
xtp(gss, grass, attend3, wtss)
```

```
=============================================
      x
y           Low    Moderate    High    Total
---------------------------------------------
LEGAL       326         149     100      575
            62.3       45.8    26.7

---------------------------------------------
NOT LEGAL   197         176     275      648
            37.7       54.2    73.3

---------------------------------------------
Total       523         325     375     1223
            42.8       26.6    30.7
=============================================
```

Clearly, the hypothesis has merit. If no relationship existed between marijuana opinions and religious attendance, then roughly equal percentages of low, moderate, and high attenders would favor legalization. Obviously, the percentages are not equal. Of the low attenders, 62.3 percent favor legalization, compared with 45.8 percent of moderate attenders and 26.7 percent of the highly observant. And note that, given the way attend3 is coded—increasing values denote increasing church attendance—a negative relationship exists between religiosity and the percentage favoring legalization. As attendance increases, the percentage favoring legalization declines. (If you interpret the cross-tab by examining the "Not legal" row, then the tendency is positive. As attendance increases, the percentage opposing legalization increases.) How strong is the relationship? You can arrive at a quick and easy measure of strength by figuring out the percentage-point change in the dependent variable across the full range of the independent variable. At one pole, 62.3 percent of low attenders favor legalization. At the other pole, 26.7 percent of high attenders are in favor. Therefore, the percentage favoring legalization drops by 62.3 – 26.7 = 35.6, or about 36 percentage points. By this rudimentary measure, the relationship's strength is 36. (In Chapter 7, we consider statistical measures of strength.)

What other factors, besides church attendance, might account for differing opinions on marijuana legalization? A plausible answer: whether the respondent has children. Regardless of religiosity, people with children may be less inclined to endorse the legalization of marijuana than are people who do not have children. And here is an interesting (if complicating) fact: People who attend church regularly are substantially more likely to have children than are people who rarely or never attend. Thus, when we compare the marijuana opinions of "High" and "Low" attenders, as we have just done, we are also comparing people who are more likely to have children ("High") with people who are less likely to have children ("Low"). It could be that secular individuals are more inclined to favor legalization, not because they are less religious, but because they are less likely to have children. By the same token, those who go to church more often might oppose legalization for reasons unrelated to their religiosity: They're more likely to have children. The only way to isolate the effect of attendance on marijuana opinions is to compare low attenders who do not have children with high attenders who do not have children, and to compare low attenders who have children with high attenders who have children. In other words, we need to control for the effect of having children by holding it constant.[4]

The xtabC function will produce the results we are after. Consider xtabC's straightforward syntax:

$$xtabC\ (\sim depvar\ +\ indepvar\ +\ controlvar,\ design.dataset)$$

Note that, unlike xtp, xtabC requires gssD, the design version of gss. Applying xtabC to the current problem:

---

[4] According to gss, 82.8 percent of high attenders have children, compared with 62.0 percent of low attenders—a 20-percentage-point difference.

```
Cross-tabulation with control variable
xtabC (~grass + attend3 + kids, gssD)
```

```
, , kids = No
            attend3
grass        Low  Moderate  High
LEGAL       71.9     55.8   36.8
NOT LEGAL   28.1     44.2   63.2
Total      100.0    100.0  100.0
Count      199.0     77.0   57.0


, , kids = Yes
            attend3
grass        Low  Moderate  High
LEGAL       56.5     42.7     25
NOT LEGAL   43.5     57.3     75
Total      100.0    100.0    100
Count      324.0    248.0    316
```

We now have two cross-tabulations—two sets of relationships to evaluate. First assess the tendency and strength of the relationship between attendance and support for marijuana legalization among respondents who do not have children. Then assess tendency and strength among respondents who have children. Among people without children, the tendency is negative. As the values of attend3 increase from low to high, support for legalization declines: 71.9 percent of the low attenders favor legalization, compared with 55.8 percent of the middle group and 36.8 percent of the high attenders. How large is the drop? Across the full range of religious attendance, the percentage favoring legalization declines from 71.9 to 36.8—an "attendance effect" of about 35 percentage points. Turn your attention to respondents with children. Note that the tendency, once again, is negative: 56.5 percent of the low attenders favor legalization, compared with 42.7 percent of moderate attenders and 25.0 percent of high attenders. Note also that the strength of the relationship is about the same for people who have children as for people who do not have children. Among respondents with kids, the percentage who favor legalization drops from 56.5 among low attenders to 25.0 among high attenders—an attendance effect of about 32 points.

To help you make correct interpretations of controlled comparisons, it is a good idea to evaluate the relationship between the control variable and the dependent variable, controlling for the independent variable. In the current example, we would determine the tendency and strength of the relationship between the control variable, kids, and marijuana attitudes, controlling for attendance. This is accomplished by jumping between the "No" cross-tabulation and the "Yes" cross-tabulation, comparing marijuana opinions of people who share the same level of attendance but who differ on the control variable, kids. You can see that "Lows" without kids are more likely to favor legalization than are "Lows" with kids. When the control variable switches from "No" to "Yes", the percentage of marijuana supporters drops, from 71.9 percent to 56.5 percent—a "kid effect" of about 15 percentage points. How about moderate attenders? As with low attenders, the kid effect is negative, 55.8 percent compared with 42.7 percent—about 13 points. This pattern reoccurs among high attenders: 36.89 percent versus 25.0 percent—a kid effect of about 12 points.

How would you characterize this set of relationships? Does a spurious relationship exist between grass and attend3? Or are these additive relationships, with attend3 helping to explain legalization opinions and kids adding to the explanation? Or is interaction going on? If the grass-attend3 relationship were spurious, then the relationship would weaken or disappear after controlling for kids. Among respondents without children, low, moderate, and high attenders would all hold the same opinion about marijuana legalization. Ditto for people with children: Attendance would not play a role in explaining the dependent variable. Because the relationship persists after controlling for kids, we can rule out spuriousness.

Now, it is sometimes difficult to distinguish between additive relationships and interaction relationships. In additive relationships, the effect of the independent variable on the dependent variable is the same or quite similar for each value of the control variable. In interaction relationships, by contrast, the effect of the independent variable on the dependent variable varies in tendency or strength for different values of the control variable.

According to the analysis, the grass-attend3 relationship has the same tendency—it "runs in the same direction"—for people with and without children: For both values of the control, as attendance goes up, pro-legalization opinions decline. Tellingly, the grass-attend3 relationships are quite similar in strength for people who do not have children and for people who do have children. For respondents without kids, the attendance effect is 35. For those with kids, the effect is 32. Notice, too, that the kid effect has the same tendency and roughly the same strength (between 12 and 15 points) at all values of attend3. To be sure, the grass-attend3-kids relationships are not paragons of symmetrical perfection—real-world relationships rarely are—but the pattern more closely approximates an additive pattern than an interactive pattern.

Additive relationships always take the same form: The relationship between the independent and dependent variables has the same tendency (direction) and the same or very similar strength at all values of the control variable. Interaction relationships are more complex—and they are probably more common. So that you can become comfortable recognizing interaction in cross-tabulations, we will present another example related to the line of analysis we have been pursuing. Does religious attendance affect attitudes toward divorce? Does the strength or tendency of the relationship depend on whether people have children?

The gss datasets contain divlaw2, which assesses attitudes toward divorce laws by two values: Laws should remain the same or make divorce easier ("Same/easier"), or laws should be changed to make it more difficult to obtain a divorce ("More difficult"). Because we have the same independent variable, attend3, and the same control variable, kids, we can easily modify our earlier xtabC syntax by replacing grass with divlaw2:

```
#Controlled cross-tabulation, interaction relationship
xtabC(~divlaw2 + attend3 +kids, gssD)
```

```
, , kids = No
               attend3
divlaw2         Low  Moderate   High
Same/easier    69.5     67.4    55.9
More difficult 30.5     32.6    44.1
Total         100.0    100.0   100.0
Count         213.0     86.0    68.0


, , kids = Yes
               attend3
divlaw2         Low  Moderate   High
Same/easier    66.1     59.3    43.3
More difficult 33.9     40.7    56.7
Total         100.0    100.0   100.0
Count         330.0    221.0   300.0
```

To ensure consistency with the analysis of marijuana opinions, we will track the more culturally permissive response, "Same/easier." Clearly enough, attendance has an effect on the dependent variable for people without children. As the independent variable changes from low to moderate to high, the percentage of respondents who think that divorce laws should be the same or easier declines by 14 points: from 69.5 percent of low attenders to 55.9 percent of high attenders. So the relationship has a negative tendency or direction, as viewed along the "Same/easier" row, and a strength equal to 14. Now shift your attention to the divlaw2-attend3 relationship among respondents who have kids. Notice that the direction of the relationship is the same. Just as with people who do not have children, as attendance increases, the percentage of "Same/easier" responses declines. However, the drop is much steeper among respondents with kids, from 66.1 percent to 43.3 percent—nearly 23 percentage points. Thus, the attendance effect is either weaker (14 points) or stronger (23 points), depending on which value of the control variable is in play. This sort of asymmetrical pattern—same tendency, different strengths—is a common form of interaction. To confirm an interaction interpretation, evaluate the kid effect separately at each value of attendance. For low attenders, the effect is only about 3 points: 69.5 percent for those without kids, compared with 66.1 percent for those with kids. Among frequent attenders, by contrast, the kid effect widens to more than 12 points, from 55.9 percent to 43.3 percent.

MULTIPLE LINE CHARTS

In Chapter 4, you learned how to obtain a line chart depicting the relationship between an independent variable and a dependent variable. For clarifying controlled comparisons, multiple line charts provide an excellent complement to cross-tabulation analysis and mean comparison analysis. Multiple line charts are simple and elegant, and they have a favorable data-ink ratio, defined as "the proportion of a graphic's ink devoted to the nonredundant display of data-information."[5] In the following guided example, we use the iplotC function to produce a multiple line chart for the additive relationship analyzed at the beginning of the chapter, the relationship between grass and attend3, controlling for kids.

Just as with Chapter 4's plotmeansC, iplotC is naturally accustomed to graphing mean values of a numeric dependent variable. (This is demonstrated below.) And, just as with plotmeansC, iplotC will gladly graph a factor—provided that we first re-express one value of the factor as an indicator variable. Here, the procedure is virtually the same as before. However, two issues make iplotC somewhat more labor-intensive. First, iplotC uses the design version of the dataset, which must be updated following the creation of the indicator variable.[6] Second, because iplotC does not produce a chart legend, the legend function must be employed for this purpose. In a nutshell: (i) create the indicator in the non-design version of the dataset; (ii) run svydesign to redefine the design version of the dataset, updating it to include the newly created indicator; (iii) run iplotC using the updated design dataset; and (iv) add a legend to the chart. This annotated script applies steps (i) and (ii) to the current example:

```
# Retrieve level names of variable to graph.
levels(gss$grass)
```

```
[1] "LEGAL"      "NOT LEGAL"
```

```
# Create the indicator in the non-design dataset, multiplied times 100.
gss$grass.legal = as.numeric(gss$grass=="LEGAL")
gss$grass.legal = 100*gss$grass.legal

#Run svydesign, updating gssD to include the new indicator.
gssD = svydesign(id=~1, data=gss, weights=~wtss)
```

Now consider iplotC's somewhat challenging syntax:

```
iplotC(~depvar,

    ~indepvar+controlvar,        # Here, indepvar is typed before controlvar:
                                 # '~indepvar + #controlvar'.
    design.dataset,
    depvar~controlvar+indepvar,  # Here, indepvar is typed after controlvar:
                                 # '~controlvar + indepvar'.
plot.options)
```

The following script will create a nicely optioned—if legend-less—multiple line chart showing the percentage favoring legalization across values of attend3, separately for respondents with and without children:

```
#Multiple line chart, controlled comparison
iplotC(~grass.legal, ~attend3+kids, gssD, grass.legal ~ kids + attend3,
    xlab="Religious attendance",
    ylab="Percent favoring legalization",
    main=list("Percentage Favoring Marijuana Legalization\n by Religious
    Attendance and Kids", cex=1))
```

---

[5] Tufte, E. R. (2001). *The visual display of quantitative information*, 2nd ed. Cheshire, CT: Graphics Press, 93.
[6] Another option is to create the indicator in the gssD as gssD$variables$grass.legal.

Figure 5.1 Multiple Line Chart with Indicator Dependent Variable (No Legend)

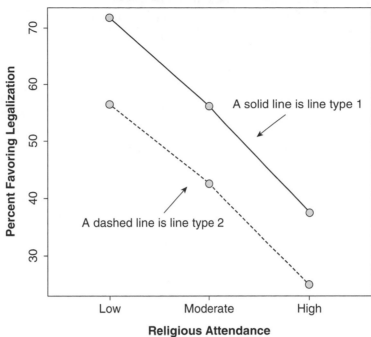

The resulting chart (Figure 5.1) provides graphic confirmation for the additive nature of these relationships. Both lines drop 32–35 points across values of attend3. And the solid line floats 12–15 points above the dashed line, depicting higher support for legalization among respondents who do not have children. (The 'cex=1' argument shrinks the main title font.)

Before adding a legend, take note of these facts: Respondents without children are represented by the solid line, which is line type 1; respondents with children are represented by the dashed line, which is line type 2. (To view R's full menu of line types, run the function lineType( ). Type the function as it appears here, with empty parentheses.)

THE legend FUNCTION

The legend function will produce a customized legend for any plot in the active graphics window. To use the legend function, therefore, you would first produce a legend-less graph in the graphics window, as we have done here, and then run the legend syntax. The generic legend syntax:

```
legend(location, legend, legend.options)
```

The legend function is extraordinarily flexible and allows many options. Type '?legend' for a comprehensive look. However, a handful of options will usually create the result you are after. For the current example:

```
legend("topright",              # Locates the legend in the plotting area
legend=c("No","Yes"),           # Labels the categories
    lty=c(1,2),                 # Makes sure the line types match the labels
    lwd=2,                      # Specifies the line weight shown in the graph
    title="Does R have kids?",  # Title in legend box
    inset=0.1,                  # Specifies distance from the plot borders
    bty="n")                    # Suppresses the box around the legend
```

The first argument, "topright", locates the legend in the plotting area. Of course, the desired location will depend on the graph and on your specific preferences. All possibilities: "bottom", "bottomleft", "left", "topleft", "top", "topright", "right", "bottomright", and "center". Experiment with the inset argument to tweak the location. Given our "topright" request, an inset equal to 0 (the default) would place the legend squarely in the upper-right corner.

Larger values of inset create more white space between the borders and the legend's edge. You can re-run the plotting command and the legend function in an iterative fashion until you find the look you like.

The legend labels—'legend=c("No", "Yes")'—and line types must match. Because, in the current example, the "No" category appears first in the legend argument, and because the "No" line is solid, the plotting value for a solid line, line type 1, appears first in the lty argument. Also, iplotC's default line weight, 'lwd=2', is echoed in the legend syntax. Finally, 'bty="n"' suppresses the default box around the legend. For short legend titles, a box works fine. But for longer multi-line titles, as in the current example, the box collides with the title's text. Go ahead and type and run the script. The finished graph appears in the graphics window (Figure 5.2).

Figure 5.2 Multiple Line Chart with Indicator Variable (Legend Added)

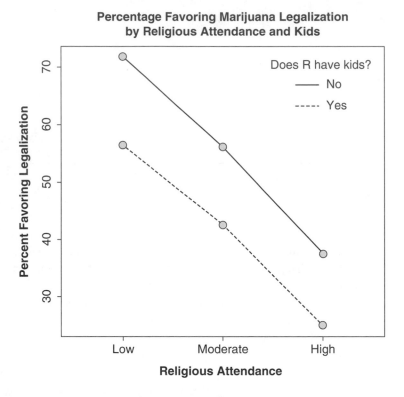

MEAN COMPARISON ANALYSIS WITH A CONTROL VARIABLE

Mean comparison analysis is used when the dependent variable is numeric class and the independent variable and the control variable are factors. We will work through two guided examples using nes and nesD and applying the imeansC function. The first example shows an interesting pattern of interaction. The second example gives you a chance to identify a set of additive relationships.

Example of an Interaction Relationship

It has become an article of faith that women are more strongly attracted to the Democratic Party than are men. Indeed, on nes's Democratic Party feeling thermometer (ft_dem), women's ratings are 5 "degrees" warmer than men's: 54 degrees versus 49 degrees. We might wonder, however, whether this gap is the same for married and unmarried people. Plausibly, shared beliefs and values (perhaps including party affiliation) are of key importance to couples who marry. And evidence suggests that married couples become politically more similar over time.[7] Let's use imeansC to investigate the relationship between Democratic ratings and gender, controlling for marital status. The imeansC syntax:

```
imeansC(~depvar, ~indepvar + controlvar, design.dataset)
```

---

[7] Stoker, L, and Jennings, M. K. (2005). Political similarity and influence between husbands and wives. In A. S. Zuckerman (Ed.), *The social logic of politics*. Philadelphia, PA: Temple University Press, pp. 51–74.

For the current problem:

```
#Controlled mean comparison
imeansC(~ft_dem, ~gender + married, nesD)
```

```
        married    No    Yes
gender
Male    svymean 53.07 46.14
Female  svymean 62.08 48.03
```

The imeansC function returns the four mean values we requested. To evaluate the controlled effect of the independent variable, gender, we would compare the mean ratings of women with the mean ratings of men for unmarried ("No") and for married ("Yes") respondents. What do these comparisons reveal? Consider respondents who are not married. The mean Democratic Party rating for unmarried men is 53.07. This mean increases to 62.08 for unmarried women. So, for the unmarried, the thermometer gets 9 degrees warmer as we move from males to females. Now shift your attention to married respondents. Here we see a gender gap of less than 2 degrees: 46.14 for men and 48.03 for women. Does the gender-Democratic thermometer relationship have the same tendency at both values of the control? Yes, for both unmarried and married respondents, women feel more warmly toward the Democratic Party than do men. Do the relationships have the same (or similar) strengths at both values of the control? No, the gender gap is almost five times larger for unmarried people than for married people. Again, a situation such as this—same tendency, different strengths—is one form of interaction.

Confirm the interaction interpretation by determining how the control variable, married, affects Democratic ratings for each gender. For males, for instance, there is a difference of about 7 degrees: 53.07 for unmarried men compared with 46.14 for married men. The marriage effect, however, is 14 degrees for women: 62.08 compared with 48.03. Again, same tendency (unmarried people rate the Democrats higher than do married people), but different strengths (the effect is substantially larger for women than for men).

Obtain a multiple line chart with iplotC and add a legend. With a numeric dependent variable, iplotC is running in its natural environment—no indicator variable required:

```
iplotC(~ft_dem, ~gender+married, nesD, ft_dem~married+gender,
    xlab="Gender", ylab="Democratic Party Rating",
    main="Democratic Party Ratings by Gender and Marital Status")

legend("topleft", legend=c("No","Yes"), lty=c(1,2), lwd=2,
    title="Is R married?", inset=0.1, bty="n")
```

You can see why line charts (Figure 5.3) are essential for correctly interpreting controlled comparisons. By tracing along each line, from male to female, you can see the effect of gender on thermometer ratings. Among married people, the line slopes up mildly, signaling a narrow gender gap. Among unmarried respondents, by contrast, the line rises more sharply—a wider gender gap. Notice, too, the relationship between marital status and the dependent variable, separately for men and women: about a 7-point marriage effect for males, compared with a 14-point effect for females.

Thus far in this chapter, we found two instances of interaction: the divlaw2-attend3-kids relationships and the ft_dem-gender-married relationships. Both cases revealed a common form of interaction. The relationship between the independent and dependent variables had the same tendency for both values of the control variable, but the relationship was stronger for one value than for the other value. Interaction can assume other forms, too. Interaction has two field marks, though, that will give it away. First, when you examine the relationship between the independent variable and the dependent variable at different values of the control variable, you may find that the relationship varies in tendency (direction), perhaps positive for one value of the control variable, zero or negative for other control values. Second, the relationship may have the same tendency for all control values but differ in strength, negative-weak versus negative-strong or positive-weak versus positive-strong. In identifying interaction, practice makes perfect. And, believe it or not, statistics can help (see Chapter 9).

Figure 5.3 Multiple Line Chart with Numeric Variable (Interaction)

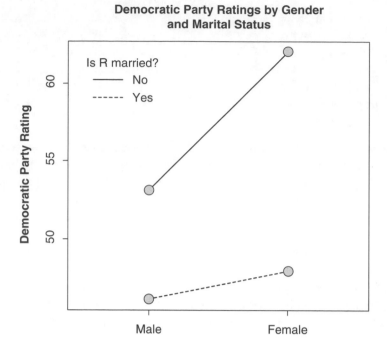

Example of an Additive Relationship

Compared with the protean complexity of interaction, additive relationships are the soul of simplicity. In a set of additive relationships, both the independent and the control variables help to explain the dependent variable. More than this, the effect of the independent variable is the same or very similar—same tendency, same strength—for all values of the control variable. Interaction relationships assume several forms. Additive relationships assume only one.

An example will illustrate this point. The nes datasets contain several measures of "linked fate," the extent to which individual members of identifiable groups feel attached to other members of the same group. For example, link_wom_scale measures the extent to which female respondents sense a connection between themselves and other women in society. Female respondents are measured as feeling "Weak", "Moderate", or "Strong" ties to other females. Nes also contains modsex_scale, which measures the extent to which individuals perceive that women are discriminated against and have few opportunities for achievement. The modsex_scale variable runs from 0 (the respondent perceives little discrimination against women and more opportunities for achievement) to 16 (a great deal of discrimination, few opportunities). It seems reasonable to hypothesize that women with a stronger sense of linked fate (higher values on link_wom_scale) will be more likely to perceive higher levels of sexism (higher values on modsex_scale) than will women with a weaker sense of linked fate. It is an interesting question, however, whether the relationship will be the same for white females and African American females. Blacks are likely to perceive greater discrimination than are whites, regardless of their feelings of link fate with other women. In this example, you will analyze the modsex_scale-link_wom_scale relationship, controlling for race (dem_raceeth2).

Deploy the imeansC function:

```
imeansC(~modsex_scale, ~link_wom_scale + dem_raceeth2, nesD)
```

link_wom_scale	dem_raceeth2	white	Black
Weak	svymean	7.99	8.99
Moderate	svymean	8.60	9.73
Strong	svymean	9.34	10.36

Does linked fate work as hypothesized? Yes. For both whites and blacks, mean values of modsex_scale ascend as we move from "Weak" to "Moderate" to "Strong." Indeed, the magnitude of the end-to-end increase is virtually identical for both races: 1.35 for white females (9.34 – 7.99) and 1.37 for black females (10.36 – 8.99). And notice the consistent effects of race. At each value of the independent variable, African American women are about 1 point higher on the discrimination scale than their white counterparts: 1 point among those having "Weak" linked fate, 1.13 points among the "Moderate" group, and 1.02 points among women who feel "Strong" ties to other women. Thus, regardless of race, the "linked-fate effect" is about 1.35. And regardless of feelings of linked fate, the "race effect" is about 1.

Top off the analysis with an accompanying line chart and legend:

```
iplotC(~modsex_scale, ~link_wom_scale+dem_raceeth2, nesD,
    modsex_scale~dem_raceeth2+link_wom_scale,
    xlab="Linked Fate Scale", ylab="Modern Sexism Scale",
    main=list("Modern Sexism Opinions by \n Linked Fate and Race", cex=1.2))

legend("topleft", legend=c("Black","White"), lty=c(2,1), lwd=2,
    title="Race",inset=0.1, bty="n")
```

You can see how this line chart (Figure 5.4) communicates the additive relationship. Moving from left to right, from weaker link to stronger link, each line rises by about 1.35 units. That's the linked-fate effect. The effect of race is conveyed by the distance between the lines. Despite a very slight widening at the middle category of the linked-fate measure, the racial difference is quite consistent. Now, you might encounter additive relationships in which the lines slope downward, imparting a negative relationship between the independent and dependent variables. And the lines might "float" closer together, suggesting a consistent but weaker effect of the control variable on the dependent variable, controlling for the independent variable. But you will always see symmetry in the relationships. The effect of the independent variable on the dependent variable will be the same or very similar for all values of the control variable, and the effect of the control variable on the dependent variable will be the same or very similar for all values of the independent variable.

Figure 5.4   Multiple Line Chart with Numeric Variable (Additive)

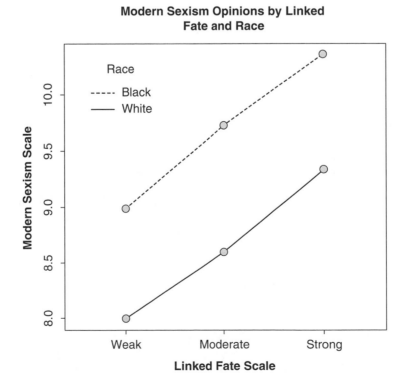

EXERCISES

1. (Datasets: world, worldD. Variables: democ_regime, frac_eth3, gdp_cap2.) Some countries have democratic regimes, and other countries do not. What factors help to explain this difference? One idea is that the type of government is shaped by the ethnic and religious diversity in a country's population. Countries that are relatively homogeneous, with most people sharing the same language and religious beliefs, are more likely to develop democratic systems than are countries having more linguistic conflicts and religious differences. Consider the ethnic heterogeneity hypothesis: Countries with lower levels of ethnic heterogeneity will be more likely to be democracies than will countries with higher levels of ethnic heterogeneity.

   A. According to the ethnic heterogeneity hypothesis, if you were to compare countries having lower heterogeneity with countries having higher heterogeneity, you should find (Check one.)

      ❑ a lower percentage of democracies among countries having lower heterogeneity.

      ❑ a higher percentage of democracies among countries having lower heterogeneity.

      ❑ no difference between the percentage of democracies among countries having lower heterogeneity and the percentage of democracies among countries with higher heterogeneity.

   B. World contains the variable democ_regime, which classifies each country as a democracy ("Yes") or a non-democracy ("No"). This is the dependent variable. World also contains frac_eth3, which classifies countries according to their level of ethnic heterogeneity: low (coded 1), medium (coded 2), or high (coded 3). This is the independent variable. Run xtp, testing the ethnic heterogeneity hypothesis. Fill in the percentages of democracies:

	Ethnic Heterogeneity		
	Low	Medium	High
Percentage of democracies	?	?	?

   C. Based on these results, does it appear that the ethnic heterogeneity hypothesis is correct or incorrect? (Circle one.)

      Correct   Incorrect

   D. Explain your answer in C, making specific reference to the percentage of democracies:

      _____

      _____

      _____

      _____

   E. A country's level of economic development also might be linked to its type of government. According to this perspective, countries with higher levels of economic development are more likely to be democracies than are countries with lower levels. The world dataset contains the variable gdp_cap2. This variable, based on gross domestic product per capita, is a measure of economic development. Countries are classified as "Low" or "High". Use xtabC to obtain a cross-tabulation analysis of the democ_regime-frac_eth3 relationship, controlling for gdp_cap2. Fill in the percentages of democracies:

| | Ethnic Heterogeneity | | |
	Low	Medium	High
Low GDP per capita percentage of democracies	?	?	?
High GDP per capita percentage of democracies	?	?	?

F. Create an indicator variable named world$democ.yes for countries coded "Yes" on democ_regime. Multiply the indicator times 100. Run the following command to update worldD: 'world=svydesign(id=~1, data=world)'. *Note*: R will issue a warning: "Warning in svydesign.default(id = ~1, data = world) : No weights or probabilities supplied, assuming equal probability." You can ignore this warning.

G. Run iplotC to obtain a multiple line chart depicting the percentage of democracies (democ.yes) for each value of frac_eth3, controlling for gdp_cap2. Suggested plot options: xlab="Fractionalization", ylab="Percentage of Democracies", main ("Percentage of Democracies by \n Fractionalization and GDP"). Use the legend function to supply a legend. Remember to match the correct line types with the legend labels. Print the chart you created.

H. Consider the evidence from parts E and G. Based on your analysis, how would you describe the relationship between ethnic heterogeneity and democracy, controlling for GDP per capita? (Circle one.)

Additive   Interaction

I. Explain your answer in H, making specific reference to the evidence in parts E and G.

_____

_____

_____

_____

2. (Datasets: nesD, nes. Variables: polknow3, dhs_threat3, ftgr_tea.) Given the tea party movement's deep skepticism of government activism, it seems plausible to hypothesize that individuals who regard the government as a threat would have warmer feelings toward the tea party than would those who do not think the government poses a threat. Of course, people would need to be reasonably well informed about politics to make the connection between their assessment of government threat and their evaluation of the tea party. When we control for political knowledge (control variable), we may find that the relationship between tea party ratings (dependent variable) and perceptions of government threat (independent variable) gets stronger as knowledge increases. In other words, interaction could be occurring in this set of relationships. Consider two propositions and an ancillary hypothesis.

Proposition 1: At all levels of political knowledge (nesD variable, polknow3), individuals who perceive the government as a threat (dhs_threat3) will give the tea party higher ratings (ftgr_tea) than will people who do not regard the government as a threat.

Proposition 2: The relationship between perceived threat and tea party ratings will be weaker for lower-knowledge respondents than for higher-knowledge respondents.

Ancillary Hypothesis: In a comparison of individuals, those with higher levels of political knowledge are less likely to regard the government as a threat than are those with lower levels of political knowledge.

The dependent variable: the tea party feeling thermometer (ftgr_tea), which runs from 0 (cold or negative feelings) to 100 (warm or positive feelings). The independent variable dhs_threat3, which captures assessments of government's threat with three ordinal levels—government represents no threat ("None"), a moderate threat ("Mod"), or an extreme threat ("Extrm"). Political knowledge is also a three-level ordinal: low ("Low know"), moderate ("Mid know"), and high knowledge ("High know").

A. Use imeansC to obtain a table of mean values of ftgr_tea for each combination of dhs_threat3 and polknow3. Record the means next to the question marks in the following table.

Ratings of Tea Party, by Perceived Government Threat and Political Knowledge			
Perceived Threat of Government (dhs_threat3)	Political Knowledge (polknow3)		
	Low know	Mid know	High know
None	?	?	?
Mod	?	?	?
Extrm	?	?	?

B. Is Proposition 1 supported or not supported by your findings? (Circle one.)

Proposition 1 is not supported.   Proposition 1 is supported.

C. Explain your answer in B, making specific reference to evidence in part A.

_____

_____

_____

_____

_____

D. Is Proposition 2 supported or not supported by your findings? (Circle one.)

Proposition 2 is not supported.   Proposition 2 is supported.

E. Explain your answer in D, making specific reference to evidence from part A.

_____

_____

_____

_____

_____

F. Use xtp (and the nes dataset) to perform a cross-tabulation analysis to test the ancillary hypothesis. Use dhs_threat3 as the dependent variable and polknow3 as the independent variable. Print the cross-tabulation table. (Remember that xtp automatically sends the cross-tab to Table.output.)

G. Is the Ancillary Hypothesis supported by your findings in part F? (Circle one.)

The Ancillary Hypothesis is not supported.   The Ancillary Hypothesis is supported.

Explain your answer in G, making specific reference to the cross-tabulation percentages.

_____

_____

_____

_____

_____

_____

H. Use iplotC and legend to create a nicely optioned multiple line chart showing means of ftgr_tea (y-axis) across values of dhs_threat3 (x-axis) for each value of polknow3. Here are some suggested labels: xlab="Perceived threat of Government", ylab="Ratings of Tea Party", main="Ratings of Tea Party, by Perceived Government Threat \n and Political Knowledge"). (*Note*: Your multiple line chart will have three lines, one for each level of polknow3. IplotC will automatically assign line type 1 [solid] to the "Low know" line, line type 2 [dashed] to the "Mid know" line, and line type 3 [dotted] to the "High know" line. In the legend command, make sure that the legend labels match the line types.)

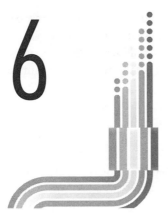

6

Making Inferences about Sample Means

Objective	Functions Introduced	Author or Source
Testing hypotheses about means	wtd.t.test {weights}	Josh Pasek[1]
Testing hypotheses about means with weighted sample data	wtd.ttestC {poliscidata}	Philip Pollock and Barry Edwards, based on Thomas Lumley's svymean and svytotal functions from survey package[2]
Testing hypotheses about proportions	prop.testC {poliscidata}	Philip Pollock and Barry Edwards, based on Jakson Aquino's compmeans function from the descr package[3]
Calculating 95% confidence intervals	CI95 {poliscidata}	Philip Pollock and Barry Edwards

Political research has much to do with observing patterns, creating explanations, framing hypotheses, and analyzing relationships. In interpreting their findings, however, researchers often operate in an environment of uncertainty. This uncertainty arises, in large measure, from the complexity of the political world. As we have seen, when we infer a causal connection between an independent variable and a dependent variable, it is hard to know for sure whether the independent variable is causing the dependent variable. Other, uncontrolled variables might be affecting the relationship, too. Yet uncertainty arises, as well, from the simple fact that research findings are often based on random samples. In an ideal world, we could observe and measure the characteristics of every element in the population of interest—every voting-age adult, every student enrolled at a university, every bill introduced in every state legislature, and so on. In such an ideal situation, we would enjoy a high degree of certainty that the variables we have described and the relationships we have analyzed mirror what is really going

---

[1] Pasek, J. (2012). *weights: Weighting and weighted statistics* (R package version 0.75). Assistance from Alex Tahk. Available at http://CRAN.R-project.org/package=weights

[2] Lumley, T. (2012). *survey: Analysis of complex survey samples* (R package version 3.28-2). Available at http://cran.r-project .org/web/packages/survey/index.html. See also: Lumley, T. (2004). Analysis of complex survey samples. *Journal of Statistical Software*, 9(1), 1–19; Lumley, T. (2010). *Complex surveys: A guide to analysis using R.* Hoboken, NJ: John Wiley & Sons.

[3] Aquino, J. (2012). *descr: Descriptive statistics* (R package version 0.9.8). Includes R source code and/or documentation written by Dirk Enzmann, Marc Schwartz, and Nitin Jain. Available at http://CRAN.R-project.org/package=descr

on in the population. Of course, we often do not have access to every member of a population. Instead we rely on a sample, a subset drawn at random from the population. By taking a random sample, we introduce random sampling error. In using a sample to draw inferences about a population, therefore, we avoid using the word *certainty.* Rather, we talk about *confidence* or *probability.* We know that the measurements we make on the sample will reflect the characteristics of the population, within the boundaries of random sampling error.

What are those boundaries? If we calculate the mean income of a random sample of adults, for example, how confident can we be that the mean income we observe in our sample is the same as the mean income in the population? The answer depends on the standard error of the sample mean, the extent to which the mean income of the sample departs by chance from the mean income of the population. If we use a sample to calculate a mean income for women and a mean income for men, how confident can we be that the difference between these two sample means reflects the true income difference between women and men in the population? Again, the answer depends on the standard error—in this case, the standard error of the *difference* between the sample means, the extent to which the difference in the sample departs from the difference in the population.

In this chapter, you will explore and apply inferential statistics. The wtd.t.test function (from the weights package) provides, among other useful statistics, a numeric variable's mean and its standard error, the essential building blocks of inferential statistics. A local function, CI95, uses the mean and standard error to determine the 95 percent confidence interval (95% CI) of the sample mean, the boundaries within which there is a .95 probability that the true population mean falls. In a natural extension of these ideas, you will also learn to use inferential statistics to evaluate the difference between two sample means. Two functions based on natural extension of these ideas, wtd.ttestC and prop.testC, permit you to use inferential statistics to evaluate the difference between two sample means or two sample proportions.

FINDING THE 95 PERCENT CONFIDENCE INTERVAL OF THE POPULATION MEAN

The nes dataset contains ftgr_gay, a measure of individuals' ratings of homosexuals. The feeling thermometer scales, as you know, range from 0 (cold or negative feelings) to 100 (warm or positive feelings). On average, where did respondents rate gays on the 0–100 scale? How much random sampling error—formally known as standard error—is contained in the average? The wtd.t.test function provides answers to both questions. Here is wtd.t.test's syntax, adapted for the task of testing hypotheses about a sample mean:

$$\texttt{wtd.t.test(}var,\ test.value,\ \texttt{weight=}optional.weight\texttt{)}$$

Inside the parentheses, one types the numeric variable of interest (in the current example, nes$ftgr_gay), a test value, and an optional sampling weight (for nes, nes$wt). The first and last arguments are familiar, but what is a test value? The wtd.t.test function is set up to compare the mean of a variable of interest, *var*, with a hypothetical mean, provided by the user in the *test.value* argument, and to see if random error could account for the difference between *var* and *test.value*. (We will discuss this application of wtd.t.test below.) To reach our current objective, the mean and standard error of a solitary sample mean, we would specify a test value equal to 0:

```
# Specify a test value equal to 0.
wtd.t.test(nes$ftgr_gay, 0, weight=nes$wt)
```

```
> wtd.t.test(nes$ftgr_gay,0,weight=nes$wt)

$test
[1] "One Sample Weighted T-Test"

$coefficients
  t.value        df   p.value
136.8418 5422.6426    0.0000

$additional
 Difference       Mean Alternative    Std. Err
 51.6268091    51.6268091   0.0000000   0.3772736
```

Respondents rated gays at 51.63, on average. How closely does this sample mean, 51.63, reflect the sentiments of the American electorate, the population from which the sample was drawn? The answer is contained in the standard error of the mean ("Std. Err"), .3772736 ≈ .38. It is an established statistical rule that 95 percent of all possible population means will fall in this interval:

Sample mean ± 1.96 (Standard error of sample mean)

By this rule, the lower 95% confidence boundary: 51.63 − 1.96(.38) = 50.89; and the upper 95% confidence boundary: 51.63 + 1.96(.38) = 52.37. There is a high probability, a 95 percent probability, that the true population mean lies in the region between 50.89 at the low end and 52.37 at the high end. The function, CI95, will return the 95% CI boundaries for any sample mean and standard error:

CI95(*mean, se.mean*)

For the example at hand, we have

```
# Calculate 95% confidence interval
CI95(51.63, .38)
```

```
> CI95(51.63,.38)

   Lower 95% CI      Upper 95% CI
      50.88521          52.37479
```

Now, we are trying to determine how much confidence to invest in our sample mean of 51.63. Is the true population mean right around 51.63? The 95% CI provides a probabilistic—not a definitive—answer. There is a high probability, a 95 percent probability, that the true population mean lies in the region between 50.89 at the low end and 52.37 at the high end. If we were to take a very large number of random samples from the population and calculate, for each sample, the mean of nes$ftgr_gay, 95 percent of those calculated means would fall in the interval between 50.89 and 52.37. To be sure, there is random "noise" in each random sample. Yet 95 percent of the time, that noise will give us a sample mean within the bandwidth of 50.89 and 52.37. On uncommon occasions—5 percent of the time—we would obtain a sample mean that falls outside those boundaries, below 50.89 or above 52.37.

The 95% CI is the inferential foundation of the widely applied *.05 test of statistical significance*. Any sample mean than falls within the 95% CI is not significantly different, in a statistical sense, from any other sample mean that falls within the interval. There is a probability of greater than .05 that both means were drawn from the same population. However, any sample mean that falls outside the interval is significantly different from any sample mean that falls inside the interval. The probability that both means were drawn from the same population is less than .05.

TESTING HYPOTHETICAL CLAIMS ABOUT THE POPULATION MEAN

You can well imagine how the .05 test of statistical significance can be used to evaluate hypothetical claims about a population mean. Suppose you hypothesize, for example, that political science majors will give gays higher ratings than will the U.S. population. To test this idea, you administer the feeling thermometer—the same question that appears in the nes dataset—to a group of political science majors. Compared with the nes dataset's mean of 51.63 on nes$ftgr_gays, you find a higher mean, 52, among the political science majors in your study. Thus, it would appear that your respondents are, on average, more positive toward gays than are the individuals in the National Election Study's random sample of adult U.S. citizens. But is this difference, 51.63 versus 52, *statistically* significant at the .05 level? No, it is not.

Why can we say this? In the method we have been applying, we know that, given a sample mean of 51.63 and a standard error of .38, there is a probability of .95 that the true population mean falls between 50.89 and 52.37. Because the political science majors' mean, 52, falls inside the interval, we must conclude that the majors' mean could have been drawn from the same population as the overall electorate. Thus, there is no significant difference.

A logically equivalent—and more common—way to apply the same idea is to work with the *difference* between the sample mean (51.63) and the hypothetical mean (52). To hypothesize that political science majors are more pro-gay than the electorate is the same thing as saying that the difference between the two means, 51.63 minus 52, is significantly different from 0. The counter-hypothesis, that any difference between the two means can be accounted for by random sampling error, says that the difference is not significantly different from 0. Thus, if the *95% CI of the difference* contains 0, then there is a probability of greater than .05 that the two means came from the same population. We would conclude that they are not significantly different. If, on the other hand, the 95% CI of the difference does not contain 0, then there is a probability of less than .05 that the two means came from the same population. In that case, we would conclude that they are significantly different.

Caveat

The 95% CI is the prevalent standard in political research, but it is *statistically conservative*; that is, it biases our decisons against inferring that two means are significantly different. You can see why this is. In applying the .05 standard, the 95% CI splits .05 in two: a .025 probability that the mean difference in the population lies below the lower boundary and a .025 probability that it lies above the upper boundary. In effect, then, the 95% CI applies a stringent .025 test for mean differences. When it comes to statistics, conservatism is a preferred philosophy. After all, we do not want to incorrectly infer that two means are different when in fact they are not. However, there is a more precise way to apply the .05 test of statistical significance. In the *P-value approach*, the researcher asks how often random sampling error would produce an observed difference between two means if, in the population, there is no true difference between them. If such an event would occur more frequently than .05 of the time, then we would conclude that, in the unseen population, the two means are not different. If such an event would occur less frequently than .05 of the time, then we would conclude that the two means are different.

Interpreting P-Values

Let's enlist wtd.t.test to produce the relevant statistics for us. The syntax is the same as before, only this time we change the test value from 0 to the majors' mean, 52:

```
# Specify a test value of 52, the political science majors' mean
wtd.t.test(nes$ftgr_gay, 52, weight=nes$wt)
```

```
> wtd.t.test(nes$ftgr_gay,52,weight=nes$wt)

$test
[1] "One Sample Weighted T-Test"

$coefficients
    t.value          df       p.value
 -0.9891784 5422.6426000     0.3226200

$additional
   Difference      Mean Alternative     Std. Err
   -0.3731909 51.6268091   52.0000000    0.3772736
```

The wtd.t.test function subtracted the test value, 52, from the nes mean, 51.63, and reported the result, −0.3731909, beneath "Difference". To obtain the 95% CI of the difference, run CI95, typing the mean difference and standard error:

```
# Calculate 95% confidence interval of difference of means
CI95(-.37, .38)
```

```
    Lower 95% CI      Upper 95% CI
     -1.1147863         0.3747863
```

The confidence boundaries encompass 0. Thus, there is a probability of greater than .05 that we would obtain a difference of −.37 if, in fact, no difference exists in the population.

But how much greater than .05? If the true population difference is equal to 0, how often will random sampling error produce a difference of −.37? The answer to this question is contained in the wtd.t.test results. The wtd.t.test function first calculates a t-statistic ("t.value"), which tells us exactly how many standard errors lie between 0 and the observed difference of −.37. A t-statistic, sometimes called a t-ratio, is equal to the mean difference divided by the standard error of the mean difference: (mean difference) / (s. e. mean difference). The function uses this calculated value, equal to −.99 in the current example, to determine a precise probability or P-value ("p.value"): .3226200. From the confidence interval test, we already knew that random processes would produce the observed difference more frequently than .05 of the time. We can now put a finer point on this probability. If, in the population, political science majors are really no different from anybody else, then random sampling error would give us a difference of −.37 about 32 percent of the time. Thus, chance processes would produce the observed difference about a third of the time—much too frequently. Conclusion: The nes mean and the majors' mean are not significantly different.

Before proceeding, consider a template for using a P-value to write an inferential statement:

If in the population there is no difference between the mean of [the test variable] and [the test value], then the observed difference of [the mean difference] would occur _____ of the time by chance.

Of course, you can embellish the template to make it fit the hypothesis you are testing. For the nes$ftgr_gay example, you could complete the sentence this way: "If in the population there is no difference between the nes mean of ftgr_gay and the political science majors' mean of 52, then the observed difference of −.37 would occur .32 of the time by chance." It is also acceptable to express the P-value as a percentage, as in: "would occur 32 percent of the time by chance." The .05 benchmark is the standard for testing your hypothesis. If the P-value is less than or equal to .05, then you can infer that the test value is significantly different from the mean of the test variable. If the P-value is greater than .05, then you can infer that the test value is not significantly different from the mean of the test variable.

MAKING INFERENCES ABOUT TWO SAMPLE MEANS

We now turn to a common hypothesis-testing situation: comparing the sample means of a dependent variable for two groups that differ on an independent variable. Someone investigating the gender gap, for example, might test a series of hypotheses about the political differences between men and women. In the next guided example, we test two gender gap hypotheses:

Hypothesis 1: In a comparison of individuals, men will give gays lower feeling thermometer ratings than will women.

Hypothesis 2: In a comparison of individuals, men will give the Republican Party higher feeling thermometer ratings than will women.

The first hypothesis suggests that when we divide the sample on the basis of the independent variable, gender, and compare mean values of the gay feeling thermometer (nes$ftgr_gay), the male mean will be lower than the female mean. The second hypothesis suggests that when we compare feeling thermometer values among Republican men and women, the male mean will be higher than the female mean.

The researcher always tests his or her hypotheses against a skeptical foil, the *null hypothesis*. The null hypothesis claims that, regardless of any group differences that a researcher observes in a random sample, no group differences exist in the population from which the sample was drawn. How does the null hypothesis explain apparently systematic patterns that might turn up in a sample, such as a mean difference between women and men on the gay feeling thermometer? It points to random sampling error. In essence, the null hypothesis says, "You observed such and such a difference between two groups in your random sample. But, in reality, no difference exists in the population. When you took the sample, you introduced random sampling error. Thus, random sampling error accounts for the difference you observed." For both hypotheses 1 and 2 above, the null hypothesis says that there are no real differences between men and women in the population, that men do not give gays lower ratings, and that they do not give the Republican Party higher ratings. The null hypothesis further asserts that any observed differences in the sample can be accounted for by random sampling error.

The null hypothesis is so central to the methodology of statistical inference that we always begin by assuming it to be correct. We then set a fairly high standard for rejecting it. The researcher's hypotheses—such as the gay thermometer and Republican Party thermometer hypotheses—are considered alternative hypotheses.

A new function, wtd.ttestC, permits us to test each alternative hypothesis against the null hypothesis and to decide whether the observed mean differences between two groups are too large to have occurred by random chance when the sample was drawn. In addition to other useful statistics, for each mean comparison, wtd.ttestC will report the 95% CI of the mean difference and it will provide a P-value, the probability of obtaining the sample difference under the working assumption that the null hypothesis is true. The wtd.ttestC syntax is as follows:

```
wtd.ttestC(~depvar, ~indepvar, design.dataset)
```

For our first gender comparison, we would type:

```
# when running wtd.ttestC, use the design version datasets
wtd.ttestC(~ftgr_gay, ~gender, nesD)
```

```
      Means and Standard Errors:
       gender ftgr_gay          se
Male     Male 47.36710 0.7033388
Female Female 55.66918 0.7379861


       t-Test Statistics:
Mean difference          Std.Err        t-statistic          P-value
  -8.302086e+00     1.019465e+00     -8.143571e+00     1.926719e-16


      Lower 95% CI     Upper 95% CI
        -10.300200        -6.303971
```

Males, on average, rated gays at 47.37, whereas females had a higher mean, 55.67—a difference equal to −8.30. The null hypothesis claims that this difference is the result of random sampling error and, therefore, that the true male-female difference in the population is equal to 0. Using the information provided by wtd.ttestC, we test the null hypothesis against the alternative hypothesis that the male mean is lower than the female mean.

If the null hypothesis is correct that, in the population, men and women do not differ, exactly how often would random chance produce an observed difference of −8.30? The upper 95% CI boundary tells us that the probability is less than .025. (Remember that, for mean differences with negative signs, as in this example, the upper 95% CI boundary will include 0 for P-values of greater than .025. For mean differences with positive signs, the lower 95% CI boundary will include 0 for P-values of greater than .025.) The P-value approach provides a poignantly precise probability. The calculated t-statistic (−8.14) has an associated P-value of 1.926719e-16, which is scientific notation for 0.0000000000000001926719, which is something on the order of 2 times in a quadrillion. Reject the null hypothesis.

All right, so men score significantly lower on the gay thermometer than do women. Are men more warmly inclined toward the Republican Party, as hypothesis 2 suggests? Let's run the script and find out:

```
# Weighted t-test, difference of means
wtd.ttestC(~ft_rep, ~gender, nesD)
```

```
Means and Standard Errors:
       gender  ft_rep          se
Male     Male 44.57382 0.6776347
Female Female 44.32298 0.7060677
```

```
   t-Test Statistics:
Mean difference        Std.Err     t-statistic      P-value
       0.2508335     0.9786319       0.2563104    0.6011443


   Lower 95% CI    Upper 95% CI
      -1.667250        2.168917
```

Again, the information on ft_rep would appear consistent with the alternative hypothesis. Men, with a mean of 44.57, score slightly higher than do women, who averaged 44.32, a mean difference of .25. Does this difference pass muster with the null hypothesis? Consider the 95% CI: −1.67 at the low end and 2.17 at the high end. Does this interval include 0, the null's talisman? Yes, the confidence interval brackets 0. Thus, we know that the mean difference would occur by chance more frequently than 5 times out of 100. There is indeed a very high probability of observing a difference of .25, if in fact the null hypothesis is correct: .601. If the null hypothesis is correct, then we would observe by chance a sample difference of .25 about 60 percent of the time. Accept the null hypothesis.

MAKING INFERENCES ABOUT TWO SAMPLE PROPORTIONS

What if the researcher is not dealing with means but rather wishes to compare proportions between groups—for example, comparing the proportion of male Democrats with the proportion of female Democrats? Following the (by now familiar) creation of an indicator variable, a different function, prop.testC, can be applied to such comparisons. Consider the following script, which converts the "Dem" category of nes$pid_3 into a numeric indicator:

```
# Create indicator variable
nes$dem – as.numeric(nes$pid_3=="Dem")
```

Here is the prop.testC syntax:

```
prop.testC(data$depvar, data$indepvar, w=data$weight)
```

Using prop.testC to evaluate gender differences in the proportion of Democrats:

```
# Difference of properties test
# The prop.testC function requires the 'data$variable' assignment.
prop.testC(nes$dem, nes$gender, w=nes$wt)
```

```
Proportions and Ns:
         Proportion      N
Male      0.3103642   2831
Female    0.3809429   3065
Total     0.3470555   5896


   Z-Test Statistics:
  Difference          Std.Err      Z-statistic          P-value
-7.057875e-02     1.235307e-02    -5.713457e+00     5.535182e-09


   Lower 95% CI       Upper 95% CI
    -0.09479033        -0.04636718
```

Among males, .31 (or 31 percent) are Democrats, compared with .38 (38 percent) for females, a difference of −.07, or about 7 percentage points. The 95% CI, which does not include 0, advises us to reject the null hypothesis. The test statistics—a difference in proportions is evaluated with a Z-test instead of a t-test—point toward a highly significant partisan gender gap: $Z = -5.71$, which has a P-value that is effectively .00. It would be an exceedingly rare event for random sampling error to have produced the observed difference. Reject the null hypothesis.

EXERCISES

1. (Dataset: gss. Variables: egalit_scale, wtss.) The 2012 General Social Survey asked people a series of questions designed to measure how egalitarian they are—that is, the extent to which they think economic opportunities and rewards should be distributed more equally in society. The gss variable egalit_scale ranges from 1 (low egalitarianism) to 35 (high egalitarianism). The 2012 GSS, of course, is a random sample of U.S. adults. In this exercise, you will analyze egalit_scale using wtd.t.test and CI95. You will then draw inferences about the population mean.

    A. Run wtd.t.test on gss$egalit_scale, with the test value set to 0. (Be sure to weight by gss$wtss.) Egalitarianism has a sample mean of (Fill in the blank.) _____.

    B. Based on the results you obtained in part A, run CI95. There is a probability of .95 that the true population mean falls between an egalitarianism score of (Fill in the blank.) _____ at the low end and a score of (Fill in the blank.) _____ at the high end.

    C. A student researcher hypothesizes that social work majors will score significantly higher on the egalitarianism scale than the typical adult. The student researcher also hypothesizes that business majors will score significantly lower on the egalitarianism scale than the average adult. After administering the scale to a number of social work majors and a group of business majors, the researcher obtains these results: Social work majors' mean, 20.1; business majors' mean, 18.8. Run wtd.t.test, specifying a test value of 20.1. Using the mean difference ("Difference") and standard error, run CI95. Run wtd.t.test again, specifying a test value of 18.8. Run CI95, using the mean difference and standard error.

    D. Based on your analyses, and applying the .05 test of significance, you can infer that (Check one.)

    ❑ Social work majors probably are not more egalitarian than most adults.

    ❑ Social work majors probably are more egalitarian than most adults.

    Explain your answer.

    _____

    _____

    _____

    Based on your analyses, and applying the .05 test of significance, you can infer that (Check one.)

    ❑ Business majors probably are not less egalitarian than most adults.

    ❑ Business majors probably are less egalitarian than most adults.

    Explain your answer.

    _____

    _____

    _____

    E. Refer to the P-value you obtained from your analysis of the business majors' mean. (Fill in the blanks.)

    If in the population there is no difference between the mean of egalit_scale and the business majors' mean, the observed difference of _____ would occur _____ of the time by chance.

2. (Dataset: gssD. Variables: age2, int_info_scale.) Are older people interested in a wider variety of social, economic, political, and scientific issues than are younger people? Or do younger people and older people not differ significantly in the scope of their interests? The gssD dataset contains int_info_scale, which measures respondents' level of interest in 10 different issue areas. Scores range from 0 to 20, with higher scores denoting higher levels of interest. The gssD also has age2, which takes on two values: "<=30" for respondents 30 years old or younger and ">=31" for respondents older than 30. Run wtd.ttestC, using int_info_scale as the dependent variable and age2 as the independent variable.

   A. Fill in the table below.

Statistics for int_info_scale	Level of Interest
Mean for younger group (<=30 years old)	?
Mean for older group (>=31 years old)	?
Mean difference	?
Lower 95% CI	?
Upper 95% CI	?
t-statistic	?
P-value	?

   B. According to the null hypothesis, in the population from which the sample was drawn, the difference between the mean for people older than 30 and the mean for people 30 or younger is equal to (Fill in the blank.) _____.

   C. In this analysis, the upper 95% CI includes 0. This fact alone tells you that the P-value (Check one.)

   ❑ must be greater than .05.

   ❑ must be greater than .025.

   ❑ must be 0.

   D. Using the .05 level of statistical significance, you can infer that (Check one.)

   ❑ The older age group and the younger age group do not differ significantly in their level of interest in current issues.

   ❑ The older age group scores significantly higher on the level of interest scale than does the younger age group.

   ❑ The older age group scores significantly lower on the level of interest scale than does the younger age group.

   E. Your inferential decision, therefore, is (Check one.)

   ❑ accept the null hypothesis.

   ❑ reject the null hypothesis.

3. (Dataset: gssD. Variables: sibs, relig2, authoritarianism, sex.) Here are two bits of conventional wisdom, beliefs that are widely accepted as accurate descriptions of the world. Conventional Wisdom 1: Catholics have bigger families than do Protestants. (Dependent variable: sibs, number of siblings; independent variable: relig2, "Protestant"/ "Catholic".) Conventional Wisdom 2: Men have stronger authoritarian tendencies than do women. (Dependent variable: authoritarianism, ranging from 0 [low authoritarianism] to 7 [high authoritarianism]; independent variable: sex.)

A. In this exercise, you will use wtd.ttestC to test these ideas and see how well they stand up to the statistical evidence. Run the analyses. Record the results in the following table.

	Conventional Wisdom 1	*Conventional Wisdom 2*
Mean difference	?	?
Lower 95% CI boundary of mean difference	?	?
Upper 95% CI boundary of mean difference	?	?
t-statistic	?	?
P-value	?	?

B. Consider the following statement: "According to the statistical evidence, we can reject the null hypothesis for Conventional Wisdom 1." Is this statement correct or incorrect? (Circle one.)

Incorrect   Correct

Explain your answer, making specific reference to the statistics in part A.

_____

_____

_____

_____

C. Consider the following statement: "The statistical evidence supports Conventional Wisdom 2." Is this statement correct or incorrect? (Circle one.)

Incorrect   Correct

Explain your answer, making specific reference to the statistics in part A.

_____

_____

_____

4. (Dataset: gss. Variables: partyid_3, sex, wtss.) In one of this chapter's guided examples, you analyzed the nes dataset and found a statistically significant difference between the proportions of males and females who are Democrats. The gss dataset also contains a measure of party identification, partyid_3 ("Dem" / "Ind" / "Rep"). However, the General Social Survey uses a different sampling frame (all U.S. adults vs. voting-eligible citizens) and somewhat different question wording for its party identification question. Will the gss dataset also reveal a statistically significant difference in the proportions of males and females who are Democrats?

A. Create a numeric indicator, named gss$dem, for the "Dem" category of gss$partyid_3. Run prop.testC. Record the results in the following table:

Statistics for gss$dem	
Proportion of males who are Democrats	?
Proportion of females who are Democrats	?
Difference	?
Lower 95% CI	?
Upper 95% CI	?
Z-statistic	?
P-value	?

B. Does the statistical evidence support the hypothesis that men are less likely than women to be Democrats? Answer yes or no and explain, making explicit reference to the evidence in part A.

_____

_____

_____

7

Chi-Square and Measures of Association

Objectives	Functions Introduced	Author or Source
Conducting a chi-square test	xtp.chi2 {poliscidata}	Quan Li[1]
Measuring association in a cross-tabulation	somersD	Philip Pollock and Barry Edwards, based on work of Eric Lecoutre[2]
	svydesign, svytable {survey}	Thomas Lumley[3]
Creating a subset sample (based on control variable)	subset {base}	R Development Core Team[4]
Using an alternative measure of association in cross-tabulation	CramersV	Philip Pollock and Barry Edwards

In the preceding chapter, you learned how to test for mean differences on a numeric dependent variable. But what if you are not dealing with numeric variables? What if you are doing cross-tabulation analysis and are trying to figure out whether an observed relationship between two factors (nominal or ordinal variables) mirrors the true relationship in the population? Just as with mean differences, the answer depends on the boundaries of random sampling error, the extent to which your observed results "happened by chance" when you took the sample. The xtp.chi2 function (based on descr's crosstab function) and svychisqC (based on Lumley's svychisq function) will provide the information needed to test the statistical significance of nominal or ordinal relationships. Two additional functions, CramersV and somersD, will yield appropriate measures of association.

[1] {survey}, Lumley, T. (2012). *survey: Analysis of complex survey samples* (R package version 3.28-2). Available at http://cran.r-project.org/web/packages/survey/index.html. See also: Lumley, T. (2004). Analysis of complex survey samples. *Journal of Statistical Software*, 9(1), 1–19; Lumley, T. (2010). *Complex surveys: A guide to analysis using R.* Hoboken, NJ: John Wiley & Sons.
[2] Pollock, P. H. (2013). *An R companion to political analysis.* Thousand Oaks, CA: SAGE/CQ Press. Based on crosstab {descr}, Aquino, J. (2012). *{descr}: Descriptive statistics* (R package version 0.9.8). Includes R source code and/or documentation written by Dirk Enzmann, Marc Schwartz, and Nitin Jain (2012). The workspace function, freqC, is a slightly modified version of freq. Available at http://CRAN.R-project.org/package=descr
[3] The somersD function implements Eric Lecoutre's tablesomersD. Available at http://tolstoy.newcastle.edu.au/R/help/05/07/9442.html#16601qlink2. The somersD function also requires svytable {survey}, written by Thomas Lumley.
[4] R Development Core Team. (2011). R: A language and environment for statistical computing. Vienna, Austria: Author. Retrieved from http://www.R-project.org/

You are familiar with using xtp and xtabC to perform cross-tabulation analysis. For analyzing datasets that contain a preponderance of factor variables—variables measured by nominal or ordinal categories—cross-tabulation is by far the most common mode of analysis in political research. In this chapter, we will use xtp.chi2 to obtain the oldest and most widely applied test of statistical significance in cross-tabulation analysis, the chi-square test. With rare exceptions, chi-square can always be used to determine whether an observed cross-tab relationship departs significantly from the expectations of the null hypothesis. In the first guided example, you will be introduced to the logic behind chi-square, and you will learn how to interpret xtp.chi2's output.

In this chapter, you will also learn how to obtain measures of association for the relationships you are analyzing. If one or both variables in the cross-tabulation are nominal level, then you need to run CramersV to obtain the Cramer's V statistic. If both are ordinal-level variables, then you will run somersD to obtain Somers' d. Cramer's V takes on a value between 0 (no relationship exists between the independent and dependent variables) and +1 (a perfect relationship). Cramer's V is based on chi-square and so, technically, it can be used to gauge the strength of any nominal- or ordinal-level relationship. For ordinal-ordinal associations, however, Somers' d is much preferred. Somers' d is a directional measure that ranges from –1 to +1. A plus (+) sign says that increasing values of the independent variable are associated with increasing values of the dependent variable. A minus (–) sign says that increasing values of the independent variable are related to decreasing values of the dependent variable. Unlike Cramer's V, Somers' d is a proportional reduction in error (PRE) measures of strength. A PRE measure tells you the extent to which the values of the independent variable predict the values of the dependent variable. A value close to 0 says that the independent variable provides little predictive leverage; the relationship is weak. Values close to the poles—to –1 for negative associations or to +1 for positive relationships—tell you that the independent variable provides a lot of help in predicting the dependent variable; the relationship is strong.

ANALYZING AN ORDINAL-LEVEL RELATIONSHIP

We will begin by using nes and nesD to analyze an ordinal-level relationship. Consider this hypothesis: In a comparison of individuals, those having higher levels of education will have stronger pro-environmental attitudes than will those having lower levels of education. Dataset nes has envjob_3, an ordinal variable that measures the extent to which respondents think that we should "regulate business to protect the environment and create jobs" or have "no regulation, because it will not work and will cost jobs." Responses are classified as pro-environment ("Envir", coded 1), a middle position ("Mid", 2), or pro-jobs ("Jobs", 3). Envjob_3 is the dependent variable. The nes variable dem_educ3 is the independent variable. Dem_educ3's ordinal categories: high school or less ("HS or less"), some college ("Some coll"), or college degree or higher ("Coll+").

Let's first test this hypothesis the old-fashioned way—by running an xtp analysis on nes and comparing column percentages.

```
xtp(nes, envjob_3, dem_educ3,wt)
```

```
  Cell Contents
|-----------------------|
|                 Count |
|        Column Percent |
|-----------------------|


==================================================
          dem_educ3
envjob_3   HS or less   Some coll   Coll+   Total
--------------------------------------------------
Envir             694         571     656    1921
                38.1%       37.8%   41.3%   39.1%

--------------------------------------------------
Mid               646         562     561    1769
                35.5%       37.2%   35.3%   36.0%

--------------------------------------------------
Jobs              482         377     370    1229
                26.5%       25.0%   23.3%   25.0%

--------------------------------------------------
Total            1822        1510    1587    4919
                37.0%       30.7%   32.3%
==================================================
```

Note: Row percentages added by authors.

Figure 7.1   Mosaic Plot of Cross-Tabulation

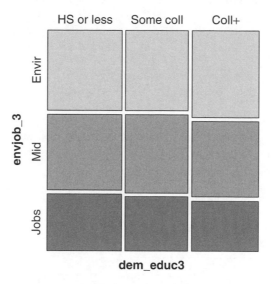

How would you evaluate the envjob_3-dem_educ3 hypothesis in light of this analysis? Focus on the column percentages in the "Envir" row. According to the hypothesis, as we move along this row, from lower education to higher education, the percentage of pro-environment respondents should increase. Is this what happens? The percentages run from 38.1 among the least educated, drop slightly, to 37.8, among the middle group, and then rise again, to 41.3, among those with a college education or higher. So there is something on the order of a 3-percentage-point difference between the least and most educated respondents, not a terribly robust relationship between the independent and dependent variables. The 3-point gradient is similar—perhaps slightly more systematic—along the "Jobs" row: 26.5 percent, 25.0 percent, and 23.3 percent. Indeed, two political analysts might offer conflicting interpretations of these results. The first analyst might conclude that, yes, as education increases, pro-environment sentiments grow stronger, and pro-jobs attitudes become weaker. The other might declare the relationship too weak to support the hypothesis. Inferential statistics, of course, is designed to settle such arguments.

Let's reconsider the envjob_3-dem_educ3 cross-tabulation in the way that the chi-square test of statistical significance would approach it. Chi-square begins by looking at the "Total" column, which contains the distribution of the entire sample across the values of the dependent variable, envjob_3. Thus, 39.1 percent of the sample is pro-environment, 36.0 percent takes a middle position, and 25.0 percent is pro-jobs. Chi-square then frames the null hypothesis, which claims that, in the population, envjob_3 and dem_educ3 are not related to each other, that individuals' levels of education are unrelated to their opinions about the environment. If the null hypothesis is correct, then a random sample of people with a high school education or less would produce the same distribution of opinions as the total distribution: 39.1 percent "Envir" / 36.0 percent "Mid" / 25.0 percent "Jobs." By the same token, a random sample of people with some college would yield a distribution that looks just like the total distribution: 39.1 percent "Envir" / 36.0 percent "Mid" / 25.0 percent "Jobs." A random sample of individuals with college or higher would produce the same result: 39.1 percent "Envir" / 36.0 percent "Mid" / 25.0 percent "Jobs." Thus, if the null hypothesis is correct, then the distribution of cases down each column of the table will be the same as the "Total" column. Of course, the null hypothesis asserts that any departures from this monotonous pattern resulted from random sampling error.

Now reexamine the table and make a considered judgment. Would you say that the observed distribution of cases within each category of dem_educ3 conforms to the expectations of the null hypothesis? For those with high school or less, the distribution is very close to the total distribution, with modest departures—for example, a somewhat lower percentage in the "Envir" category than the null would expect and a slightly higher percentage in the "Jobs" category. The distribution for those with some college corresponds quite well to the total distribution, as does the distribution for the most-educated respondents. Thus, for each value of dem_educ3, there is fairly close conformity to what we would expect to find if the null hypothesis is true. The small departures from these expectations, furthermore, might easily be explained by random sampling error, the null's explanation for everything.

Let's run xtp.chi2 and find out if our considered judgment is borne out by the chi-square test. Aside from the function's name, xtp.chi2 shares xtp's syntax:

```
xtp.chi2(data, depvar, indepvar, weight)
```

```
xtp.chi2(nes, envjob_3, dem_educ3, wt)
```

```
|-----------------------|
|                 Count |
|       Expected Values |
|-----------------------|
```

	x			
y	HS or less	Some coll	Coll+	Total
Envir	694	571	656	1921
	711.5	589.7	619.8	
Mid	646	562	561	1769
	655.2	543.0	570.7	
Jobs	482	377	370	1229
	455.2	377.3	396.5	
Total	1822	1510	1587	4919

Statistics for All Table Factors

Pearson's Chi-squared test

Chi^2 = 7.449319   d.f. = 4   p = 0.1

Minimum expected frequency: 377.2698

The xtp.chi2 produces a cross-tabulation featuring two numbers in each cell, followed by a table of statistics, labeled "Pearson's Chi-squared test." (The mosaic plot does not change and is not shown.) The cross-tab data reveal the building blocks of the chi-square test of significance. The top number, labeled "Count", is the actual or *observed* number of cases in the cell. For example, 694 "HS or less" respondents fall into the "Envir" category of envjob_3. The bottom number, labeled "Expected Values", is the number of respondents that we *expect* to fall into the cell, under the assumption that the null hypothesis is correct. Thus, the null hypothesis predicts that 711.5 low-education respondents—about 712 people—should fall into the "Envir" category. The chi-square test statistic is based on a comparison of the observed and expected frequencies for every cell in the table. The chi-square test asks, "Overall, how closely do the null's expectations fit the observed data?" If the answer is "Quite closely," then the chi-square statistic is a small number with a large P-value. If the answer is "Not closely at all," then the chi-square statistic is a large number with a small P-value.

Consider the statistics in the test table. The entry labeled "Chi^2" provides the chi-square test statistic. Again, the larger the magnitude of this test statistic—or any test statistic—the less likely that the observed data can be explained by random sampling error. The smaller the test statistic, the more likely that the null's favorite process—random chance—accounts for the observed data. So, if the observed data perfectly fit the expectations of the null hypothesis, then the chi-square test statistic would be 0. As the observed data depart from the null's expectations, this value grows in size, allowing the researcher to begin entertaining the idea of rejecting the null hypothesis.

For the envjob_3-dem_educ3 cross-tabulation, xtp.chi2 calculated a chi-square test statistic equal to 7.449319. Is this number, 7.45, statistically different from 0, the value we would expect to obtain if the null hypothesis were true? Put another way: If the null hypothesis is correct, how often will we obtain a test statistic of 7.45 by chance? The answer is contained in the value labeled "p", the P-value. In our example, xtp.chi2 reports a P-value of .1. If the null hypothesis is correct in its assertion that no relationship exists between the independent and dependent variables, then we will obtain a test statistic of 7.45, by chance, about 10 percent of the time. Because .10 exceeds the .05 standard, the null hypothesis is on safe ground. From our initial comparison of percentages, we suspected that the relationship might not defeat the null hypothesis. The chi-square test has confirmed that suspicion. Accept the null hypothesis.

How strong is the relationship between the independent and dependent variables? How accurately can we predict the dependent variable by knowing the independent variable? Given that the null hypothesis prevailed in the current example, it is probably safe to say that education is a very weak predictor of environmental opinions. To find out how weak, let's obtain Somers' d, a measure of strength for ordinal relationships. The somersD syntax:

$$somersD(\sim indepvar + depvar, \ design.dataset)$$

Notice that the independent variable is typed first and that somersD uses the design version of the dataset. The following expression will give us the Somers' d statistic for the relationship between dem_educ3 (independent variable) and envjob_3 (dependent variable):

```
somersD(~dem_educ3+envjob_3, nesD)
```

```
    Somers'dyx:
[1] -0.02905914
```

What does this value, −.029, tell us about the relationship? Because the statistic is negative, it tells us that increasing codes on dem_educ3 are associated with decreasing codes on envjob_3. We can discern a faint pattern: More educated respondents are slightly more likely to fall into the "Envir" category, and less educated respondents are slightly more likely to fall into the "Jobs" category. Because the statistic is puny—it has a magnitude (absolute value) of .029 on a scale that runs from 0.000 to 1.000—it tells us that the relationship is weak. More specifically, because Somers' d is a PRE measure of association, we can say this: Compared to how well we can predict environmental opinions without knowing respondents' levels of education, we can improve our prediction by 2.9 percent by knowing respondents' levels of education.

Not much going on there. Obviously, we need to frame another hypothesis, using different variables, and see if our luck changes. But before moving on, let's review the interpretation of the chi-square statistic and Somers' d. This is also a good place to introduce templates that will help you describe your findings.

Summary

Values of the chi-square test statistic that are close to 0 are within the domain of the null hypothesis. As chi-square increases in magnitude (the chi-square statistic cannot assume negative values), the null's explanation for the observed data—"it all happened by chance"—becomes increasingly implausible. The chi-square statistic is accompanied by a P-value, "p". Here is a template for writing an interpretation of the P-value:

"If the null hypothesis is correct that there is no relationship between [independent variable] and [dependent variable], then random sampling error will produce the observed data [P-value] of the time."

For our example: "If the null hypothesis is correct that, in the population from which the sample was drawn, there is no relationship between education and environmental opinions, then random sampling error will produce the observed data .114 of the time." (If you prefer percentages, you can make this substitution: " . . . will produce the observed data 11.4 percent of the time.") Use the .05 benchmark. If the P-value is less than or equal to .05, then reject the null hypothesis. If the P-value is greater than .05, accept the null hypothesis.

For ordinal-by-ordinal relationships, run somersD. Somers' d is a directional measure, ranging from −1 to +1. Somers' d has a PRE interpretation. Here is a template for writing an interpretation of Somers' d or, for that matter, any PRE measure:

"Compared to how well we can predict [dependent variable] by not knowing [independent variable], we can improve our prediction by [value of PRE measure] by knowing [independent variable]."

Our example: "Compared to how well we can predict environmental opinions by not knowing respondents' levels of education, we can improve our prediction by .029 by knowing respondents' levels of education." (Actually, percentages may sound better here: " . . . we can improve our prediction by 2.9 percent by knowing respondents' levels of education.") Note that a negative sign on a PRE measure imparts the direction of the relationship, but it does not affect the PRE interpretation.

ANALYZING AN ORDINAL-LEVEL RELATIONSHIP WITH A CONTROL VARIABLE

The education-environmental attitudes hypothesis did not fare well against the null hypothesis. Here is a hypothesis that sounds more promising: In a comparison of individuals, liberals will be more supportive of gay rights than will conservatives. For the dependent variable, we will use gay_rights3, which measures attitudes toward gay rights by three categories: "Low" support, a middle position ("Mid"), and "High" support. The independent variable is libcon3: liberal ("Lib"), moderate ("Mod"), and conservative ("Cons"). Because education might also affect attitudes toward gay rights, we will use dem_educ3 (from the previous example) as the control variable. We are running a controlled cross-tabulation, so we can deploy xtabC:

```
xtabC(~gay_rights3+libcon3+dem_educ3, nesD)
```

```
, , dem_educ3 = HS or less

          libcon3
gay_rights3   Lib    Mod   Cons
Low          20.9   44.4   51.6
Mid          33.9   33.7   33.8
High         45.2   21.8   14.6
Total       100.0   99.9  100.0
Count       292.0  243.0  500.0

, , dem_educ3 = Some coll

          libcon3
gay_rights3   Lib    Mod   Cons
Low          17.5   33.8   53.8
Mid          30.8   32.5   34.7
High         51.7   33.8   11.5
Total       100.0  100.1  100.0
Count       263.0  157.0  409.0

, , dem_educ3 = Coll+

          libcon3
gay_rights3   Lib    Mod   Cons
Low           9.7   20.4   49.6
Mid          24.5   41.6   38.7
High         65.7   38.1   11.7
Total        99.9  100.1  100.0
Count       318.0  113.0  403.0
```

It would appear that, at all levels of education, ideology plays a big role in gay rights attitudes. Among the least educated group, there is about a sizable 30-point decline in the percentages professing "High" support across the values of libcon3, from 45.2 percent among liberals to 14.6 percent among conservatives. Yet the drop is even steeper among those with some college: from 51.7 percent to 11.5 percent, a 40-point drop. The gap increases to over 50 points among the most highly educated: 65.7 percent for liberals and 11.7 percent for conservatives. Thus, the "ideology effect" is either 30 points, 40 points, or over 50 points, depending on education level. Although the direction of the gay_rights3-dem_educ3 relationship is the same at all levels of education—conservatives are less supportive than liberals—the relationship becomes stronger as education increases. Interaction would seem the best way to describe this set of relationships.[5]

---

[5] Notice that the "education effect" is quite pronounced for liberals, yet virtually nonexistent for conservatives. For liberals, gay rights support increases from 45.2 percent, to 51.7 percent, to 65.7 percent—about 20 points from low education to high education. By contrast, education has practically no effect for conservatives: 14.6 percent, 11.5 percent, and 11.7 percent.

Reading tables and discussing patterns are familiar tasks. But do chi-square and Somers' d support our interpretation? Xtp.chi2 only works for bivariate relationships, and xtabC does not report chi-square or Somers' d. As is often the case with R, an additional step is needed. The additional step, in this case, requires that we create three subsets of the nesD dataset, one of each value of the control variable, dem_educ3. Consider the syntax for the subset function:

$$subset(data, \ subset.expression)$$

The subset function makes more sense when illustrated with a specific example. Here is the script that will create the three data subsets for our current analysis:

```
nesD.led = subset(nesD, dem_educ3=="HS or less")
nesD.med = subset(nesD, dem_educ3=="Some coll")
nesD.hed = subset(nesD, dem_educ3=="Coll+")
```

To create the low-education dataset, nesD.led, we specify the expression "dem_educ3== "HS or less""; for the middle-education subset, nesD.med, "dem_educ3== "Some coll""; and for the high-education subset, nesD.hed, "dem_educ3== "Coll+"". We then can apply somersD and a new function, svychisqC, to each subset. The syntax for svychisqC:

$$svychisqC(\sim depvar+indepvar, \ design.dataset)$$

Now obtain chi-square and Somers' d for each design dataset:

```
svychisqC(~gay_rights3+libcon3, nesD.led)
somersD(~libcon3+gay_rights3, nesD.led)

svychisqC(~gay_rights3+libcon3, nesD.med)
somersD(~libcon3+gay_rights3, nesD.med)

svychisqC(~gay_rights3+libcon3, nesD.hed)
somersD(~libcon3+gay_rights3, nesD.hed)
```

```
> svychisqC(~gay_rights3+libcon3, nesD.led)

        Pearson's X^2: Rao & Scott adjustment

data:  survey::svychisq(formula, design, statistic = "Chisq", na.rm = TRUE)
X-squared = 225.29, df = 4, p-value = 3.009e-12

> somersD(~libcon3+gay_rights3, nesD.led)
        Somers' dyx:
[1] -0.2765834


> svychisqC(~gay_rights3+libcon3, nesD.med)

        Pearson's X^2: Rao & Scott adjustment

data:  survey::svychisq(formula, design, statistic = "Chisq", na.rm = TRUE)
X-squared = 355.1, df = 4, p-value < 2.2e-16

> somersD(~libcon3+gay_rights3, nesD.med)
        Somers' dyx:
[1] -0.3834642


> svychisqC(~gay_rights3+libcon3, nesD.hed)

        Pearson's X^2: Rao & Scott adjustment

data:  survey::svychisq(formula, design, statistic = "Chisq", na.rm = TRUE)
X-squared = 557.89, df = 4, p-value < 2.2e-16

> somersD(~libcon3+gay_rights3, nesD.hed)
        Somers' dyx:
[1] -0.5149742
```

Judging from the chi-square tests at all values of the control, it is extremely unlikely that the observed patterns were produced by random sampling error. So the chi-square statistics invite us to reject the null hypothesis. Again note the negative signs on the Somers' d statistics. At each education level, as the values of libcon3 increase from "Lib" to "Cons", gay_rights3's values decline from "High" support to "Low" support. Thus, the negative signs are consistent with the hypothesis that conservatives are less supportive of gay rights than are liberals. Focus on the Somers' d magnitudes. Somers' d has a magnitude (absolute value) of .277 for the least educated, .384 for the middle group, and .515 for the most educated. So the values of Somers' d capture the strengthening relationship between gay_rights3 and libcon3 as education increases. Plus, because Somers' d is a PRE measure, we can give a specific answer to the "how strong?" question. For least educated respondents, we would say that, compared to how well we can predict their opinions on gay rights without knowing their ideology, we can improve our prediction by 27.7 percent by knowing their ideology. The predictive leverage of the independent variable strengthens to 38.4 percent for the middle group, and increases to 51.5 percent for those at the highest level of educational attainment.

ANALYZING A NOMINAL-LEVEL RELATIONSHIP WITH A CONTROL VARIABLE

All of the variables analyzed thus far have been ordinal level. Many social and political characteristics, however, are measured by nominal categories—gender, race, region, or religious denomination, to name a few. In this example, we will use nesD variables dem_raceeth2 and pid_3 to frame the following hypothesis: In a comparison of individuals, blacks are more likely to be Democrats than are whites. To make this remarkably pedestrian hypothesis marginally more interesting, we will control for another variable that might also affect partisanship, whether the respondent resides in the South (nesD variable south). Would the racial difference on partisanship be the same for southerners and non-southerners? Or might the racial divide be stronger in the South than the non-South? Let's investigate, starting with an xtabC run:

```
xtabC(~pid_3+dem_raceeth2+south, nesD)
```

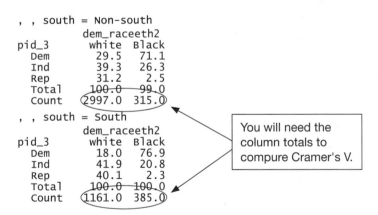

Before subsetting and running svychisqC and computing Cramer's V, consider the substantive relationships depicted in the cross-tabulations. Are there inter-regional differences in the patterns of the relationships? Among non-southerners, 29.5 percent of whites are Democrats, compared with 71.1 percent of blacks—more than a 40-percentage-point gap. What happens when we switch to respondents who reside in the South? Among southerners, the percentage of black Democrats increases to 76.9, while the percentage of white Democrats drops by about 11 points, to 18.0 percent. These dynamics produce a racial gap that is considerably wider in the South (about 60 points) than in the non-South (about 40 points). Because the effect of race on partisanship is stronger in the South than in the non-South, we can conclude that interaction best describes this situation.

Create two data subsets, nesD.NS for non-southern respondents and nesD.S for respondents who reside in the South:

```
nesD.NS=subset(nesD,south=="Non-south")
nesD.S= subset(nesD,south=="South")
```

Mobilize svychisqC:

```
svychisqC(~pid_3+dem_raceeth2, nesD.NS)
svychisqC(~pid_3+dem_raceeth2, nesD.S)
```

```
        Pearson's X^2: Rao & Scott adjustment

data:  svychisq(formula, design, statistic = "Chisq", na.rm = TRUE)
X-squared = 288.2588, df = 2, p-value < 2.2e-16

> svychisqC(~pid_3+dem_raceeth2, nesD.S)

        Pearson's X^2: Rao & Scott adjustment

data:  svychisq(formula, design, statistic = "Chisq", na.rm = TRUE)
X-squared = 606.8145, df = 2, p-value < 2.2e-16
```

According to the chi-square statistics, the party identification-race relationship defeats the null hypothesis in the non-South cross-tab (chi-square = 288.2588, P-value ≈ .000) and in the South cross-tab (chi-square = 606.8145, P-value ≈ .000).

What measure of association is appropriate for gauging the strength of these relationships? For nominals, the menu of choices is limited. However, Cramer's V is a satisfactory go-to for cross-tabs in which one or both variables are nominal level. Unlike Somers' d, Cramer's V is not a PRE measure. However, V is bracketed by 0 (no relationship) and +1 (perfect relationship), making it particularly useful for comparing the strength of a relationship across values of a control. The syntax for the CramersV function:

```
CramersV(chi2.statistic, #rows, #columns, N)
```

Inside the parentheses, enter the chi-square statistic for the cross-tabulation, followed by the number of rows in the table, the number of columns, and the number of cases. Ask R to calculate N by summing the column totals from each cross-tab. N for the non-southern cross-tabulation:

```
> 2997+315
[1] 3312
```

For the Southern cross-tab:

```
> 1161+385
[1] 1546
```

Plug in the numbers:

```
CramersV(288.2588,3,2,3312) # Non-south

CramersV(606.8145,3,2,1546) # South
```

```
> CramersV(288.2588,3,2,3312)
[1] 0.2950164

> CramersV(606.8145,3,2,1546)
[1] 0.6265031
```

For the non-South, we obtain a V of .295; for the south, .627. Cramer's V does not have a PRE interpretation. However, it varies between 0 (weak relationship) and 1 (strong relationship). V is particularly useful in interpreting controlled comparisons. In reassuring support of our interaction interpretation, the V for Southern respondents is much stronger than the V for non-Southern respondents.

EXERCISES

1. (Dataset: statesD. Variables: abort_rank3, gun_rank3, cook_index3.) Pedantic Pontificator is pondering a potential partisan paradox of public policy.

"Think about two sorts of policies that figure prominently in cultural debate: laws restricting abortion and laws restricting guns. For both policies, fewer restrictions mean more choices and greater freedom, while more restrictions mean fewer choices and less freedom. Because choice and freedom are the touchstone values, one would think that partisan elites would be consistent in their positions on these policies. If Republicans favor fewer gun restrictions, then they ought to favor fewer abortion restrictions, too. By the same logic, if Democrats favor fewer abortion restrictions, then they should also support less gun control. As a keen observer of state politics, however, it is my impression that Republican-controlled states have less restrictive gun laws but more restrictive abortion laws. Democrat-controlled states are just the reverse: less restrictive abortion laws and more restrictive gun laws. I am sure that when you analyze the states dataset, you will discover this odd partisan paradox."

The statesD dataset contains these two policy measures, which will serve as dependent variables: abort_rank3 and gun_rank3. Both variables are identically coded three-category ordinals, with higher codes denoting fewer abortion restrictions ("More restr" / "Mid" / "Less restr") and fewer gun restrictions ("More restr" / "Mid" / "Less restr") Another three-category ordinal, cook_index3, measures states' partisan balance in three ascending codes, from Republican to Democrat ("More Rep", "Even", or "More Dem"). This is the independent variable.

A. If Pedantic Pontificator is correct, as you compare states across increasing values of cook_index3—from Republican states, to even states, to Democratic states—the percentage of states having more restrictive abortion policies should (Circle one.)

decrease.   stay the same.   increase.

The percentage of states having more restrictive gun policies should (Circle one.)

decrease.   stay the same.   increase.

B. If Pedantic Pontificator is correct, you should find that states having higher codes on cook_index3 will have (Circle one.)

lower codes on abort_rank3.   higher codes on abort_rank3.

You should also find that states having higher codes on cook_index3 will have (Circle one.)

lower codes on gun_rank3. higher codes on gun_rank3.

C. Think about how R calculates Somers' d. If Pedantic Pontificator is correct, the Somers' d statistic for the abort_rank3-cook_index3 relationship will have a (Circle one.)

negative sign.   positive sign.

The Somers' d statistic for the gun_rank3-cook_index3 relationship will have a (Circle one.)

negative sign.   positive sign.

D. Using statesD, run xtabC, svychisqC, and somersD on the abort_rank3-cook_index3 relationship. Run the same suite of functions on the gun_rank3-cook_index3 relationship. In the table below, enter the percentage of Democratic states, even states, and Republican states having more restrictive ("More restr") policies. For each relationship, record chi-square, chi-square's P-value, and Somers' d.

Dependent Variable	More Rep	Even	More Dem	Chi-Square	P-Value	Somers' d
Abort_rank3 % more restrictive	?	?	?	?	?	?
Gun_rank3 % more restrictive	?	?	?	?	?	?

E. Consider Somers' d for the gun_rank3-cook_index3 relationship. This value of Somers' d means that, compared to how well we can predict gun_rank3 without knowing cook_index3, (Complete the sentence.)

_____.

F. Consider the chi-square P-value for the abort_rank3-cook_index3 relationship. This P-value means that, under the assumption that the null hypothesis is correct, (Complete the sentence.)

_____.

Therefore, you should (Circle one.)

reject the null hypothesis.   not reject the null hypothesis.

G. Consider all the evidence from your analysis. The evidence suggests that Pedantic Pontificator is (Circle one.)

correct.   incorrect.

Explain your reasoning.

_____

_____

_____

_____

_____

2. (Dataset: gssD. Variables: sex, femrole2, abhlth.) Interested student has joined Pedantic Pontificator in a discussion of the gender gap in U.S. politics.

Interested student: "On what sorts of issues or opinions are men and women most likely to be at odds? What defines the gender gap, anyway?"

Pedantic Pontificator: "That's easy. A couple of points seem obvious, to me anyway. First, we know that the conflict over abortion rights is the defining gender issue of our time. Women will be more likely than men to take a pro-choice position on this issue. Second—and pay close attention here—on more mundane cultural questions, such as whether women should be homemakers or pursue careers outside the home, men and women will not be significantly different."

A. Pedantic Pontificator has suggested the following two hypotheses about the gender gap: (Check two.)

❑ In a comparison of individuals, women will be less likely than men to think that abortion should be allowed.

❑ In a comparison of individuals, women and men will not differ in their abortion opinions.

❑ In a comparison of individuals, women will be more likely than men to think that abortion should be allowed.

❑ In a comparison of individuals, women will be less likely than men to think that women should pursue careers outside the home.

❑ In a comparison of individuals, women and men will not differ in the opinions about female roles outside the home.

❑ In a comparison of individuals, women will be more likely than men to think that women should pursue careers outside the home.

B. The gssD dataset contains two variables that will serve as dependent variables: abhlth, which records whether the respondent thinks that a woman should be able to obtain an abortion if the woman's health is seriously endangered ("YES" or "NO"); and femrole2, which gauges respondents' opinions on the appropriate female role ("Traditional" / "NonTrad"). The independent variable is sex. Perform xtabC and svychisqC on the abhlth-sex and femrole2-sex relationships. Run CramersV. (Calculate N by summing the column totals from the xtabC analyses.) In the abhlth-sex cross-tabulation, focus on the percentage saying "YES". In the femrole2-sex cross-tabulation, focus on the "NonTrad" category. Record your results in the table that follows.

Dependent Variable	Male	Female	Chi-Square	P-Value	Cramer's V
Percent "YES" (abhlth)	?	?	?	?	?
Percent "NonTrad" (femrole2)	?	?	?	?	?

C. Based on these results, you may conclude that (Check three.)

❑ A statistically significant gender gap exists on abortion opinions.

❑ Pedantic Pontificator's hypothesis about the femrole2-sex relationship is not supported by the analysis.

❑ Under the assumption that the null hypothesis is correct, the abhlth-sex relationship would occur by chance more frequently than 5 times out of 100.

❑ Pedantic Pontificator's hypothesis about the abhlth-sex relationship is supported by the analysis.

❑ A higher percentage of females than males think that women belong in non-traditional roles.

D. The P-value of the chi-square statistic in the abhlth-sex cross-tabulation tells you that, under the assumption that the null hypothesis is correct, (Complete the sentence.)

_____

_____

3. (Dataset: gssD. Variables: partyid_3, egalit_scale3, educ_2.) Certainly you would expect partisanship and egalitarian attitudes to be related: In a comparison of individuals, those with stronger egalitarian beliefs are more likely to be Democrats than are those with weaker egalitarian beliefs. Yet it also seems reasonable to hypothesize that the relationship between egalitarianism (independent variable) and party identification (dependent variable) will not be the same for all education groups (control variable). It may be that, among people with less education, the party identification-egalitarianism relationship will be weaker than among those with higher levels of education. This idea suggests a set of interaction relationships: As education increases, the relationship between the independent variable and the dependent variable becomes stronger. In this exercise, you will test for this set of interaction relationships.

GssD contains partyid_3, which measures party identification: "Dem", "Ind", and "Rep". This is the dependent variable. (For this exercise, treat partyid_3 as an ordinal-level variable, with higher codes denoting stronger Republican identification.) The independent variable is egalit_scale3: "Less egal", "Middle", or "More egal". The control variable is educ_2: "0–12 yrs" and "13+ yrs".

A. Use the subset function to create two datasets: gssD.led for respondents in the "0-12 yrs" category of educ_2, and gssD.hed for those in the "13+ yrs" category of educ_2. Run xtabC, svychisqC, and somersD for each subset. Focus on the percentages of Democrats across the values of egalit_scale3. Fill in the table that follows.

Education Level	Less egal (% Dem)	Middle (% Dem)	More egal (% Dem)	Chi-Square	P-Value	Somers' d
0–12 years	?	?	?	?	?	?
13+ years	?	?	?	?	?	?

B.   Which of the following inferences are supported by your analysis? (Check all that apply.)

   ❑   At both levels of education, people with stronger egalitarian beliefs are more likely to be Democrats than are people with weaker egalitarian beliefs.

   ❑   For the less educated group, random sampling error would produce the observed relationship between egalitarianism and partisanship less frequently than 5 times out of 100.

   ❑   The partisanship-egalitarianism relationship is stronger for the more educated group than for the less-educated group.

C.   Focus on the value of Somers' d for those who have 13 or more years of education. This value of Somers' d says that, compared to how well you can predict, (Complete the sentence.)

   _____

   _____

D.   Based on your analysis of these relationships, you can conclude that (Check one.)

   ❑   the partisanship-egalitarianism-education relationships are not a set of interaction relationships.

   ❑   the partisanship-egalitarianism-education relationships are a set of interaction relationships.

   Explain your reasoning, making specific reference to the statistical evidence in part A.

   _____

   _____

   _____

   _____

   _____

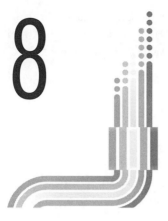

8

Correlation and Linear Regression

Objective	Functions Introduced	Author or Source
Analyzing correlation	wtd.cor {weights} cbind {base}	Josh Pasek[1] R Development Core Team[2]
Estimating linear regression models	lm {stats} summary {base} relevel {stats}	R Development Core Team R Development Core Team R Development Core Team
Conducting regression analysis with weighted data	svyglm {survey} svyglm.fit {rcompanion} update {stats}	Thomas Lumley[3] Philip Pollock and Barry Edwards R Development Core Team

This chapter introduces you to some powerful and flexible techniques that political scientists frequently use to analyze variables measured at the interval level. (R classifies interval-level variables as numerics.)

In the first part of this chapter, you will learn how to conduct correlation analysis. Researchers often use correlation techniques in the beginning stages of analysis to get an overall picture of the relationships between interesting variables. We will focus on the wtd.cor() function. As its name suggests, wtd.cor() was developed for weighted data, but it can also be used with unweighted data.

Regression is more specialized than correlation. Researchers use regression analysis to model causal relationships between one or more independent variables and a dependent variable. Regression analysis produces a statistic, the regression coefficient, that estimates the effect of an independent variable on a dependent variable. In regression analysis, the dependent variable is measured at the interval level, but the independent variable can be of any variety—nominal, ordinal, or interval. The lm() function can be used to estimate many linear regression models. For unweighted data, such as states and world, the classic lm function (from the stats package) produces a full array of regression statistics.

---

[1] Pasek, J. (2012). *weights: Weighting and weighted statistics* (R package version 0.75). With some assistance from Alex Tahk and some code modified from R-core. Available at http://CRAN.R-project.org/package=weights

[2] R Development Core Team. (2011). *R: A language and environment for statistical computing*. Vienna, Austria: Author. Available at http://www.R-project.org/

[3] Lumley, T. (2012). *survey: Analysis of complex survey samples* (R package version 3.28-2). Available at http://cran.r-project.org/web/packages/survey/index.html. See also: Lumley, T. (2004). Analysis of complex survey samples. *Journal of Statistical Software*, 9(1), 1–19; Lumley, T. (2010). *Complex surveys: A guide to analysis using R*. Hoboken, NJ: John Wiley & Sons.

For regression analysis, however, you will learn different functions for unweighted and weighted data. For weighted data, such as nes and gss (more accurately, their design versions, nesD and gssD), you will learn svyglm (from the survey package). A workspace function, svyglm.fit, returns the appropriate R-square value for svyglm output.

CORRELATION ANALYSIS

Pearson's correlation coefficient (Pearson's r) measures the strength and direction of the relationship between two interval-level variables. Pearson's r is not a proportional reduction in error (PRE) measure, but it does gauge strength by an easily understood scale—from –1, a perfectly negative association between the variables, to +1, a perfectly positive relationship. A correlation of 0 indicates no relationship.

Correlation analysis is often used to explore relationships among variables. Let's explore some of the issues associated with liberals in the NES dataset. We will use the wtd.cor() function to estimate correlation coefficients.[4] The function's basic syntax calls for two interval-level variables:

$$\text{wtd.cor}(\textit{var1, var2}, \text{weight}=\textit{optional.weight})$$

Because the correlation coefficient is a symmetric measure, the order of var1 and var2 does not matter. This function does not allow us to specify the dataset as an argument, so we need to fully specify our variables in the form dataset$variable. If we wanted to estimate the correlation coefficient between variables in the states or world datasets without survey weights, we could replace var1 and var2 in the example above and omit the weights argument.

To estimate the Pearson's correlation coefficient between NES respondents' feelings about liberals and their feelings about feminists (using survey weights), we can enter:

```
# Calculates Correlation Coefficient with (optional) weighted data
wtd.cor(nes$ftgr_liberals, nes$ftgr_feminists, weight=nes$wt)
```

```
        correlation    std.err   t.value  p.value
v1.v1     0.5611043  0.0113539  49.41953        0
```

The results show a strong, positive correlation between these two variables: 0.561. How strong is the relationship? We know that Pearson's r is bracketed by –1 and +1, so we could say that this relationship is a fairly strong positive association.

We can go further and not just consider the relationship between individuals' views of liberals and feminists, but we can also examine the correlations among multiple political opinions. Feelings about liberals appear to be highly correlated to feminist views, but what about attitudes about big business, the military, atheists, and gays? Let's use correlation analysis to explore a small constellation of political beliefs.

To obtain a matrix that displays the correlations among more than two variables, we need to pass the variables of interest to the wtd.cor() function in a particular format. This is a two-step process. We'll use the column bind function, cbind(), to organize our variable set in the proper format and then pass our variable set to the wtd.cor function.

```
# Estimates a Correlation Coefficient Matrix Among Set of Variables
variableSet = cbind(nes$ftgr_liberals, nes$ftgr_feminists, nes$ftgr_bigbus,
                    nes$ftgr_military, nes$ftgr_atheists, nes$ftgr_gay)
wtd.cor(variableSet, weight=nes$wt)
```

For the sake of brevity, we'll show just the matrix of correlation coefficients rounded to three decimal places. Somewhat confusingly, wtd.cor's row and column labels follow the order in which variables appear in the variable set. In this example, v1 = liberals, v2 = feminists, v3 = big business, v4 = military, v5 = atheists, and v6 = gays.

---

[4] The cor() function yields the same correlation coefficient without the additional inferential statistics. The wtd.cor() function may be more useful because it allows the user to specify sample weights for survey data and removes missing data by default.

	V1	V2	V3	V4	V5	V6
V1	1.000	0.561	-0.133	-0.106	0.324	0.437
V2	0.561	1.000	0.000	0.018	0.273	0.398
V3	-0.133	0.000	1.000	0.341	-0.065	-0.078
V4	-0.106	0.018	0.341	1.000	-0.145	-0.023
V5	0.324	0.273	-0.065	-0.145	1.000	0.452
V6	0.437	0.398	-0.078	-0.023	0.452	1.000

Because wtd.cor substitutes generic variable labels for their actual names, you may want to make the re-substitutions yourself. The diagonal of 1's tells you that each variable is perfectly correlated with itself (this is not surprising, but it helps orient you to the matrix results). Each of the correlation coefficients appears twice in the table: once above the diagonal of 1's and again below the diagonal. The correlation between the liberal (v1) and feminist (v2) thermometers is 0.561, and we see this figure in row 1, column 2 as well as row 2, column 1 (remember that correlation coefficients are symmetrical and you can see this symmetry in the sample matrix above).

Let's use these results to explore the political belief system of NES respondents. Feelings about feminists (0.561) have the strongest positive correlation to liberals, then it's sentiment toward gays (0.437), atheists (0.324), the military (-0.106), and big business (-0.133). How about the relationship between opinions about the military and other issues? Based on this matrix, feelings about the military are positively correlated to big business (0.341) but negatively correlated to sentiments about atheists (-0.145). With data like these, you can begin to map out how closely related people view different political issues, institutions, and politicians.

BIVARIATE REGRESSION WITH A DUMMY VARIABLE

Correlation analysis is a good place to start when analyzing interval-level relationships. Even so, a correlation coefficient is agnostic on the question of which variable is the cause and which is the effect. Regression analysis is more powerful than correlation, in part because it helps us investigate causal relationships—relationships in which an independent variable is thought to affect a dependent variable. Bivariate regression analysis, which is regression analysis with one independent variable, will (1) reveal the precise nature of the relationship between an independent variable and a dependent variable, (2) test the null hypothesis that the observed relationship occurred by chance, and (3) provide a PRE measure of association between the independent variable and the dependent variable. Regression also produces a PRE measure of association, R-square, which indicates how completely the independent variable (or variables) explains the dependent variable.

We'll start by looking at the basic syntax used to estimate a bivariate regression model in R:

```
lm(depvar ~ indepvar, data=dataset)
```

The lm() command estimates the expected value of the dependent variable as a function of the independent variable. It is important to write the function in the correct order. Your dependent variable goes on the left side of the formula and the independent variable goes on the right side; unlike correlation analysis, regression analysis does not yield a symmetrical measure. You don't need to add an intercept term to the function; the lm() function will automatically estimate an intercept term. If you prefer, you can fully specify the dependent variable and the independent variable using the form dataset$depvar and dataset$indepvar and omit the data argument.

To illustrate how to estimate and interpret a bivariate regression model using R, let's use a simple dummy variable to explain variation in an interval-level dependent variable. Recall from Chapter 3 that a dummy variable can take on only two values, 1 or 0. Each case being analyzed either has the characteristic being measured (a code of 1) or does not have it (a code of 0). For example, a dummy variable for gender might code females as 1 and males as 0. Everybody who is coded 1 has the characteristic of being female, and everybody who is coded 0 does not have that characteristic. To appreciate why this 0 or 1 coding is the essential feature of dummy variables, consider the following regression model, which is designed to test the hypothesis that women will give Barack Obama higher feeling thermometer ratings than will men:

```
nes$female = as.numeric(nes$gender == "Female")   # create dummy variable
lm(obama_therm ~ female, data=nes)                # dummy variable regression
```

```
Call:
lm(formula = obama_therm ~ female, data = nes)

Coefficients:
(Intercept)          female
     57.024           7.239
```

When we estimate this model, R reports two regression coefficients. We can express our bivariate regression results as a line equation in the general form y = a + b·x. This equation tells us what dependent variable value (y) we should expect based on the value of the independent variable (x). In this case:

$$\text{Obama Thermometer} = a + b*\text{Female}$$

or more specifically,

$$\text{Obama Thermometer} = 57.024 + 7.239*\text{Female}$$

Since males are coded 0 on the dummy, the constant or intercept, a, will tell us the average Obama rating among men (57.024). Why so? Substituting 0 for the dummy yields: a + b*0 = a. In the language of dummy variable regression, males are the "omitted" category, the category whose mean value on the dependent variable is captured by the intercept, a. The regression coefficient, b, will tell us how much to adjust the intercept for women—that is, when the dummy switches from 0 to 1. Thus, just as in any regression, b will estimate the average change in the dependent variable for a unit change in the independent variable. In this case, a unit change in the independent variable adds, on average, 7.239 points to the Obama sentiment. It is important to be clear on this point: The coefficient, b, *does not* communicate the mean Obama rating among females. Rather, it estimates the *mean difference* between males and females. Of course, an estimated value of the dependent variable among females can be arrived at easily by summing a and b: a + b*1 = 57.024 + 7.239 = 64.263.

Bivariate regression with a dummy variable should remind you of the mean comparison analysis you learned in Chapter 4. Both methods will tell us that the mean Obama thermometer score is 57.024 for males and 64.263 for females. Regression analysis makes more efficient use of the sample and makes it easier to add control variables, as we will soon see. As with any regression coefficient, we can rely on the coefficient's t-statistic and P-value to test the null hypothesis that there is no statistically meaningful gender difference in thermometer ratings of Obama. We need to access the summary statistics of our linear model for this and we'll do that in the next example.

BIVARIATE REGRESSION WITH AN INTERVAL-LEVEL INDEPENDENT VARIABLE

In this section, we will use bivariate regression to explain variation in an interval-level dependent variable with an interval-level independent variable. We will continue to use the lm() function introduced in the preceding section. If you followed the example with bivariate regression with a dummy variable, you'll have no problem executing the R code in this section. However, interpreting the results can be a challenge because of the flurry of numbers generated by R, so pay close attention to how we interpret regression coefficients and inferential statistics.

Suppose you are interested in the gender composition of state legislatures. Before launching into regression analysis, it's a good idea to use descriptive methods to acquaint yourself with the relevant dependent variable, states$womleg_2015, and correlation analysis to explore relations in the dataset. Using the freq() function to analyze the variable states$womleg_2015, you would find that state legislatures range from 12.5% to 42% female. Why is there such variation in the female composition of state legislatures? Try using correlation analysis to get an overview of the relationship between women in state legislatures and other interval-level variables in the states dataset.

Perhaps states with lower percentages of college graduates have lower percentages of women legislators than do states with more college-educated residents. We can estimate a bivariate regression that explains variation in women legislators as a function of state college graduation rates.

```
lm(womleg_2015 ~ college, data=states)        # bivariate regression example
lm(states$womleg_2015 ~ states$college)       # alternate syntax, same results
```

```
Coefficients:
(Intercept)        college
     0.3703         0.9203
```

According to these results, the expected percentage of women legislators in a state equals 0.370 percent plus 0.920 times the percentage of the state population that graduated from college. More formally, we write an algebraic formula that summarizes this relationship:

Percent women legislators = 0.370 + 0.920*(College Graduation Percent)

On average, a 1-percent increase in the college graduation rate increases the percentage of women legislators nearly 1 percent. These results allow us to make informed predictions about the percentage of women legislators we would expect in a state based on its college graduation rate. The intercept value, 0.370, represents the expected percentage of women legislators when the independent variable, a state's college graduation rate, is equal to 0. No state has a college graduation rate near zero so the intercept value isn't particularly interesting in this model, but it is statistically necessary. Your estimate for a state with, say, a 25 percent college graduation rate would be 0.370 + 0.920*(50) = 0.370 + 23 = 23.37 percent female legislators. The main statistic of interest, then, is the regression coefficient, 0.920, which estimates the average change in the dependent variable for each unit change in the independent variable.[5]

The lm function, when run by itself, will not return complete information about the regression model. To see all of the model's statistics, nest your lm call inside the summary function, or store the model estimated by lm as an object and summarize this object.

When we summarize the bivariate regression model of women in state legislatures, R outputs considerably more information than the bare lm() function call does. The section labeled Residuals summarizes the differences between the values we would expect from our regression equation and the actual data points. We'll discuss residuals more later, but we can see initially that linear regression yields a typical/median residual close to zero with some expected values that are too low and others that are too high.

```
summary(lm(womleg_2015 ~ college, data=states))          # summarize results

biVarModelWomLeg = lm(womleg_2015 ~ college, data=states) # alternate syntax
summary(biVarModelWomLeg)                                  # has same result
```

```
Residuals:
    Min       1Q    Median       3Q      Max
-12.9035  -3.1945  -0.5043   3.5059  13.3841
```

Here are the intercept and slope estimates we saw above when we called lm() without the summary

```
Coefficients:
             Estimate Std. Error t value Pr(>|t|)
(Intercept)    0.3703     4.7130    0.079    0.938
college        0.9203     0.1797    5.122 5.31e-06 ***
---
```

Model estimates

```
Signif. codes:  0 '***' 0.001 '**' 0.01 '*' 0.05 '.' 0.1 ' ' 1

Residual standard error: 5.693 on 48 degrees of freedom
Multiple R-squared:  0.3534,  Adjusted R-squared:  0.3399
F-statistic: 26.24 on 1 and 48 DF,  p-value: 5.311e-06
```

The "Coefficients" section reports the intercept and slope estimates we saw from the bare lm() call. R's Estimate for the intercept, 0.370, is listed first, followed by the estimated effect for a one-unit change in the college variable, 0.920. These estimates are now supplemented with vital inferential statistics: standard errors, t-values, and P-values (based on two-tailed t-tests). These supplementary statistics are particularly important for testing the hypothesized relationship between graduation rates and women in the legislature.

---

[5] Sometimes, it is a good idea to center the independent variable (see Chapter 3 for how to do this) so the intercept term represents the expected value of the dependent variable for a typical case, like a state with an average college graduation rate, and the slope coefficient stays the same.

We are not analyzing a random sample here, since we have information on the entire population of 50 states, but let's assume, for illustrative purposes, that we have just analyzed a random sample. What would the null hypothesis have to say about the relationship between graduation rates and women in the legislature? The null hypothesis would say what it always says: In the population from which the sample was drawn, there is no relationship between the independent variable (in this case, the percentage of college graduates) and the dependent variable (the percentage of female legislators). According to the null hypothesis, the true regression coefficient is equal to 0 and the regression coefficient that we obtained, 0.920, occurred by chance.

In lm regression results, you test the null hypothesis by examining two columns in the Coefficients table—the column labeled "t value", which reports t-statistics, and the column labeled "Pr(>|t|)", which reports P-values. Informally, to safely reject the null hypothesis, you generally look for t-ratios with magnitudes (absolute values) of 2 or greater. According to the results of our analysis, the regression coefficient for college has a t-statistic of 5.122, well above the informal |2|-or-greater rule. A P-value, which tells you the probability of obtaining the results if the null hypothesis is correct, helps you to make more precise inferences about the relationship between the independent variable and the dependent variable. If "Pr(>|t|)" is *greater* than .05, then the observed results would occur too frequently by chance, and you must *not reject* the null hypothesis. By contrast, if "Pr(>|t|)" is *less than* .05 (or equal to .05), then you should *reject* null hypothesis. The t-statistic for college (which is equal to the coefficient 0.920 divided by the standard error 0.180) has a corresponding P-value of 5.31e-06, scientific notation for .00000531. If the null is correct, the probability of observing this relationship purely by chance is about 5 in 1 million. Although we're saying that there's a chance, it's a very, very small chance. Reject the null hypothesis. It depends on the research problem at hand, of course, but for most applications you can ignore the t-ratio and P-value for the constant.

How strong is the relationship between college and womleg_2015? Some of the most relevant information about this bivariate regression model is reported in the second-to-last row of the summary. R reports both "Multiple R-squared" and "Adjusted R-squared" values. Like any proportion, these statistics range between 0 and 1. The Multiple R-squared value is the traditional R-squared model fit statistic (for multiple predictors). Here, this statistic tells us that 0.353 (equal to 35.3%) of the variation in the dependent variable, states$womleg_2015, is explained by our bivariate regression model. The rest of the variation in womleg_2015, 64.7 percent, remains unexplained by the independent variable. Most research articles also report the Adjusted R-squared value, which is meant to correct for artificially inflating R-squared statistics. The Adjusted R-squared statistic is equal to .340. Pay attention to the Adjusted R-squared statistics when you estimate different regression models of the same dependent variable, because they can tell you whether your explanations are getting better or worse.

MULTIPLE REGRESSION ANALYSIS

Social systems are complicated, so we are often interested in the effect of several variables on political opinions, state policies, world politics, or some other outcome of interest. In our bivariate regression analysis of the prevalence of female state legislators, we found that the higher a state's graduation rate, the greater the percentage of women in its legislature. Could there be more to the story? Perhaps states with high college graduation rates differ from states with low graduation rates in ways that affect the success of women in politics. Multiple regression analysis is a technique used to control for alternative explanations and obtain better estimates of the effect of an independent variable on the outcome of interest.

Maybe a cultural variable, such as the percentage of a state's residents who frequently attend religious services, plays a role in the gender composition of a state legislature. Perhaps states with higher percentages of frequent attenders have lower percentages of female lawmakers. It's tempting to simply substitute attendance at religious services in place of college graduation rates and use bivariate regression analysis to test the hypothesis that this cultural variable also plays a role in the prevalence of women in state politics, but this may cause misleading results. Why? The two explanations we're proposing, college graduation rates and church attendance, are negatively related to each other (correlation coefficient = −0.531). Do states with more college graduates have higher percentages of female legislators because they have more college graduates or because they have fewer religious attenders? How much of the "college effect" is attributable to the "attendance effect"? Multiple regression analysis is designed to disentangle the confounding effects of two (or more) independent variables. Multiple regression will estimate the effect of each independent variable on the dependent variable, controlling for the effects of all other independent variables in the model.

The general syntax for multiple regression should look familiar:

```
lm(depvar ~ indepvar1 + indepvar2 + … indepvarn, data=data)
```

To analyze the effect of several different independent variables on a dependent variable, we add them to the right side of the formula (as indepvar1, indepvar2, and so on). Use the plus sign to separate your independent variables. The transition from bivariate regression to multiple regression in R is a simple one. In the sample code below, the only change we're making is adding "+ attend_pct" on the right side of the function that the lm function estimates.

```
# estimate and summarize multiple regression model
summary(lm(womleg_2015 ~ college + attend_pct, data=states))
```

```
Coefficients:
            Estimate  Std. Error  t value  Pr(>|t|)
(Intercept)  28.42575     6.84000    4.156  0.000136  ***
college       0.46216     0.17358    2.663  0.010584    *
attend_pct   -0.41640     0.08384   -4.967  9.42e-06  ***
---
Signif. codes:   0 '***' 0.001 '**' 0.01 '*' 0.05 '.' 0.1 ' ' 1

Residual standard error: 4.659 on 47 degrees of freedom
Multiple R-squared:       0.576,      Adjusted R-squared:   0.5579
```

This analysis provides the information we need to isolate the partial effect of each independent variable on the dependent variable. According to our multiple regression results, the relationship can be summarized by the following equation:

$$\text{Percent women legislators} = 28.43 + 0.46*(\text{College Grad \%}) - 0.42*(\text{Church Attendance \%})$$

Let's focus on the regression coefficients for each of the independent variables. The coefficient on college, .46, tells us the effect of the college variable on womleg_2015, controlling for attend_pct. Recall that in the bivariate analysis, a 1-percentage-point increase in college was associated with a 0.92 increase in the percentage of female legislators. When we control for attend_pct, however, we find a reduction in this effect—to 0.46. This means that part of the effect we attributed to college graduation rates in the bivariate regression analysis can be explained by the more infrequent attendance at religious services in states with higher college graduation rates. Even so, the regression coefficient on college, with a t-statistic of 2.663 and a P-value of 0.011, remains statistically significant.

In multiple regression analysis, the R-squared statistic communicates how well *all* of the independent variables explain variation in the dependent variable. So by knowing two things about states (the percentage of frequent church attenders and the percentage of college graduates), we can account for 57.6 percent of the variation across states in the percentage of female legislators. This is a noticeable improvement over the R-squared statistic of 0.353 in the bivariate regression model with just college as an explanatory variable. An even better option for comparing regression models with the same dependent variable is the Adjusted R-square statistic, which is also higher in the multiple regression model than the bivariate regression model (0.558 compared to 0.340).

MULTIPLE REGRESSION WITH ORDINAL OR CATEGORICAL VARIABLES

Let's look at how we estimate regression models when one of our independent variables is an ordinal or categorical variable. (A categorical variable is simply a nominal variable with more than two values.) In this situation, we compare the effect of values of the independent variable using multiple regression analysis. The R code is a simple twist on what we've already used, but interpreting the results can be tricky and it's good to know how to tweak the default output to make your results easier to digest.

The world dataset contains an interval-level measure of gender inequality in countries around the world, gender_unequal (this variable ranges from 0 to 1, with higher values signifying greater inequality). Suppose we want to explain variation in gender inequality in different countries. One factor we might consider, at least as a starting point, is regional differences. Let's take a look at the values of the categorical variable regionun in the world dataset using the levels function:

```
levels(world$regionun)              # get levels of categorical variable
```

```
[1]  "Africa"                      "Asia"
[3]  "Australia/New Zealand/Oceania"  "Europe"
[5]  "Latin America/Caribbean"     "USA/Canada"
```

As you can see, the countries of the world are divided into six different regions. When we incorporate a categorical or ordinal variable with k different values in a linear model, R will automatically create $k-1$ dummy variables and the partial regression coefficient for each one of them. Let's use the lm() function to examine regional differences in gender inequality to see how R handles categorical or ordinal variables in regression analysis.[6]

```
# multiple regression with categorical independent variable
summary(lm(gender_unequal ~ regionun, data=world))
```

Coefficients:

	Estimate	Std. Error	t value	Pr(>|t|)	
(Intercept)	0.69992	0.01858	37.669	< 2e-16	***
regionunAsia	-0.12116	0.02610	-4.642	8.36e-06	***
regionunAustralia/New Zealand/Oceania	-0.23325	0.06699	-3.482	0.000681	***
regionunEurope	-0.37471	0.02666	-14.055	< 2e-16	***
regionunLatin America/Caribbean	-0.08957	0.02976	-3.010	0.003145	**
regionunUSA/Canada	-0.35542	0.08099	-4.388	2.35e-05	***

Signif. codes: 0 '***' 0.001 '**' 0.01 '*' 0.05 '.' 0.1 ' ' 1

Residual standard error: 0.1115 on 129 degrees of freedom
  (32 observations deleted due to missingness)
Multiple R-squared: 0.6313, Adjusted R-squared: 0.617

In our multiple regression results, we find estimates for the intercept and five different regions. Your first impression may be that R left out Africa. Let's write out the algebraic equation for gender inequality to tease out our finding:

$$\text{Gender inequality} = 0.70 - 0.12*(\text{Asia}) - 0.23*(\text{Australia/New Zealand/Oceania})$$
$$- 0.37*(\text{Europe}) - 0.09*(\text{Latin America/Caribbean}) - 0.36*(\text{USA/Canada})$$

The intercept, 0.70, tells us the expected value of gender inequality when the value of all the independent variables is zero; in other words, it's the expected value for a country that's not in Asia, Australia/New Zealand/Oceania, Europe, Latin America/Caribbean, or USA/Canada. What countries are left? 0.70 is the expected value of gender inequality in African countries. When you estimate a multiple regression model with a categorical- or ordinal-level independent variable, R makes a dummy variable for each unique value of your independent variable, except for one of them. This omitted category serves as

---

[6] If your ordinal or categorical independent variable has numeric values but you want R to create $k-1$ dummy variables rather than treat the independent variable as an interval-level variable in the regression model, use the factor() function. Make your independent variable the argument to the factor() function and insert that function as an indepvar argument in your lm() function call. When lm (or the svyglm function we'll use for weighted regressions) encounters the factor function, it will temporarily convert the numeric variable to a factor and create a set of dummy variables that treat each numeric value as a separate level.

the baseline or reference category. The expected value of the dependent variable for the baseline/reference category is the intercept.

Now that we've figured out how to interpret the intercept term, let's figure out what our results tell us about gender inequality in other regions of the world. Each partial regression coefficient (b_1–b_5) will communicate the average change in gender inequality for a one-unit change in the corresponding independent variables. So what's the expected level of gender inequality in a country in Asia? It's not −0.12 (remember, the dependent variable doesn't go lower than 0). For a country in Asia, the value of the automatically created dummy variable regionunAsia equals 1, and the values of all the other dummy variables are equal to 0 (because a country in Asia is not in those other regions). Referring again to our algebraic equation for gender inequality, the expected value for gender inequality in an Asian country = 0.70 − 0.12*1 − 0.23*0 − 0.37*0 − 0.09*0 − 0.36*0, which simplifies to 0.70 − 0.12, which is simply 0.58. You evaluate all of the partial regression coefficients relative to the omitted value. These results tell us that gender inequality is 0.12 lower in Asia *than it is in Africa* and 0.23 lower in Australia/New Zealand/Oceania *than it is in Africa*.

When you interpret the inferential statistics in the summary of a multiple regression model that has an ordinal- or interval-level independent variable, you need to keep the omitted category in mind. In our analysis of gender inequality around the world, African countries served as the reference category and the expected value of gender inequality in Africa is equal to the intercept value, 0.70. The t-statistic for the intercept term is used to test the null hypothesis that the intercept is really equal to 0. Given the extremely small P-value, we are on safe ground to believe that there really is gender inequality in Africa. What about the interferential statistics for the partial regression coefficients? Remember, the partial regression coefficients express the difference between a region and the omitted category, Africa. So the inferential statistics help us decide whether any of the difference in gender inequality we observe between Africa and another region could be the result of random sampling error. For example, the inferential statistics indicate that the difference in gender inequality between Asia and Africa is statistically significant (P-value much less than .05). In fact, these results indicate that gender inequality is significantly different in all regions than it is in Africa.

These inferential statistics in our sample analysis of gender inequality around the world don't tell us whether the differences between USA/Canada and regions other than Africa are statistically significant. From a statistical standpoint, any value of the ordinal or categorical independent variable can serve as the baseline category for reference purposes, but it's sometimes helpful to change the reference category to the one that facilitates the most natural, intuitive interpretation of the data.

If you're from the United States, a comparative analysis might make more sense to you if the USA/Canada region is the reference category to which other regions are compared. Let's override the default levels of the world$regionun variable to make the USA/Canada region our point of reference for statistical analysis. As it stands, R will make "Africa" the omitted category—not "USA/Canada". Use the relevel function to change the reference category. The basic relevel syntax:

$$newvar = \text{relevel}(oldvar, \text{ref="omitted.level"})$$

Creating a new variable is not a requirement, just a good practice. The ref argument is an abbreviation for "reference category," which is synonymous with omitted category. Applied to the example:

```
# change reference value of factor
world$regionun.usref = relevel(world$regionun, ref="USA/Canada")

levels(world$regionun.usref)                      # check the result
```

```
[1] "USA/Canada"              "Africa"
[3] "Asia"                    "Australia/New Zealand/Oceania"
[5] "Europe"                  "Latin America/Caribbean"
```

This sample code creates a new variable, world$regionun.usref, and leaves the original variable, world$regionun, unchanged in the dataset. Now let's re-estimate our statistical model of global gender inequality with the independent variable we just created.

```
summary(lm(gender_unequal ~ regionun.usref, data=world))
```

Coefficients:

	Estimate	Std. Error	t value	Pr(>|t|)	
(Intercept)	0.34450	0.07883	4.370	2.53e-05	***
Africa	0.35542	0.08099	4.388	2.35e-05	***
Asia	0.23426	0.08093	2.894	0.00446	**
Australia/New Zealand/Oceania	0.12217	0.10177	1.200	0.23218	
Europe	-0.01929	0.08112	-0.238	0.81237	
Latin America/Caribbean	0.26585	0.08219	3.235	0.00155	**

Signif. codes: 0 '***' 0.001 '**' 0.01 '*' 0.05 '.' 0.1 ' ' 1

Residual standard error: 0.1115 on 129 degrees of freedom
  (32 observations deleted due to missingness)
Multiple R-squared: 0.6313, Adjusted R-squared: 0.617

These results look similar to the regression model we estimated with the original world$regionun variable (we've shortened the variable names to fit the page), but the USA/Canada region is now the reference category where the expected gender inequality is equal to the new intercept value, 0.34. Our new coefficient estimates are simply a rearrangement of our earlier estimates; before, we found a −0.36 difference in the USA/Canada region compared to Africa, and now we're finding a +.36 difference in gender inequality in Africa compared to the USA/Canada region. The expected values of gender inequality in each region are the same and our model fit statistics are unchanged, but now we're judging each region compared to the USA/Canada. Before, every region was significantly different from Africa. Now we have two regions, Europe and Australia/New Zealand/Oceania, that are not significantly different from our reference category in terms of gender inequality.

WEIGHTED REGRESSION WITH A DUMMY VARIABLE

We now turn to regression analysis with weighted data, an increasingly common situation, especially in survey research. The general concepts are the same. We are still using regression analysis to estimate equations that summarize the relationship between an independent variable (or variables) and an interval-level dependent variable. We'll also interpret the results the same way. The difference is somewhat technical; we don't want R to treat all observations the same. We want to estimate a regression model in a way that reflects the sample weights of our observations.

For weighted regression, we enlist the svyglm function to analyze the design versions of the big survey sets, nesD and gssD. These design datasets are created as a preliminary step to estimating our weighted regression models. For convenience, nesD and gssD have already been created and are part of the poliscidata package. The general syntax of the svyglm function is similar to that of the lm function but requires specifying the design to use[7]:

```
svyglm(depvar ~ indepvar, design=design.dataset, na.action=na.options)
```

The na.action argument is not required, but we like to set this to "na.omit". You can run svyglm on the design version of any dataset, weighted (nesD and gssD) or unweighted (statesD and worldD).

Let's start by estimating a weighted bivariate regression model with a dummy variable. We'll use the same example we used demonstrating (unweighted) bivariate regression with a dummy variable: the gender difference in Obama sentiment.

```
# weighted bivariate regression with a dummy variable
# the svyglm function works with special "design" dataset
svyglm(obama_therm ~ gender, design=nesD, na.action=na.omit)
```

---

[7] Somewhat confusingly, the lm function we used to estimate unweighted regression models has an option "weights" argument but the lm function's weights are inverse variance weights used to correct certain statistical issues, not sampling weights that we want to use with our survey data.

```
Independent Sampling design (with replacement)
svydesign(id = ~1, data = nes, weights = ~wt)

Call: svyglm(formula = obama_therm ~ gender, design = nesD, na.action = na.omit)

Coefficients:
  (Intercept)     genderFemale
       53.441            5.777

Degrees of Freedom: 5494 Total (i.e. Null);  5493 Residual
   (421 observations deleted due to missingness)
Null Deviance:      6453000
Residual Deviance: 6408000     AIC: 56660
```

The svyglm results are formatted a little differently than the lm results we generated earlier. We'll discuss the model fit statistics in a moment, but let's look at the coefficients. According to these results, the intercept (expected Obama thermometer ratings for males) is 53.4 and we expect females to rate Obama 5.8 higher on a feeling thermometer than males. In the unweighted bivariate regression mode, we estimated an intercept of 57.0 and a gender difference of 7.2. Weighting observations seems to make a noticeable difference here.

Just as we had to use the summary() function to see the inferential statistics for regression models estimated with the lm() function, we'll have to do the same with weighted regression models we estimate with svyglm(). Let's take a look at the summary of our weighted bivariate regression with a dummy variable.

```
# summary for weighted bivariate regression with a dummy variable
summary(svyglm(obama_therm ~ gender, design=nesD, na.action=na.omit))
```

```
Coefficients:

              Estimate  Std. Error  t value  Pr(>|t|)
(Intercept)    53.4405      0.8619   62.001   < 2e-16   ***
genderFemale    5.7769      1.2349    4.678  2.97e-06   ***
---
Signif. codes:  0 '***' 0.001 '**' 0.01 '*' 0.05 '.' 0.1 ' ' 1
```

You may have noticed that we didn't create an indicator variable for female NES respondents this time. When you insert a factor on the right-hand side of a svyglm or an lm model, R automatically "dummifies" the factor into zeroes and ones, choosing the first-named level as the omitted category. You can run levels(nes$gender) to see which factor value will be the default reference category.[8]

Unfortunately, applying the summary function to the svyglm model does not generate the model fit statistics we've used to evaluate other regression models, such as R-squared and Adjusted R-squared. To estimate these model fit statistics from a weighted regression model, we created the svyglm.fit() function and applied it to the output of the svyglm() function to obtain model fit statistics.

```
# summary for weighted bivariate regression with a dummy variable
svyglm.fit(svyglm(obama_therm ~ gender, design=nesD, na.action=na.omit))
```

```
$R2
[1] 0.007

$adjR2
[1] 0.007
```

---

[8] You can change the omitted category with the levels function, as described in Chapter 3.

These model fit statistics seem pretty modest compared to other R-squared and Adjusted R-squared values we've encountered in this chapter. Low R-squared values are common when you analyze individual-level political behavior. As you can plainly see, the partial regression coefficient for gender in the model of Obama sentiment is clearly statistically significant, even though a lot of variance in how people feel about Obama is not explained by this variable alone.

MULTIPLE REGRESSION ANALYSIS WITH WEIGHTED DATA

We will invoke the svyglm function again to estimate a weighted multiple regression model. Just as we saw with the lm function, the transition from estimating a bivariate regression model to a multiple regression model is relatively minor, but properly interpreting the results usually requires a bit of practice. The generic syntax for weighted multiple regression analysis with svyglm:

svyglm(*depvar* ~ *indepvar1* + *indepvar2* + … + *indepvarn*, design=*design.dataset*)

As was the case with weighted bivariate regression, the svyglm function allows the user to specify how to handle observations with missing data, the na.action argument, that we'll set to "na.omit".

Let's use weighted multiple regression to gain a better understanding of public support for federal spending problems. We begin with a simple weighted bivariate regression analysis of the relationship between nes$fedspend_scale (the dependent variable), an interval-level measure of support for federal spending, and nes$ft_dem, sentiment toward the Democratic Party on a feeling thermometer. Because we're going to execute two functions on our weighted regression model, summary and svyglm.fit, we might save the output of the svyglm call as an object called "fedspend.model1".

```
# start with weighted bivariate regression model
fedspend.model1 = svyglm(fedspend_scale ~ ft_dem, design=nesD,
                         na.action=na.omit)
summary(fedspend.model1)
svyglm.fit(fedspend.model1)
```

```
Coefficients:
            Estimate  Std. Error  t value  Pr(>|t|)
(Intercept) 6.609057  0.122382    54.00    <2e-16  ***
ft_dem      0.063402  0.001944    32.61    <2e-16  ***

---
Signif. codes:  0 '***' 0.001 '**' 0.01 '*' 0.05 '.' 0.1 ' ' 1

$R2
[1] 0.291

$adjR2
[1] 0.291
```

Starting with the simplest possible regression model and adding independent variables is a good way to avoid coding errors and can help you better understand your results. According to these results, we would expect someone who gives the Democrats a 0 on a feeling thermometer to score 6.61 on the federal spending scale; for each unit increase in the Democratic feeling thermometer, we'd expect the support for federal spending programs to increase by 0.06. With a whopping t-statistic of 32.61 and a vanishingly small P-value, we can safely reject the null hypothesis. This relationship almost certainly did not occur by chance when the random sample was drawn. About 29 percent of the variation in the fedspend_scale can be explained by ratings of the Democratic Party. Perhaps by adding political knowledge to the mix, we can improve the completeness of our explanation.

In svyglm, just as with lm, additional independent variables follow a plus sign. To estimate a weighted regression model of support for federal spending as a function of both ft_dem and polknow_combined, the number of political questions NES respondents answered correctly, we could execute the following lines of code:

```
# estimate weighted multiple regression model
fedspend.model2 = svyglm(fedspend_scale ~ ft_dem + polknow_combined,
                     design=nesD, na.action=na.omit)


# summary model results, model fit statistics
summary(fedspend.model2)
svyglm.fit(fedspend.model2)
```

```
Coefficients:
                  Estimate  Std. Error  t value  Pr(>|t|)
(Intercept)       7.325183    0.257525   28.445   < 2e-16   ***
ft_dem            0.062086    0.002363   26.269   < 2e-16   ***
polknow_combined -0.180406    0.040241   -4.483  7.57e-06   ***

---
Signif. codes:  0 '***' 0.001 '**' 0.01 '*' 0.05 '.' 0.1 ' ' 1


$R2
[1] 0.308


$adjR2
[1] 0.308
```

The weighted multiple regression estimates:

$$\text{Support for federal spending} = 7.33 + 0.06 * (\text{Dem. therm.}) - 0.18 * (\text{Political knowledge})$$

Controlling for political knowledge, a one-unit increase in Democratic ratings occasions a .06-point increase in the dependent variable, a statistically significant effect (t-statistic = 26.27, P-value ≈ Pollock and Edwards's chance of playing in the NBA). Notice that this controlled effect is virtually identical to the uncontrolled relationship in the bivariate model, confirming that little of the "Democratic thermometer effect" can be attributed to a confounding relationship between the Democratic thermometer and political knowledge. The "income effect" shows up, too: Controlling for sentiment about the Democratic Party, support for federal spending programs decreases by .18, on average, for each one-unit increase in the political knowledge score (t-statistic = −4.48, P-value ≈ Cleveland Browns' chances of winning the next five Super Bowls).

Do both variables, working together, explain a lot of variation in the fedspend_scale? Yes, the model fit statistics are impressive. Political knowledge increases the Adjusted R-squared statistic by nearly 2% (in the context of individual political behavior, this is an impressive contribution). But there is still room for improvement and you've seen how to add independent variables to a weighted multiple regression model. Perhaps before you begin the exercises, you could identify additional variables, re-run the analysis, and try to improve the model's performance. A good thing about assigning svyglm output to an object and then applying the summary and svyglm.fit functions to that object is you can produce different results by changing just one line of code.

WEIGHTED REGRESSION WITH ORDINAL OR CATEGORICAL INDEPENDENT VARIABLES

To demonstrate weighted bivariate regression with a dummy variable, we examine the gender difference in sentiment toward Obama. Although we found a statistically significant gender difference, the overall model fit was relatively modest, leaving lots of room for improvement. Let's pick the Obama thermometer analysis back up and incorporate an ordinal-level variable into the model to estimate a weighted multiple regression model.

It's a safe bet that how someone feels about Obama is influenced by whether he or she identifies as a Democrat, an Independent, or a Republican. This three-value partisanship scale appears in the nesD design dataset as pid_3. Because gender and partisanship may be correlated, it's important to control for partisanship to accurately estimate the effect of gender on expected values of the dependent variable.

```
# weighted multiple regression with ordinal or categorical indep. variable
obama.model2 = svyglm(obama_therm ~ gender + pid_3, design=nesD,
                      na.action=na.omit)

summary(obama.model2)
svyglm.fit(obama.model2)
```

```
Coefficients:
               Estimate   Std. Error   t value   Pr(>|t|)
(Intercept)     81.5101       0.8410    96.925    < 2e-16   ***
genderFemale     2.8973       0.9529     3.041    0.00237   **
pid_3Ind       -29.4888       1.0969   -26.884    < 2e-16   ***
pid_3Rep       -56.7039       1.1071   -51.216    < 2e-16   ***

---

Signif. codes:  0 '***' 0.001 '**' 0.01 '*' 0.05 '.' 0.1 ' ' 1

$R2
[1] 0.428

$adjR2
[1] 0.428
```

The svyglm automatically created $k-1$ dummy variables out of the three-category party identification variable. Now our weighted multiple regression model of Obama sentiment estimates the gender difference controlling for the difference that being an Independent or Republican makes. As always, the intercept represents the expected value of the dependent variable when the values of all the independent variables are zero. So 81.5 is the expected Obama thermometer rating for someone who is not female, not an Independent, and not a Republican. Who's left as the reference group? Male Democrats. So the expected value of the dependent variable for females isn't 2.9; that's the difference between females and males. It's tempting to say that the expected Obama sentiment for females is 84.4 (81.5 + 2.9), but it depends on partisanship too now. We would expect female Democrats to give Obama a warm 84.4 rating, but the expected rating drops to 54.9 for female Independents (81.5 + 2.9 – 29.5) and a cold 27.7 (81.5 + 2.9 – 56.7) for female Republicans. It's interesting to note that we're still seeing a statistically significant gender difference in this weighted multiple regression model, but the coefficient is smaller now than in our weighted bivariate regression model (2.9 compared to 5.8), which indicates that some of what we saw as a gender difference before was really a partisanship effect. Our model fit statistics have also shot up considerably.

What if we wanted to make Independents, rather than Democrats, our reference category in our multiple regression analysis of Obama sentiments? Changing the reference category with the relevel function was relatively easy when we used the lm function to estimate a multiple regression model using the nes dataset. Now that we're using the svyglm function to estimate a weighted multiple regression model using the special nesD design dataset, working with new variables (such as a releveled pid_3 variable) presents some complications, but it's really just a matter of running a couple additional lines of code.

There are two ways to insert a new variable into a design dataset. The first method is to make changes to the non-design dataset, and then re-run the svydesign function, replacing the "old" design set with the "new" design set.

```
# first, create new independent variable with "Ind" as reference category
nes$pid_3.indref = relevel(nes$pid_3, ref="Ind")

levels(nes$pid_3.indref)                              # check the result

# then, recreate the nesD design dataset with new variable added
nesD = svydesign(id=~1, data=nes, weights=~wt)
```

Alternatively, you can nest the relevel expression inside the survey package's update function. This will update the nesD design dataset with the new, releveled variable.[9]

```
# update nesD with new independent variable with "Ind" as reference category
nesD = update(nesD, pid_3.indref = relevel(nes$pid_3, ref="Ind"))
```

This is the procedure you would use to incorporate any new or transformed variable into one of the design datasets in the polyscidata package. We're tried to include all the variables you need in the design datasets from the start, but it's impossible to foresee all the different ways students will analyze these datasets.

Which way is better to add a new variable to a design dataset? It's your call. Both achieve the desired goal. We can now estimate our weighted multiple regression model.

```
# weighted multiple regression with ordinal or categorical indep. variable
obama.model3 = svyglm(obama_therm ~ gender + pid_3.indref, design=nesD,
                      na.action=na.omit)

summary(obama.model3)
svyglm.fit(obama.model3)
```

```
Coefficients:
                 Estimate  Std. Error  t value  Pr(>|t|)
(Intercept)       52.0213      0.9853   52.797  < 2e-16  ***
genderFemale       2.8973      0.9529    3.041  0.00237  **
pid_3.indrefDem   29.4888      1.0969   26.884  < 2e-16  ***
pid_3.indrefRep  -27.2151      1.2775  -21.303  < 2e-16  ***
---
Signif. codes:  0 '***' 0.001 '**' 0.01 '*' 0.05 '.' 0.1 ' ' 1

$R2
[1] 0.428

$adjR2
[1] 0.428
```

The regression equation is as follows:

$$\text{Obama thermometer rating} = 52.02 + 2.90 * \text{Female} + 29.49 * \text{Dem} - 27.22 * \text{Rep}.$$

You would interpret these multiple regression results the same way we did when male Democrats were the reference category, except that male Independents are now the reference category. You may find it easier to interpret these results because the intercept is now pretty close to the mean observation.

---

[9] Additionally, once can create this new variable in the design dataset as nesD$variables$pid-3.indref.

CREATING TABLES OF REGRESSION RESULTS

By this point, you've invested a lot of time into learning how to use R to estimate different regression models. You've worked with both weighted and unweighted datasets, multiple independent variables, and different types of independent variables. Sometimes, copying console output is a fine way to share your results. Other times, however, you'll want to organize your regression results in a table that makes your results easier for others to read and interpret.

You can use the printC function to output a table of regression coefficient estimates to your working directory. You'll recall that the printC function exports html-style tables to a file in your working directory called "Table.Output.html". The printC function shouldn't generate any output in your R Console window; it writes to the "Table.Output.html" in your working directory.

Let's use the printC function to produce a table from our multiple regression model of the percentage of women in state legislatures. You can nest the lm function call inside the printC function to accomplish the same result in one line rather than two.

```
# estimate multiple regression model, assign result to object
womleg.model = lm(womleg_2015 ~ college + attend_pct, data=states)

# print table of results to file in working directory
printC(womleg.model)
```

After you execute the printC command, look in your working directory for a file called "Table.Output.html" that should look something like the image in Figure 8.1. If you're not sure what your working directory is, enter the command "getwd()" for the path to your current working directory.

Figure 8.1   The Table.Output.html File

    Table.Output.html   7/29/2016 11:19 AM   Firefox HTML Doc...   1 KB

When you open this file, which is in a web page–type mark-up, it will appear in a web browser (not in R or a word processor). You can copy and paste the html table you see into a word-processing document, like so:

	Estimate	*Std. Error*	*t value*	*Pr(>|t|)*
(Intercept)	28.4258	6.8400	4.16	0.0001
college	0.4622	0.1736	2.66	0.0106
attend_pct	−0.4164	0.0838	−4.97	0.0000

Getting this much of our multiple regression results in a table is very helpful because we can easily resize the table, edit the text, and modify the properties. You'll notice that this table doesn't include the model fit statistics or report the number of observations analyzed. You'll want to add these essential pieces of information when you report results of your regression analysis. For maximum effect, try formatting your regression results tables like those you see published in leading political science journals such as the *American Political Science Review*, *American Journal of Political Science*, or *Journal of Politics*. With a few modifications in a word processor, we can create professional-looking results:

The printC function works with the output of the svyglm function too. Well-organized tables are a great way to present multiple regression results. Raw regression results can look more confusing than enlightening, particularly if you're not looking at your own work. A lot of people are afraid of numbers and statistics, so it's a good idea to make your work clear and presentable in order to communicate effectively to a wide audience.

TABLE. REGRESSION MODEL OF PERCENTAGE
WOMEN IN STATE LEGISLATURES

Variable	Estimate
College Graduation Rate	0.46*
	(0.17)
Religious Service Attendance	–0.42***
	(0.08)
Intercept	28.43***
	(6.84)
N	50
R^2	0.58
Adjusted-R^2	0.56

Note: standard errors in parenthesis.
***$p<0.001$, **$p<0.01$, *$p<0.05$ (two-tailed tests)

> Title: Make sure the dependent variable is clear and use smallcaps font.

> Keep table borders simple; use just a few horizontal lines to separation.

> t-statistics and P-values generally omitted. You can calculate t-statistics from coefs and SE and star significant variables.

> Two or three decimal places is usually enough; avoid all zero estimates.

> The intercept term is generally listed last.

> Use plain words, not computer code, to identify independent variables.

> Decimal places should be vertically aligned; it makes a big difference visually.

Visual representations of regression results can also help communicate the relationships you identify in datasets. In the next chapter, we'll learn different ways of visualizing the results of regression analysis.

EXERCISES

1. (Dataset: states. Variables: demhr11, demstate13, union10.) Consider a plausible scenario for the relationships between three variables: the percentage of a state's U.S. House delegation who are Democrats, the percentage of state legislators who are Democrats, and the percentage of workers in the state who are unionized. We could hypothesize that, compared with states with fewer Democrats in their state legislatures, states having larger percentages of Democratic legislators would also have greater proportions of Democrats in their U.S. House delegations. Furthermore, because unions tend to support Democratic candidates, we would also expect more heavily unionized states to have higher percentages of Democratic legislators at the state legislative and congressional levels. States contains three variables: demhr11, the percentage of House members who are Democrats; demstate13, the percentage of state legislators who are Democrats; and union10, the percentage of workers who are union members.

   A. Run wtd.cor to find the Pearson correlation coefficients among demhr11, demstate13, and union10. Fill in the six empty cells of this correlation matrix:

	Percent U.S. House Delegation Democratic	*Percent State Legislators Democratic*	*Percent Workers Who Are Union Members*
Percent U.S. House delegation Democratic correlation	1	?	?
Percent state legislators Democratic correlation	?	1	?
Percent workers who are union members correlation	?	?	1

B. According to the correlation coefficient, as the percentage of Democratic state legislators increases, the percentage of Democratic U.S. representatives (Circle one.)

increases.   decreases.

C. According to the correlation coefficient, as the percentage of Democratic state legislators decreases, the percentage of Democratic U.S. representatives (Circle one.)

increases.   decreases.

D. Consider this argument: Unions are more important in U.S. House races than in state legislative races. Does your analysis support this argument? (Circle one.)

No   Yes

Explain your reasoning.

_____

_____

_____

2. (Dataset: States. Variables: abortlaw10, permit, womleg_2015.) As you are no doubt aware, in its momentous decision in *Roe v. Wade* (1973), the U.S. Supreme Court declared that states may not outlaw abortion. Even so, many state legislatures have enacted restrictions and regulations that, while not banning abortion, make an abortion more difficult to obtain. Other states, however, have few or no restrictions. What factors might explain these differences in abortion laws among the states? We know that the mass public remains divided on this issue. Public opinion in some states is more favorable toward permitting abortion and in other states is less favorable. Does public opinion guide state policy on this issue? What about the direct role of state lawmakers? Are state legislatures with fewer female legislators more likely to enact restrictive abortion laws than are legislatures with more female legislators?

States contains abortlaw10, which measures the number of abortion restrictions a state has enacted into law. Values on abortlaw10 range from 0 (least restrictive) to 10 (most restrictive). This is the dependent variable. States also has the variable permit, the percentage of the mass public saying that abortion should "always" be permitted. And states has womleg_2015, the percentage of female legislators. First you will run a bivariate regression with abortlaw10 and permit. Then you will run a multiple regression that includes permit and womleg_2015.

A. Think about how abortlaw10 and permit are coded. If you were to use regression analysis to test the idea that public opinion on abortion affects state abortion policy, then you would expect to find (Check one.)

❑ a negative sign on permit's regression coefficient.

❑ a positive sign on permit's regression coefficient.

B. Analyze the abortlaw10-permit relationship using lm. According to the results, the regression equation for estimating the number of abortion restrictions is (Fill in the blanks.)

_____ + _____ *permit.

(constant)   (regression coefficient)

C. Run a multiple regression analysis of abortlaw10, specifying permit and womleg_2015 as independent variables. Based on your results, the multiple regression for estimating the number of abortion restrictions is (Fill in the blanks.)

14.21 + _____ *permit + _____ *womleg_2015.

D. The P-value for the regression coefficient on permit is (Fill in the blank.) _____, and the P-value for the regression coefficient on womleg_2015 is (Fill in the blank.) _____.

E. Suppose someone claimed that, after controlling for womleg_2015, the relationship between abortlaw10 and permit turns out to be spurious. Does your analysis support this claim? Answer yes or no and briefly explain your answer:

_____

_____

_____

3. (Dataset: gssD. Variables: femrole, authoritarianism, age.) Two scholars are discussing why some people are more likely than others to accept women in non-traditional roles.

Scholar 1: "The main thing to know about people is how old they are. Older people were socialized in a more traditional time and are not as willing to accept women in roles outside the home. Younger people, by contrast, are being socialized during an era of greater female empowerment outside the home. I'll bet that if you perform a regression analysis using a variable measuring the level of acceptance of women outside the home as the dependent variable, and you use age as the independent variable, the regression coefficient on age will be negative and statistically significant."

Scholar 2: "You are on the right track, but you're not really addressing the question of *why* age and gender-role attitudes are negatively related. That 'more traditional time' to which you referred was, more specifically, a time of greater authoritarianism. Authoritarianism is significantly related to gender-role attitudes: As authoritarianism goes up, support for non-traditional roles goes down. Thus, the older generation's objection to non-traditional gender roles arises from their greater authoritarianism, not simply their age. Go ahead and run your simple bivariate regression using age as the independent variable. Then run a multiple regression, using age *and* authoritarianism as independent variables. The multiple regression will show that authoritarianism is strongly related to gender-role attitudes. But the coefficient on age will be statistically insignificant."

The design dataset, gssD, contains femrole, a metric that runs from 0 (women belong in the home) to 9 (women belong outside the home). So higher values of femrole indicate greater acceptance of non-traditional roles. The dataset also has age, respondent age in years. The variable, authoritarianism, ranges from 0 (low authoritarianism) to 7 (high authoritarianism).

A. Run the bivariate regression suggested by Scholar 1. To obtain complete model statistics, run summary(svyglm), svyglm, and fit.svyglm. Record the statistics next to the question marks in the following table:

	Regression Coefficient	t-Statistic	P-Value
(Intercept)	?		
Age	?	?	?
Adjusted R-square	?		

B. According to the results of your analysis, Scholar 1's idea is (Circle one.)

correct.   incorrect.

Explain how you know.

_____

_____

_____

C. Run the multiple regression suggested by Scholar 2. Record the statistics next to the question marks in the following table:

	Regression Coefficient	t-Statistic	P-Value
(Intercept)	?		
Age	?	?	?
Authoritarianism	?	?	?
Adjusted R-square	?		

D. Scholar 2 claimed that authoritarianism is negatively and significantly related to greater acceptance of non-traditional gender roles. This claim is (Circle one.)

correct.   incorrect.

Explain how you know.

_____

_____

_____

E. Scholar 2 claimed that, after controlling for authoritarianism, the age-femrole relationship will be insignificant. This claim is (Circle one.)

correct.   incorrect.

Explain how you know.

_____

_____

_____

4. (Dataset: nes. Variables: owngun_owngun, fedspend_scale.) In this question, we'll examine the political views of gun owners. Do gun owners have distinct political opinions compared to non-gun owners? While groups like the National Rifle Association certainly represent distinct, special interests, there are many gun owners in the United States. Let's use bivariate regression analysis to examine whether gun owners believe the federal government should cut spending programs. The fedspend_scale variable in the nes summarizes respondents' sentiment about federal spending on different programs, with higher values representing more support for federal spending.

   A. Using the nes dataset, estimate a bivariate regression model that explains individual support for the federal spending programs as a function of gun ownership (owngun_owngun). Based on these results, what is a gun owner's expected support for federal spending on this scale? What is a non-gun owner's expected support for federal spending on this scale?

   _____

   B. Write an equation in the form y = a + bx that expresses an individual's support for federal spending programs (y) as a function of gun ownership (x).

   _____

   C. Do gun owners express significantly different opinions about federal spending programs than non-gun owners do? Use the summary function to view the inferential statistics for your bivariate regression model. Based on the inferential statistics reported by R, assess whether any differences in the opinions of gun owners you observed could be the result of random chance in a relatively small sample, rather than a real political difference between gun owners and non-gun owners.

   _____

   _____

   D. What percentage of the variation in nes respondents' sentiment about federal spending on different programs is explained by whether these respondents own a gun?

   _____%

9

Visualizing Correlation and Regression Analysis

Objective	Functions Introduced	Author or Source
Visualizing correlation analysis	plot {graphics}	R Development Core Team[1]
	pairs {graphics}	R Development Core Team
Plotting bivariate regression results	abline {graphics}	R Development Core Team
	expand.grid {base}	R Development Core Team
	predict.lm {stats}	R Development Core Team
	segments {graphics}	R Development Core Team
	axis {graphics}	R Development Core Team
	box {graphics}	R Development Core Team
	symbols {graphics}	R Development Core Team
	text {graphics}	R Development Core Team
	Colors {rcompanion}	Philip Pollock and Barry Edwards
	plotChar {rcompanion}	Philip Pollock and Barry Edwards
	scatterplot {car}	Jon Fox and Sanford Weisberg
Plotting multiple regression results	plot3d {rgl}	Daniel Adler and Duncan Murdock
	scatterplot3d {scatterplot3d}	Uwe Ligges, Martin Maechler, and Sarah Schnackenberg[2]
Dealing with limited unique values	svyplot {survey}	Thomas Lumley[3]
	jitter {base}	R Development Core Team

[1] R Development Core Team. (2011). *R: A language and environment for statistical computing*. Vienna, Austria: Author. Available at http://www.R-project.org/

[2] *rgl: 3D visualization using openGL* (R package version 0.96.0). Available at https://r-forge.r-project.org/projects/rgl

[3] Lumley, T. (2012). *survey: Analysis of complex survey samples* (R package version 3.28-2). Available at http://cran.r-project.org/web/packages/survey/index.html. See also: Lumley, T. (2004). Analysis of complex survey samples. *Journal of Statistical Software*, 9(1), 1–19; Lumley, T. (2010). *Complex surveys: A guide to analysis using R*. Hoboken, NJ: John Wiley & Sons.

In the previous chapter, we showed how to conduct correlation analysis and estimate regression models using R. These are powerful and flexible methods that you can apply to different research situations. In many situations, you can supplement your statistical results with visualizations of the relationships among the variables of interest.

Visualizing relationships in data is at least as much an art as it is a science. In most cases, there is not a single, right way to visualize data. The variety of graphics you can produce using R is staggering. There's lots of room for creativity and personal expression. It can be helpful to think of R's graphics window as a canvas on which you layer visual representations of data. At the same time, you want to be aware of some basic design principles. You should try to strike a happy medium between presenting too much and too little information in your graphics. You don't want your graphics to seem cluttered or overdone, but there's no reason to make a graphic that simply shows a line you could more succinctly express in y = a + b*x form. Essential features should be clearly labeled. If you incorporate text in graphics, the text should be readable; you don't want the font size to be too small or words to be printed on top of each other. Where possible, make effective use of different colors, shapes, and line types. If you know your figure will ultimately be rendered in black and white, you can still make effective use of different shades of gray. Your eyes can see patterns quickly and clearly. If you can produce effective visual representations of your analysis, you'll be able to communicate your findings to a wide audience.

There are a few different general approaches to generating graphics. One approach applies low-level plotting functions to build figures in the graphics window one step at a time. Another approach selects the most appropriate plotting function from any one of a number of R packages.

Creating effective graphics is usually an iterative process. We like to start by executing the most basic function call possible. This can give you a rough idea of what the data look like. If you're on the right track, then start refining the figure.

We also introduce hexagonal scatterplots, an innovative bivariate graphing technique for large, weighted survey datasets. With the scatterplot function and symbols (from the graphics package), you will learn to visualize bivariate and multivariate relationships.

As in Chapter 8, you will learn to use different functions for unweighted data and weighted data. You will use lm for unweighted data and svyglm for weighted data. You will find that, in adapting these functions to accommodate dummy variables and interaction effects, R is remarkably user-friendly. Indeed, it is almost as if R's main purpose in life is to run general linear models.

In some cases, you might suspect that the effect of one independent variable on the dependent variable is not the same for all values of another independent variable—in other words, that interaction is going on in the data. In this chapter, you will learn how to model and interpret interaction effects in multiple regression.

VISUALIZING CORRELATION

As discussed in the previous chapter, correlation analysis is used to characterize the relationship between a pair of interval-level variables. When you analyze the correlation between two variables, you want to know the strength and direction of the relationship. A scatterplot is a simple visualization of the observations in a dataset, placed according to the values that define the x-axis and y-axis. R's plotting functions have many optional arguments that allow R users to fine-tune graphics. Because we're just getting started, we'll keep things simple and just specify which variables define the x-axis and y-axis and label both axes as follows.

```
# Simple scatterplot of two interval level variables
plot(x=nes$ftgr_liberals, y=nes$ftgr_feminists,
    xlab="Feeling Thermometer: Liberals",
    ylab="Feeling Thermometer: Feminists")
```

The plot shown in Figure 9.1 could communicate the relationship between these two thermometer scores more clearly, but it conveys the positive correlation between NES respondents' sentiments toward liberals and feminists (r = 0.56).

In Chapter 8, we generated a correlation matrix to explore the relationship between respondents' sentiment on a variety of political subjects. The pairs() function can produce a scatterplot matrix that allows one to visualize correlations among several variables. We'll use the same set of thermometers we used in Chapter 8 and create a vector of labels (called variableNames) to make the final product clearer. This time, we'll customize the look of our scatterplots a bit by setting the optional arguments of the pairs() function.[4]

---

[4] Thankfully, plotting functions tend to adopt the same argument keywords. Optional arguments like "col", "xlab", "ylab", "pch", and "cex" work the same way with most plotting functions, so you don't have to learn a whole new set of arguments with each plotting function you encounter.

Figure 9.1 Scatterplot Showing the Correlation of Two Variables

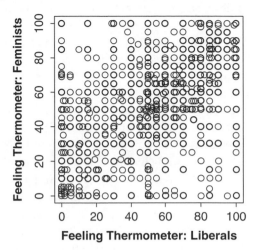

```
# Estimates a Correlation Coefficient Matrix Among Set of Variables
variableSet = cbind(nes$ftgr_liberals, nes$ftgr_feminists,
                nes$ftgr_bigbus, nes$ftgr_military,
                nes$ftgr_atheists, nes$ftgr_gay)

variableNames = c("Liberals", "Feminists", "Big Business", "Military",
             "Atheists", "Gays")

pairs(variableSet, labels=variableNames, cex=.8, cex.labels=1.5,
     col="#00000010")
```

Figure 9.2 Scatterplot Matrix of Correlations among Multiple Variables

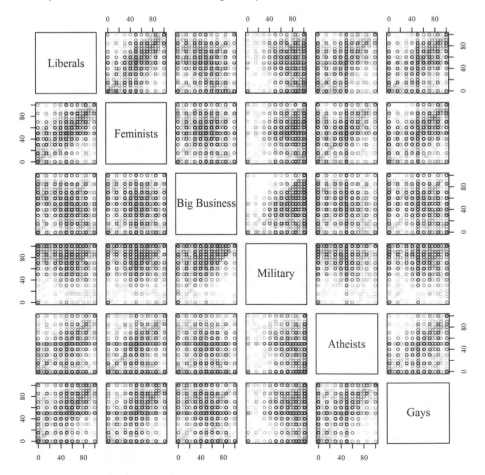

The 6 × 6 scatterplot matrix shown in Figure 9.2 presents a massive amount of information in visual form. With so many data points, some optional arguments are used to simplify the scatterplots and help us see patterns.

The "cex" and "cex.labels" arguments adjust the size of the points and labels, respectively (cex is short for character expansion/extension). The default expansion value is 1.0; cex values greater than that make things bigger, whereas cex values less than 1 make things smaller. If you think a plot element would look better bigger or smaller, adjust cex values up or down. It usually seems to take some trial and error to achieve the desired effect.

The "col" argument specifies the color of the dots that represent observed values in the nes dataset. There are several ways to specify colors in R plots. You can put the name of the color in quotation marks (e.g., col="black"). You can also specify the color with a number between 1 and 657. Enter the command "Colors()" to see the palette of colors and their corresponding numbers. For the scatterplot matrix in Figure 9.2, we used a third method of selecting colors in order to implement a simple technique for visualizing a large number of points more clearly: the "hex code" of the color. Hex codes are six characters long, but R allows you to set the opacity of a color by appending two additional numbers to the hex code.[5] In this case, col= "#000000" is black and col= "#00000010" is also black, but only 10% opaque (so it's 90% transparent). When you're plotting points with a lot of overlap, it's a simple way to see the actual pattern of observations more clearly.

What about survey weights? We could vary the size of plotting characters in the simple scatterplot by setting the cex argument equal to the sampling weight (or the square root of the sampling weight so the plotting character area is proportional to weight). Weighting observations doesn't change the x and y values, just the emphasis placed on them for statistical purposes. We'll illustrate this approach below with state-level data; with a large number of observations, like we have with NES data, the effect may be more confusing than enlightening.

GENERAL COMMENTS ABOUT VISUALIZING REGRESSION RESULTS

When you use multiple regression analysis, you can use more than one independent variable to explain variation in the dependent variable and the independent variables can be measured at different levels. This flexibility is great but presents some challenges when it comes to visualizing results. By convention, values of the independent variable define the x-axis, or horizontal dimension of a plot.

If your independent variable is measured at the interval level, scatterplots are a great way to show the relationship you're analyzing. Our bivariate regression of the percentage of women in state legislatures from Chapter 8 is a good example of this approach. We'll plot each observation and then use the abline command to superimpose the regression line. The resulting plot allows us to see not only the bivariate regression results but also how well the model fits the data (Figure 9.3).

```
# Visualizing bivariate regression with interval independent variable
womleg.model1 = lm(states$womleg_2015 ~ states$college)

plot(x=states$college, y=states$womleg_2015)
abline(womleg.model1)
#  abline(a=0.3703, b=0.9203)  # same line, specifying intercept and slope
```

There are lots of ways to fine-tune and improve this plot, but it's generally best to get a basic model working first before commencing to fine-tune your figure. Using the text function to add two-digit state codes in place of or adjacent to the circular points works well with the states dataset because the number of observations is relatively small. This is a good way to make the plot more informative without making it more cluttered.

R developers have published a number of scatterplot functions that offer different ways of visualizing the same basic relations. We could also use the scatterplot function from the car package. The basic scatterplot syntax identifies the dependent (y-axis) variable, the independent (x-axis) variable, and the dataset[6]:

---

[5] There is an rgb function (in the grDevices package) that takes red, blue, and green values as inputs and outputs the corresponding hex code. This function also allows a fourth argument for opacity.

[6] Another alternative is producing the scatterplots using the survey package, which also works with unweighted data (as discussed in this chapter).

```
scatterplot(depvar ~ indepvar, data=data, plot.options)
```

Notice that the dependent variable and the independent variable are specified as a function using the ~ symbol, rather than as x and y arguments. As with most R graphics functions, the scatterplot function makes many optional arguments available for customizing the plot's appearance. Using the scatterplot function from the car package, let's look at a basic version of the relationship between the percentage of women in state legislatures and the college graduation rate:

Figure 9.3   Scatterplot Showing Bivariate Regression Estimates

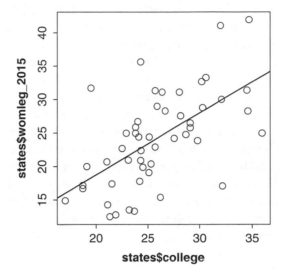

```
# Visualizing bivariate regression with interval independent variable
scatterplot(womleg_2015 ~ college, data=states)
```

Figure 9.4   Enhanced Scatterplot with Bivariate Regression Estimates

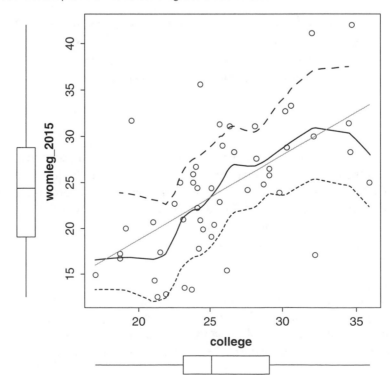

As you can see in Figure 9.4, the basic scatterplot function call produces an information-rich graphic. In addition to plotting the observations and the regression line estimate, the function also produces box plot summaries of both variables, adds a background grid, and shows the results of non-parametric local regression (with the crooked line and the dashed crooked lines on either side, it's like a moving average). These enhancements look good, but they obscure the essence of what we're trying to convey about this relationship. If you don't know what non-parametric local regression is (and it's an advanced topic beyond the scope of this book), you probably don't want to feature it in your work even though it looks pretty cool. You can set the scatterplot function's optional "smooth" and "boxplots" arguments to FALSE to suppress these features.

If you are estimating a bivariate regression model with a nominal- or ordinal-level independent variable, effectively visualizing results is a bit more challenging. If your independent variable is a nominal or ordinal variable, it will have relatively few different values and many observations will have the same value of the independent variable. When you plot the actual values of observations, they'll look like vertical stripes or dotted lines on a scatterplot.

Our suggested approach to visually depicting regression analysis with a nominal- or ordinal-level independent variable is similar to the methods used to graphically represent mean comparison analysis, with the distinct values of the independent variable marked as ticks on the x-axis. Rather than plot the standard deviation of the dependent variable for observations with each value of the independent variable, however, we want to show the standard error of the expected mean based on the regression results.

Recall our analysis of gender inequality in different regions of the world. To create our visualization of results, we'll estimate the model again, this time saving our results as a new object. Next, we'll create a prediction frame that contains all the different values of the independent variable for which our regression model estimates an expected value of gender inequality. We'll then use the regression model we estimated from observations in the world dataset to calculate the expected value of gender inequality in each region, along with the standard error of these expected values. Finally, we'll plot the expected value of gender inequality and the corresponding standard error for each region (represented as vertical line segments). The result is not the same as plotting the coefficient estimates.[7]

```
# visualizing bivariate regression with nominal IV
gender.model = lm(gender_unequal ~ regionun, data=world)

# use model results to generate predicted DV for each value of IV
prediction.frame = expand.grid(regionun = levels(world$regionun))
predictions = predict.lm(gender.model, newdata = prediction.frame,
                        interval="confidence", level=.95)

# plot the results
plot(x=1:6, y=predictions[,"fit"], ylim=c(0, 1), axes=F, xlab="Region",
    ylab="Gender Inequality", pch=16)
segments(x0=1:6, y0=predictions[,"lwr"], x1=1:6, y1 = predictions[,"upr"])
axis(side=1, at=1:6, labels=prediction.frame[,1], cex.axis=.7)
axis(side=2, las=2)
box()
```

If you are unsure what the expand.grid and predict.lm functions did in this example, type "prediction.frame" and then "predictions" in the R Console command to see the contents of the objects the sample code creates (Figure 9.5). Rather than rely on the plot function's default axis labels, we're suppressing the default axes and customizing the x- and y-axes by calling the axis function. The box function simply outlines the plotting area. We'll expand on this plotting technique shortly to visualize the results of multiple regression analysis with two independent variables measured at the nominal or ordinal level.

---

[7] If your ordinal or categorical independent variable has numeric values but you want R to create k–1 dummy variables rather than treat the independent variable as an interval-level variable in the regression model, use the factor() function. Make your independent variable the argument to the factor() function and insert that function as an indepvar argument in your lm() function call. When lm (or the svyglm function we'll use for weighted regressions) encounters the factor function, it will temporarily convert the numeric variable to a factor and create a set of dummy variables that treat each numeric value as a separate level.

If you've estimated a multiple regression model with an ordinal-level independent variable, it can make sense to add a line connecting the expected means because there is a logical order to the independent variable values. In the preceding example, the order of regions on the x-axis is arbitrary and it doesn't make sense to suggest the expected value of gender inequality between x-axis values.

PLOTTING MULTIPLE REGRESSION RESULTS

In multiple regression, the variable that defines the x-axis is part of the equation, but there are multiple independent variables, each defining different dimensions in a visual representation of the data. We can estimate many partial regression coefficients, but it's hard to visualize how an expected value changes along multiple dimensions on a two-dimensional page or three-dimensional space.

Figure 9.5   Expected Values from Regression with a Nominal-Level Independent Variable

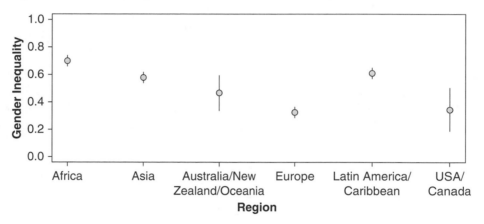

When we present multiple regression results with graphics, we frequently have to decide what are the most relationships to communicate. As a rule of thumb, it's hard to visualize the effect of more than two independent variables on a dependent variable in a single figure because we're used to seeing things in three dimensions. It may be possible to represent additional dimensions using color or varying shapes/sizes, but it's difficult to make sense of all of it at once. We may need to make some simplifying assumptions, such as assuming fixed values of some independent variables, to show how varying levels of two independent variables affect expected values of the dependent variable.

Since we were generally limited to depicting the effect of two independent variables at once, we'll discuss approaches to plotting multiple regression results in three different situations: two nominal/ordinal-level independent variables, one nominal/ordinal-level independent variable and one interval-level independent variable, and two interval-level independent variables.[8]

As an example of a multiple regression model with two nominal/ordinal-level independent variables, recall from Chapter 8 our analysis of individuals' sentiment toward President Obama as a function of gender and party identification. There are two possible values of gender (male and female) and three possible values of party identification (Democrat, Independent, and Republican). This means our multiple regression results enable us to predict the Obama sentiment for *six* different cases: female Democrats, male Democrats, female Independents, male Independents, female Republicans, and male Republicans. To visually represent these estimated values, we follow the approach we used above of estimating the regression model, creating a prediction frame for all possible combinations of the independent variables, generating expected values for each case based on our model results, and, finally, plotting the estimates. As we see in the example below, this approach works with the svyglm() function we've used with weighted survey data.

---

[8] Another approach, not discussed here, is to plot regression coefficients and their standard errors. This is a versatile way to represent the results of regression analysis, particularly with many independent variables. When you plot regression coefficients, the x- and y-axes do not represent values of the independent and dependent variables; instead, the x-axis represents the values of the regression coefficient and the y-axis ticks correspond to the independent variable labels. The coefplot function in the arm package works well.

```
# weighted multiple regression with nominal/ordinal indep. variables
obama.model = svyglm(obama_therm ~ gender + pid_3, design=nesD,
                     na.action=na.omit)

# use model results to generate predicted DV for each value of IV
prediction.frame = expand.grid(gender = levels(nes$gender),
                               pid_3 = levels(nes$pid_3))
predictions = predict.lm(obama.model, newdata = prediction.frame,
                         interval="confidence", level=.95)

# plot the results
plot(x=1:6, y=predictions[,"fit"], ylim=c(0, 100), axes=F,
     xlab="Individuals", ylab="Feeling about Obama", pch=16)
segments(x0=1:6, y0=predictions[,"lwr"], x1=1:6, y1 = predictions[,"upr"])
axis(side=1, at=1:6, labels=c("Male Dem","Female Dem","Male Indep",
     "Female Indep","Male Rep","Female Rep"), cex.axis=.7)
axis(side=2, las=2)
box()
```

Figure 9.6 Visualizing Multiple Regression Results with Nominal-Level Independent Variables

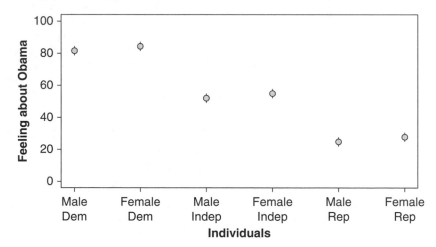

Consistent with the multiple regression model, the gender difference is the same for each party identification (Figure 9.6). The vertical line segments that represent 95% confidence intervals of the mean estimates are relatively short because the sample size is large.

If you estimate a multiple regression model with an interval-level independent variable and an independent variable measured at the nominal or ordinal level, you can visually represent your results in a scatterplot with parallel regression lines. Let the interval-level independent variable define the x-axis and let the nominal- or ordinal-level independent variable define the upward or downward intercept shifts. To illustrate this approach, we'll take a look at the variation in sin taxes in the United States.

To begin our examination of sin taxes, let's estimate a multiple regression model that explains the variation in the amount of taxes imposed on cigarettes in different states as a function of the partisan composition of their legislatures (an interval-level independent variable) and whether the state is in the South (a nominal variable). When you estimate a multiple regression model like this, list the interval-level independent variable first on the right-hand side of the equation, followed by the nominal or ordinal variable (this will make plotting the results easier). We'll summarize the model to take a look at the partial regression coefficients before we attempt to visualize the results.

```
# multiple regression with an interval IV and a nominal IV
cigtax.model = lm(states$cig_tax12 ~ states$demstate09 + states$south)
summary(cigtax.model)
```

```
Coefficients:
                 Estimate Std. Error t value Pr(>|t|)
(Intercept)      -0.033539   0.397517  -0.084 0.933127
states$demstate09 0.032746   0.006781   4.829 1.56e-05 ***
states$southSouth -0.904202  0.216548  -4.176 0.000131 ***
---
Signif. codes:  0 '***' 0.001 '**' 0.01 '*' 0.05 '.' 0.1 ' ' 1

Residual standard error: 0.7102 on 46 degrees of freedom
  (1 observation deleted due to missingness)
Multiple R-squared:  0.4808,  Adjusted R-squared:  0.4583
```

According to these results, a 1-percent increase in Democrats in the legislature increases state cigarette taxes by $.03 and states in the South impose $.90 less tax on cigarettes per pack. Our visualization should reflect these results. Our plot should have two positively sloped regression lines: one that shows the expected values in the South and one that shows the higher average tax in non-Southern states. According to our results, Democratic representation in state legislatures has the same effect in all states ($.03), so these lines should be parallel to one another. We should make the lines look different so our eyes can tell them apart. To visually reinforce the regional difference, let's use a different plotting character for Southern states and, finally, add a simple legend that identifies the points and lines.

```
# visualize multiple regression with an interval IV and a nominal IV
plot(x=states$demstate09, y=states$cig_tax12, xlim=c(0,100),
ylim=c(0,max(states$cig_tax12)),
    xlab="Percentage Democrats in Legislature",
    ylab="Cigarette Tax Per Pack ($)")
abline(cigtax.model, lty=2)                    # this is the dashed line

# distinct points and regression line for Southern States
states.south = subset(states, south=="South")
points(x=states.south$demstate09, y=states.south$cig_tax12, pch=16)
abline(a=-0.033539 -0.904202, b=0.032746, lty=1) # this is the solid line

# legend identifying lines and point
legend(x=0, y=4.3, lty=c(2,1), pch=c(1,16), cex=0.8, bty="n",
       legend=c('Non-Southern States','Southern States'))
```

Figure 9.7 Multiple Regression Results with Interval-Level and Nominal-Level Independent Variables

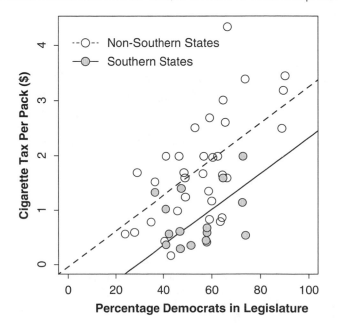

This visual representation of the relationship between partisanship in state legislatures, region, and cigarette taxes complements the statistical results you would report in a table. You can also look at Figure 9.7 to get a sense of how much the values of these variables vary from state to state.

Take a close look at the two abline function calls that add the estimated regression lines to the plot. The first one, abline(cigtax.model, lty=2), uses the intercept from the multiple regression model (−.03) and the first partial regression coefficient (0.03), which is why we listed the demstate09 variable first on the right-hand side of the regression equation. So if we pay attention to detail, we can plot the regression line for the omitted value of the dummy variable automatically, but we need to specify the intercept and slope values to show the partial effect of the dummy variable. If we just plot the line for the omitted category, it won't fit the points or accurately represent the findings. According to our results, we expect cigarette taxes to drop by 0.90 in the South, but the effect of Democrats in the legislature is the same. So to add the regression prediction for Southern states, we set abline's "a" argument to −.03 −.90 (just copy and paste the values from the multiple regression results and let R do the arithmetic) and the "b" argument is the partial regression coefficient that corresponds to the x-axis variable, .03.

If you're working with a nominal variable with more than two values or an ordinal variable (which by definition has more than two values), you'll want to add a distinct line for each group to your plot. So if we estimate the amount of cigarette taxes imposed in different states as a function of partisan representation in their legislatures and a nominal variable with four different region values, we could effectively represent these results in a scatterplot with four parallel lines, one line for each region. Changing the plotting characters for different values of the nominal/ordinal variable and adding a legend are some nice finishing touches on a plot like this.

Let's turn now to plotting the results of a multiple regression model with two interval-level independent variables. In Chapter 8, we estimated a multiple regression model that explained the percentage of women in state legislatures as a function of the states' college graduation rates and the attendance at religious services. This multiple regression analysis is based on two interval-level independent variables and we have several options for visually representing our results.

One way to accurately depict the relationship between an interval-level dependent variable and two interval-level independent variables is to vary the size of the points on a scatterplot based on the values of a second interval-level independent variable. The higher the value of the second independent variable, the larger the points appear. We can use the symbols function to create a bubble plot. Instead of representing states with uniform-sized dots, each state is represented by a circle. The size of each circle represents the second independent variable, attend.pct—the bigger the circle, the higher the state's percentage of frequent attenders. To create this figure, we'll first create the basic scatterplot and then add the circle-shaped symbols. For full effect, we'll add the estimated regression line and abbreviated state names to the figure.

```
# Visualizing multiple regression with two interval IV
# first, create basic scatterplot
plot(x=states$college, y=states$womleg_2015,
  xlab="Percent college or higher",
  ylab="Percent state legislators who are women",
  main="Percent Female State Legislators, \n by Percent Population
  College or Higher", pch=16)

# partial effect of one interval IV with other interval IV at mean value
abline(lm(womleg_2015 ~ college + scale(attend_pct), data=states))

# then, add varying-size symbols on scatterplot
symbols(x=states$college, y=states$womleg_2015,
  add=T, inches=0.25, fg="black", bg=416,
  circles=states$attend_pct)

# finally, label the symbols with state postal abbreviations
text(states$college, states$womleg_2015, states$stateid, cex=.6,
  offset=-1, pos=2)
```

Take a few minutes to examine the bubble plot in Figure 9.8. To visualize the womleg.2010-attend.pct relationship, imagine collapsing the circles onto the y-axis, stacking them up as they would fall, from low values of womleg_2015 to high values of womleg_2015. The lower range of the dependent variable would be populated with larger circles, and the higher range with smaller ones. Now imagine collapsing the circles onto the x-axis. As college increases, from left to right, the circles decrease in size, from high-attending states to low-attending states. Thus, when we compare states having lower percentages of college graduates with states having higher percentages of college graduates, we are also comparing states having higher percentages of frequent religious service attenders with states having lower percentages of religious service attenders. Some of the variation in the percentage of women in state legislatures can be attributed to variation in religious service attendance rather than college graduation rates.

Figure 9.8 Multiple Regression Results with Two Interval-Level Independent Variables

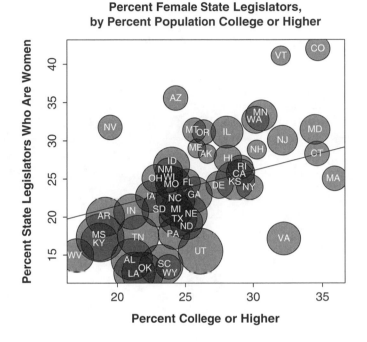

The problem you run into superimposing regression lines on a scatterplot when working with the results of multiple regression analysis is specifying intercept values. Although the partial effect, or slope, of the x-axis variable remains the same regardless of the value of the second independent variable, the value of the independent variable that doesn't define the x-axis can raise or lower the intercept. As discussed, by default, the abline plots a regression line with an intercept equal to the intercept of the multiple regression results and a slope equal to the first partial regression coefficient. So it would show the partial effect of college graduation rates on the percentage of women in state legislatures when the percentage attending religious services is equal to 0, an unrealistic situation. A nice solution to this problem is plotting the expected effect of the x-axis variable with the second independent variable fixed at its mean value, which is a realistic assumption and will raise or lower the intercept so that the regression line goes through the center of the observations. We accomplish this by substituting scale(attend_pct) for attend_pct in our demonstration code above. Recall from Chapter 3 that the scale function standardizes interval-level variables, thus centering our regression line intercept on the mean value of attend_pct.

You can also create three-dimensional figures to depict the relationship between an interval-level dependent variable and two interval-level independent variables. To create three-dimensional figures, we'll use a couple of R functions specifically designed for this purpose. Be aware that these specialized functions refer to vertical dimension (which was the y-axis in our two-dimensional plots) as the z-axis.

The plot3d function from the rgl package (this package isn't automatically installed as part of the rcompanion package, so you would need to install it) creates a three-dimensional scatterplot that you can interact with to see the relationship among variables from different perspectives. The scatterplot3d function from the package with the same name allows the user to easily plot regression lines in two dimensions (which defines a regression plane). We'll illustrate basic renditions of both of these three-dimensional figures using our example of the percentage of women in state legislatures explained by college graduate rates and attendance at religious services (Figures 9.9 and 9.10).[9]

```
# interactive 3d scatterplot in new window (RGL device)
install.packages("rgl")
library(rgl)
plot3d(x=states$college, y=states$attend_pct, z=states$womleg_2015,
       col="red", type="s",
       xlab="% College Graduates",
       ylab="% Attend Religious Services",
       zlab="% Women in Legislature")
```

Figure 9.9 Three-Dimensional Representation of Multiple Regression Results with Two Interval-Level Independent Variables

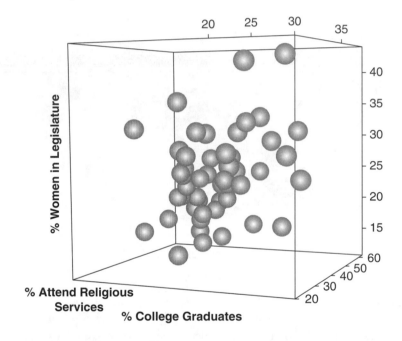

```
# 3d scatterplot with regression plane superimposed
install.packages("scatterplot3d")
library(scatterplot3d)

s3d = scatterplot3d(x=states$college, y=states$attend_pct,
                    z=states$womleg_2015,
                    pch=16, highlight.3d=TRUE, type="p", cex.symbols=2,
                        xlab="% College Graduates",
                        ylab="% Attend Religious Services",
                        zlab="% Women in Legislature")
fit <- lm(states$womleg_2015 ~ states$college + states$attend_pct)
s3d$plane3d(fit)
```

---

[9] Plotting the bivariate regression results for the expected effect of college graduation on the percentage of women in state legislatures also doesn't make much sense because we see that the bivariate regression model omits the significant variable attend_pct and overstates the effect of variation in college graduation.

Figure 9.10 Three-Dimensional Scatterplot of Multiple Regression Results with Two Interval-Level Independent Variables

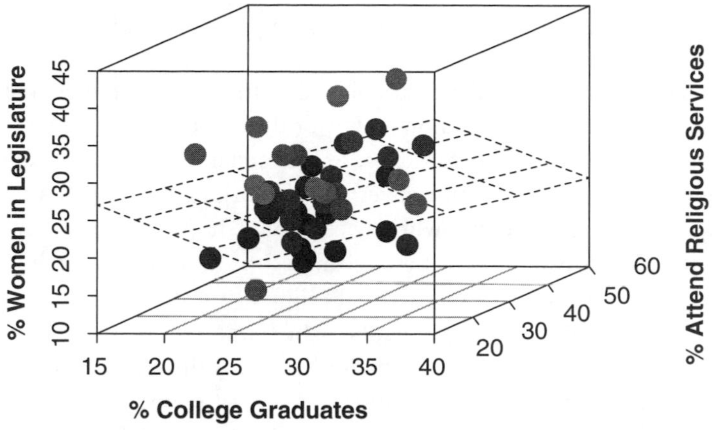

Box 9.1   Visualizing Multiple Regressions with Many Independent Variables

If your multiple regression model has more than two independent variables, you should think about which relationships are the most important to visualize because you are generally limited to visualizing relationships in three dimensions (i.e., one dependent variable and two independent variables).

Although you can sometimes use the size and/or color of plotting characters to represent varying values of additional independent variables, such complicated visualizations may be more confusing than helpful. Generally, you want to focus your work on the variables you have hypothesized about. You might want to make some simplifying assumptions about the expected values of other explanatory variables in order to plot a regression line with a realistic and appropriate intercept. You rarely want to assume that the values of all other independent variables are zero; assuming that other independent variables have their mean values is more realistic. Consider using the scale function discussed in Chapter 3 to mean-center independent variables that appear in your multiple regression model that you don't want to feature in your visualization of results; your plot will then show how the two featured independent variables affect the dependent variable when other independent variables are at their mean values.

INTERACTION EFFECTS IN MULTIPLE REGRESSION

Multiple regression is a linear and additive technique. It assumes a linear relationship between the independent variables and the dependent variable. It also assumes that the effect of one independent variable on the dependent variable is the same for all values of the other independent variables in the model. This assumption works fine for additive relationships. However, if interaction is taking place—if, for example, the effect of one independent variable depends on the value of another independent variable—then multiple regression will not capture this effect. Before researchers model interaction effects by using multiple regression, they usually have strong reasons to believe that such effects are occurring in the data.

To illustrate how to estimate and visualize interaction effects, let's consider public opinion about abortion, a controversial and politically important issue. Because some people take a pro-life position on the abortion issue for religious reasons, it seems reasonable to hypothesize that individuals with more positive sentiments toward Christians as measured on a feeling thermometer may adopt more pro-life positions on the abortion issue than those with less positive feelings about Christians. At the same time, however, religious values are more important to some people than others. Perhaps the policy views of those who say religion plays an important role in their lives are more influenced by their feelings about Christians compared to those who say religion is not important to them. Thus, the strength of the relationship between abortion attitudes and evaluations of Christians may depend on the importance of religion to the individual.

Consider the following algebraic expression of the hypothesized relationship between the sentiment toward Christians and the importance of religion:

$$\text{Abort. Scale} = a + b_1 {}^*\text{Christian Therm.} + b_2 {}^*\text{Relig. Imp.} + b_3 {}^*\text{Christian Therm.} {}^*\text{Relig. Imp.}$$

The notation for two of these independent variables, Christian thermometer score and religious importance, should look familiar to you based on our prior discussions of multiple regression analysis. The third variable is the product of the first two variables, so it is equal to 0 for respondents who say religion is not important to them (any Christian thermometer score multiplied by 0 is 0) and it is equal to the Christian thermometer score for respondents who say religion is important to them (any score multiplied by 1 is equal to that score). The constant, "a", then, estimates the anti-abortion scale for respondents who rate Christians 0 on a feeling thermometer and say that religion is not important to them (the value of the interactive term would also be 0 for these respondents). The parameter b_1 estimates the effect of each unit increase in Christian thermometer score. The parameter b_2 tells us the effect of a one-unit increase in the religious importance variable (in other words, the difference that the importance of religion makes, since this is a nominal-level variable). The parameter b_3 estimates how much believing religion is important has on the effect of feelings about Christians.

The nes dataset contains a variable named abort_scale, an interval-level variable that measures respondents' anti-abortion sentiment (the higher the number, the more pro-life the respondent's views on abortion). The nes dataset also includes a variable named ft_xian, an interval-level variable that records respondents' feeling thermometer ratings of Christians, and relig_import, a nominal-level variable that indicates whether religion is important to the respondent. The R code we've used to estimate multiple regression models accommodates interactive terms fairly easily; we simply add the interactive term following both base terms. To create an interaction term, you multiply one independent variable by the other independent variable. Consider the interaction term for the problem at hand: ftgr_xian*(relig_import=="1 . Important").[10]

```
# Multiple regression with interaction effect

summary(svyglm(abort_scale ~ ftgr_xian + (relig_import=="1. Important")
                    + ftgr_xian*(relig_import=="1.Important"),
            design=nesD, na.action=na.omit))
```

```
Coefficients:
                                      Estimate  Std. Error  t value  Pr(>|t|)
(Intercept)                            13.974      1.422      9.836    <2e-16  ***
Christian Therm.                        0.093      0.024      3.794    0.0002  ***
Religion Important                      5.053      2.177      2.321    0.020   *
Christian Therm. x Religion Important   0.096      0.032      3.020    0.003   **
---
Signif. codes:   0 '***' 0.001 '**' 0.01 '*' 0.05 '.' 0.1 ' ' 1
```

Note: R output edited for format.

Let's consider the results of this multiple regression analysis. Recall that the survey respondents reported either that religion is or is not important in their lives. For respondents who said religion was *not important*, for whom the indicator variable is equal to 0, the model reduces to:

---

[10] We're creating an indicator variable, relig_import=="1. Important", in the svyglm call to estimate the multiple regression model with interactive term in one line. Alternatively, we could generate the indicator variable and interactive term before calling the svyglm command, which would make the code clearer but require us to update the nesD design dataset before estimating the model.

$$\text{Abort. Scale} = a + b_1 * \text{Christian Therm.} + b_2 * 0 + b_3 * \text{Christian Therm.} * 0, \text{ or}$$

$$\text{Abort. Scale} = a + b_1 * \text{Christian Therm.}$$

Referring to our multiple regression results above, we see that our estimate of a is 13.974 and our estimate of b_1 is equal to 0.093.

Now consider how the multiple regression model would estimate the anti-abortion scale for respondents who reported that religion was important to them. For this group, the indicator variable is equal to 1:

$$\text{Abort. Scale} = a + b_1 * \text{Christian Therm.} + b_2 * 1 + b_3 * \text{Christian Therm.} * 1, \text{ or}$$

$$\text{Abort. Scale} = (a + b_2) + (b_1 + b_3) * \text{Christian Therm.}$$

The coefficient b_2 adjusts the constant, a, for the group that considers religion important. If b_2 is positive, we can say that this group is *more* pro-life, on average, than those who say religion is not important to them. A negative sign on b_2 will mean that this group is *less* pro-life, on average, than those who say religion is not important to them. In this case, our estimate of b_2 is 5.053 and the inferential statistics tell us that this coefficient is statistically significant. Thus, the intercept for the regression line for the religion-is-important group is 13.974 + 5.053 = 19.027.

The coefficient b_3 adjusts for the different effect that sentiment toward Christians has on abortion opinions among those who consider religion important compared to the effect sentiment toward Christians has among those who say religion is not important to them. While a one-unit increase in the Christian thermometer score correlates to a b_1 change in the abortion scale for the religion-not-important respondents, a one-unit increase in the Christian thermometer score correlates to a $b_1 + b_3$ change for the religion-is-important group. While b_2 tells us by how much to adjust the intercept for the religion-is-important group, b_3 tells us by how much to adjust the *effect* of the Christian thermometer for those in this group. Because the positive relationship between the anti-abortion scale and the Christian thermometer gets stronger as the importance of religion increases, we are expecting a positive sign on b_3. The t-statistic and P-value on b_3 will allow us to test the null hypothesis that the effect of the Christian thermometer on the anti-abortion scale is the same no matter how important religion is to someone. In this case, our estimate of b_3 is 0.096 and, reading across the row of inferential statistics, this coefficient is significantly greater than zero. According to our results, for this group, a one-unit increase in the Christian thermometer corresponds to a 0.093 + 0.096 = 0.189 increase in the anti-abortion scale.

We can visualize this interactive relationship using a scatterplot with two regression lines superimposed on the actual observations. (It's similar to visualizing the results of a multiple regression with one interval-level independent variable and one independent variable measured at the nominal or ordinal level.) It's helpful to use distinct points and lines for the two groups being analyzed.

```
# visualizing multiple regression with interaction term

plot(x=nes$ftgr_xian, y=nes$abort_scale, ylab="Anti-Abortion Scale",
    xlab="Feeling Thermometer: Christians", ylim=c(0,80), cex=.5)

# regression line for religion-low-importance group
abline(a=13.974, b=0.093, lty=3)          # this is a dotted line

# distinct points and regression line for religion-is-important group
nes.religious = subset(nes, relig_import=="1. Important")
points(x=nes.religious$ftgr_xian, y=nes.religious$abort_scale, pch=16,
    cex=.5)
abline(a=13.974 + 5.053, b=0.093 + 0.096, lty=1)    # this is a solid line

# legend identifying lines and points
legend(x=0, y=80, lty=c(3,1), pch=c(1,16), cex=0.8, bty="n",
    legend=c('Religion Not Important', ' Religion Is Important'))
```

The plot in Figure 9.11 helps to clarify the relationship between sentiment toward Christians, the importance of religion, and anti-abortion opinions. The interaction between the feeling thermometer and the importance placed on religion is seen in comparing the regression lines; for those who feel religion is important, the mean anti-abortion scale is higher and the effect of sentiment toward Christians is greater.

Still, we may not be fully satisfied with this representation of the data. When we work with large datasets, like the NES with its 5,916 observations, it can be hard to make effective use of all the information without cluttering our figures. Feeling thermometer data present additional challenges. Although respondents can respond with any number between 0 and 100, they tend to answer in multiples of 5 and 10. When you plot thermometer data, the observations may look like vertical or horizontal stripes on a scatterplot. In the next section, we'll discuss some techniques to effectively visualize large numbers of observations and thermometer data.

VISUALIZING REGRESSION RESULTS WITH WEIGHTED DATA

Weights don't change the observed values of dependent and independent variables, so the points on the scatterplot are in the same locations regardless of whether one analyzes weighted or unweighted data. However, you might want to visually represent the relative weight of observations by varying the size of scatterplot points. Moreover, the regression coefficients estimated from a weighted dataset will be different than those estimated from unweighted data. If you estimate a regression model with sampling weights and want to superimpose the regression line on a scatterplot, you want to use the slope and intercept values from the weighted regression results.

Figure 9.11 Visualizing Interactive Terms in Multiple Regression

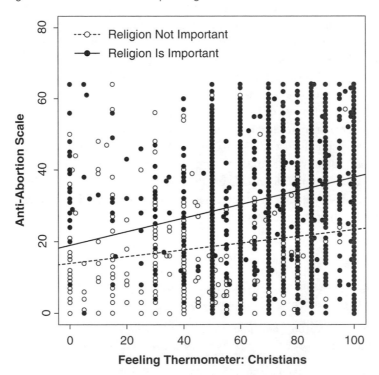

The simplest way to visually represent the relative weight of observations in a scatterplot is by setting the character expansion argument, cex, equal to sampling weight. To illustrate, let's look at a population-weighted scatterplot of the percentage of adults who smoke cigarettes and the cigarette taxes imposed in the 50 states. To weight these observations by population, we'll divide each state's population by the mean state population, so that a state with twice the population of an average state has double sampling weight (Figure 9.12).

Figure 9.12 Scatterplot of Regression with Weighted Data

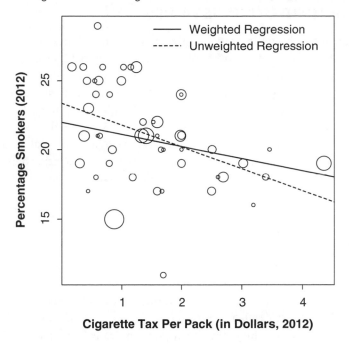

```
# visualizing regression analysis with weighted observations

# create population weight for each state
states$pop_weights = states$pop2010/mean(states$pop2010)

plot(x=states$cig_tax12, y=states$smokers12,
     xlab="Cigarette Tax Per Pack (In Dollars, 2012)",
     ylab="Percentage Smokers (2012)",
     cex=sqrt(states$pop_weights))

# regression lines superimposed
abline(a=21.9689,b=-0.8755, lty=1)     # from weighted analysis
abline(a=23.3889,b=-1.5909, lty=3)     # from unweighted analysis

# legend identifying lines and points
legend(x=2.75, y=max(states$smokers12), lty=c(1,3), cex=0.8, bty="n",
       legend=c('Weighted Regression', 'Unweighted Regression'))
```

A technical note is in order here. The cex argument's value is proportional to the radius of a scatterplot point, which means that doubling the cex value will quadruple the area of a point. Therefore, you should set the cex argument equal to the square root of the sampling weight as in the example.

One alternative to varying the expansion value of plotting characters is the svyplot function in the survey package. The svyplot function is readymade for weighted data and also has some nice options for representing large numbers of observations. In the next section, we'll use the svyplot function to illustrate some special approaches to visually representing a large number of observations and feeling thermometer data.[11]

---

[11] The svyplot function's bubble plots have the same effect as setting the cex of standard points equal to the square root of weights, but they don't allow the user to superimpose regression lines.

SPECIAL ISSUES WHEN PLOTTING OBSERVATIONS WITH LIMITED UNIQUE VALUES

We conclude this chapter with a discussion of issues that arise when we work with variables that have a limited number of unique values. We often work with interval-level variables that have relatively few unique values. For example, if you ask someone how many days a week he or she talks about politics, the person's answer will be an integer between 0 and 7. We also encounter this problem with feeling thermometer data. For example, when asked to rate their feelings about the middle class using any value between 0 and 100, over 80% of NES respondents picked one of five responses (50, 60, 70, 85, or 100 degrees). A standard scatterplot does not do justice to the relationship between variables that have a limited number of unique values; the standard plot may make a significant relationship appear nonexistent. When this happens, it's useful to represent the number of observations with the same values; the default plot may look too neat and obscure patterns in the data.

One solution to the problem of plotting observations with many tied values is "binning" observations together.[12] This method counts the number of observations in a defined space, such as a square area on a grid superimposed on a scatterplot, and visually represents that count rather than the actual observations directly. As an example of this method, consider the relationship between the fedspend_scale and ft_dem variables in the nes dataset. The variable fedspend_scale is a count of the number of federal programs respondents want increased and it ranges from 0 to 16. The ft_dem variable measures respondents' feelings about the Democratic Party on a scale from 0 to 100, but most respondents give values that end in 0 or 5. A "hexagonal scatterplot" produced using the svyplot function clearly communicates the direction and strength of the relationship. It also provides a good idea of the number and distribution of respondents at each value of the independent variable.

Figure 9.13 Hexagonal Scatterplot to Better Visualize Limited Unique Values

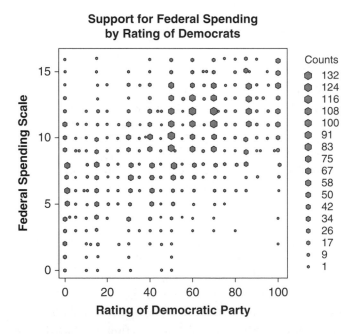

```
# hexagonal scatterplot helps display observations with tied values

svyplot(fedspend_scale ~ ft_dem, design=nesD, style="hex",
        xlab="Rating of Democratic Party", ylab="Federal Spending Scale",
        main="Support for Federal Spending\nby Rating of Democrats")
```

---

[12] For an alternative method of binning observations, see the hexbin function in the hexbin package.

As you can see in Figure 9.13, the smaller the hexagon, the fewer the cases, and the larger the hexagon, the more numerous the cases. We can now see than many respondents give the Democrats ratings that end in 0 or 5, but there is a strong positive correlation between Democrat thermometer scores and support for federal spending, a relationship that is not apparent in the standard scatterplot. The "hex" style is one of several styles available for plotting observations with the svyplot function and we encourage you to consult the function's help file and experiment with different methods.

Another approach to visually representing variables that have a limited number of unique values is to "jitter" the placement of actual observations in a standard scatterplot to show how many observations are actually in a particular area. When you jitter observations, you add some "noise" to randomly vary the x and y coordinates of the observations so they spread out slightly on the scatterplot rather than overlap in the same location. To illustrate, we'll plot the relationship between the fedspend_scale and ft_dem variables again, this time jittering the points to better represent the data.

```
# jittering points helps display observations with tied values

# create new variables with an amount of noise added
nes$ft_dem.j = jitter(nes$ft_dem, amount=2)
nes$ft_fedspend_scale.j = jitter(nes$fedspend_scale, amount=2)

plot(x=nes$ft_dem.j, y= nes$ft_fedspend_scale.j, cex=.25, pch=16,
    xlab="Rating of Democratic Party",
    ylab="Federal Spending Scale",
    main="Support for Federal Spending\nby Rating of Democrats")
```

Figure 9.14   Scatterplot with Jittered Observed Values

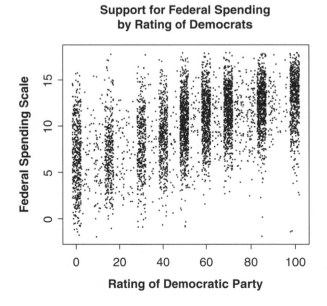

Like the hexagonal scatterplot, the jittered scatterplot in Figure 9.14 helps reveal the strong positive relationship between Democrat thermometer ratings and support for federal spending programs. There was no inherent reason we set the amount of jittering to 2 or the character expansion value to .25; we actually experimented with several different values of each before settling on these values. As we noted at the outset of this chapter, creating effective visualizations is often an iterative process. Think about the essential qualities you hope to convey, start with the basic plot, and refine your script until you are satisfied your plot communicates the essential qualities you hope to convey in an effective manner.

EXERCISES

1. (Dataset: states. Variables: hr_conserv11, conpct_m.) Two congressional scholars are discussing the extent to which members of the U.S. House of Representatives stay in touch with the voters in their states.

   Scholar 1: "When members of Congress vote on important public policies, they are closely attuned to the ideological makeups of their states. Members from states having lots of liberals will tend to cast votes in the liberal direction. Representatives from states with mostly conservative constituencies, by contrast, will take conservative positions on important policies."

   Scholar 2: "You certainly have a naïve view of congressional behavior. Once they get elected, members of Congress adopt a 'Washington, D.C., state of mind,' perhaps voting in the liberal direction on one policy and in the conservative direction on another. One thing is certain: The way members vote has little to do with the ideological composition of their states."

   Think about an independent variable that measures the percentage of self-described conservatives among the mass public in a state, with low values denoting low percentages of conservatives and high values denoting high percentages of conservatives. And consider a dependent variable that gauges the degree to which the state's House delegation votes in a conservative direction on public policies. Low scores on this dependent variable tell you that the delegation tends to vote in a liberal direction, and high scores say that the delegation votes in a conservative direction.

   A. Below is an empty graphic shell showing the relationship between the independent variable and the dependent variable. Draw a regression line inside the shell that depicts what the relationship should look like if Scholar 1 is correct.

   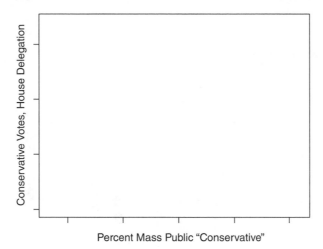

   B. Below is another graphic shell showing the relationship between the independent variable and the dependent variable. Draw a regression line inside the shell that depicts what the relationship should look like if Scholar 2 is correct.

   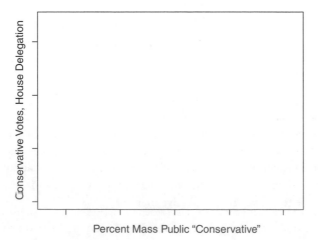

C. The states dataset contains the variable conpct_m, the percentage of the mass public calling themselves conservative. This is the independent variable. States also contains hr_conserv11, a measure of conservative votes by states' House members. Scores on this variable can range from 0 (low conservatism) to 100 (high conservatism). This is the dependent variable. Run Regression to analyze the relationship between cons.hr and conpct_m.

According to the regression equation, a 1-percentage-point increase in conservatives in the mass public is associated with (Check one.)

❑ about a 66-point decrease in House conservatism scores.

❑ about a 3-point increase in House conservatism scores.

❑ about a 6-point increase in House conservatism scores.

D. If you were to use this regression to estimate the mean House conservatism score for states having 30 percent conservatives, your estimate would be (Circle one.)

a score of about 30.　　　　a score of about 45.　　　　a score of about 95.

E. The adjusted R-square for this relationship is equal to (Fill in the blank.) _____. This tells you that about (Fill in the blank.) _____ percent of the variation in hr_conserv11 is explained by conpct_m. Follow the syntax rules described in this chapter. Provide axis labels, such as "Percent Mass Public Conservative" for the x-axis and "Conservative Votes, House Delegation" for the y-axis. Provide a main title. Print the scatterplot.

F. Create a scatterplot of the relationship between hr_conserv11 and conpct_m. Follow the syntax rules described in this chapter. Provide axis labels, such as "Percent Mass Public Conservative" for the x-axis and "Conservative Votes, House Delegation" for the y-axis. Provide a main title. Print the scatterplot.

G. Based on your inspection of the graph, the regression line, and the adjusted R-square, which congressional scholar is more correct? (Fill in the appropriate blank.)

Scholar 1 is more correct because　_____

_____

Scholar 2 is more correct because　_____

_____

2. (Dataset: states. Variables: blkleg, blkpct10, south.) In this question, we'll examine the demographics of state legislatures and the citizens they serve. In particular, we'll use multiple regression analysis to examine the determinants of African American representation in state legislatures. In the states dataset, you'll find a variable called blkleg, which records the percentage of black state legislators in the 50 U.S. states.

A. We will estimate a multiple regression model, but let's start with a simple bivariate regression model before adding an additional explanatory variable. Estimate a bivariate regression model that explains variation in the percentage of African American state legislators in the 50 U.S. states as a function of the African American percentage of each state's population (blkpct10 in the states dataset). Include a summary of your results in your answer.

B. Now let's consider regional differences in African American representation in state legislatures by incorporating a variable identifying Southern states into our analysis. You can use the south variable in the states dataset. Estimate a multiple regression model that explains variation in the percentage of African American state legislators as a function of states' African American populations and whether the state is in the South. Include a summary of these results in your answer.

C. Compare the multiple regression results you obtained in part B with the bivariate regression results you obtained in part A. Based on your analysis, how does incorporating a variable identifying Southern states affect the expected impact of the African American population in a state on African American representation in state legislatures? Does the partial regression coefficient for the blkpct10 variable increase or decrease?

_____

_____

D. Create a graphic that visually represents your multiple regression results. The y-axis should correspond to states$blkleg and the x-axis should correspond to states$blkpct10. Plot the observed values of these variables in the states dataset as points on the plot. Add two distinct lines to your plot: one line that represents the relationship between the x- and y-axis variables in the South and another line that represents the relationship in non-Southern states. For clarity, add a legend to your plot that identifies each line.

3. (Dataset: world. Variables: free_labor, regionun.) Workers of the world, unite! Let's examine labor freedom around the world. In the world dataset, you'll find an index of labor freedom (free_labor), originally published by the Heritage Foundation, that rates the degree to which employees and employers are free from undue government interference. For this question, we will use regression analysis to compare the labor policies of governments around the world and produce a visualization of the results.

A. Estimate a linear regression model that explains variation in labor freedom (world$free_labor) as a function of region of the world (world$regionun). When you estimate this model, you'll notice that R automatically creates five dummy variables to allow you to compare labor freedom in six different regions (the sixth region is the omitted, or reference, category). Include a summary of these results in your answer.

B. According to your results, which region of the world enjoys the greatest labor freedom? Which region of the world has the least labor freedom?

greatest freedom _____

least freedom _____

C. Create a graphic that visually represents your regression results. The y-axis should correspond to the expected value of the labor freedom index and the x-axis should have six tick marks, one for each region of the world. Plot the expected value of labor freedom corresponding to each region and use vertical line segments to display the 95% confidence interval for each expected value.

4. (Dataset: nes. Variables: ftgr_unions, incgroup_prepost, dem_unionhh.) In this problem, we'll take a closer look at public sentiment about labor unions in the United States. Labor politics is a complex subject, but many view unions as an important vehicle for protecting the interests of working-class people from rich and powerful employers. Union membership in the United States peaked in the 1950s and has been steadily declining since that time. Yet many workers are union members or have at least one family member who belongs to a union. How are attitudes about unions shaped by income and personal experience with unions? Let's use multiple regression analysis with an interaction term to answer this question.

A. To begin, estimate a multiple regression model that explains variation in individuals' feelings about unions (use the ftgr_unions variable in the nes dataset) as a function of their income and whether anyone in their household belongs to a union (dem_unionhh). Individual income is included in the nes dataset as the incgroup_prepost variable but it's in the form of an ordered factor, so it becomes unwieldy when incorporated in a multiple regression model. Therefore, transform the incgroup_prepost variable into a numeric class variable by using the as.numeric function. You can simply enter as.numeric(incgroup_prepost) directly into your lm function call. Include a summary of these results in your answer.

B. Based on the results of your analysis in part A, what is the expected effect of increasing income on someone's sentiment toward unions? How does having a member of one's household in a union affect one's sentiment toward unions?

_____

_____

C. Now let's consider how one's personal experience with unions interacts with personal income in shaping sentiment toward unions. To analyze the interaction between personal experience and income, add an interaction term to the multiple regression model you estimated in part A. Be sure to keep both base terms, dem_unionhh and as.numeric(incgroup_prepost), in your multiple regression model. Include a summary of these results in your answer.

D. Based on the results of your analysis in part C, does the expected effect of increasing income on someone's sentiment toward unions depend on whether there's a union member in one's household? In answering this question, indicate whether income has a greater effect on someone without a household connection to a union or someone with a household connection to a union.

_____

_____

E. Create a graphic that visually represents the results of the multiple regression model of union sentiment with an interaction term that you estimated to answer part D. The y-axis should correspond to the union feeling thermometer scores and the x-axis should demarcate the income groups represented in the nes dataset. Plot the actual observations as points on the plot. Add two distinct lines to the plot: One line should represent the expected effect of income on union sentiment for those in households with union members, and the other line should represent the expected effect of income on union sentiment for those in households without union members. If, in answering part D, you found that personal experience interacts with income, these two lines should have different slopes.

F. The visualization you created for part E may not illuminate the relationships in these data because the observations are numerous and people often give a limited number of unique responses when asked to rate something on a feeling thermometer. Enhance your visualization of the relationship between personal experiences with unions, income, and sentiment about unions using one or more of the following techniques described in this chapter: reducing the character expansion values of the points in the plot, plotting points with semi-transparent colors, binning observations, or jittering points to avoid overlaps. As a final touch, add a legend to your plot that distinguishes the two lines you created to answer E.

10

Logistic Regression

Objective	Functions Introduced	Author or Source
Introducing odds, logged odds, probabilities	log {base} exp {base}	R Development Core Team[1] R Development Core Team
Estimating logistic regression models	glm {stats} svyglm(family=quasibinomial) {survey}	R Development Core Team Thomas Lumley[2]
Interpreting logistic regression results	orci {companion}	Philip Pollock and Barry Edwards
Evaluating model fit	logregR2 {companion} pchisqC {companion}	Philip Pollock and Barry Edwards Philip Pollock and Barry Edwards
Visualizing predicted probabilities	inverse.logit {companion} lineType {companion} persp {graphics}	Philip Pollock and Barry Edwards Philip Pollock and Barry Edwards R Development Core Team

As you've learned in the preceding two chapters, bivariate and multiple regression analysis are powerful techniques for studying an interval-level dependent variable. What about dependent variables measured at the nominal or ordinal level? In its most specialized application, logistic regression is designed to analyze the effect of independent variables on a dependent variable measured at the nominal or ordinal level. In this chapter, we'll focus on how you can use R to estimate logistic regression models with binary dependent variables.

A binary variable, as its name suggests, can assume only two values. Binary variables are just like the dummy variables and indicator variables you created and analyzed earlier in this book. Either a case has the attribute or behavior being measured or it does not. Voted/did not vote, married/not married, favor/oppose same-sex marriage, and South/non-South are examples of binary variables.

In this chapter, you will use svyglm (from the survey package) to learn the basics of logistic regression in R. A local function, orci, re-expresses the coefficients as odds ratios, which facilitate interpretation.

[1] R Development Core Team. (2011). *R: A language and environment for statistical computing.* Vienna, Austria: Author. Available at http://www.R-project.org/

[2] Lumley, T. (2012). *survey: Analysis of complex survey samples* (R package version 3.28-2). Available at http://cran.r-project .org/web/packages/survey/index.html. See also: Lumley, T. (2004). Analysis of complex survey samples. *Journal of Statistical Software*, 9(1), 1–19; Lumley, T. (2010). *Complex surveys: A guide to analysis using R.* Hoboken, NJ: John Wiley & Sons.

The function, logregR2 (based on the descr package's LogRegR2 function), returns a host of model summary statistics, including several "pseudo R-square" measures that help gauge the strength of the relationships. You will learn to estimate predicted probabilities, which can be visualized using predicted probability curves. You will then exercise and extend these skills, enlisting the classic glm function (from the stats package) to analyze one of the unweighted datasets.

THINKING ABOUT ODDS, LOGGED ODDS, AND PROBABILITIES

Consider a binary dependent variable of keen interest in American politics: whether someone votes to re-elect the president. When the value of this variable is recorded in a survey of individuals, there are only two possible values: Either the survey respondents voted for the president (coded 1 on the binary variable) or they did not vote for the president (coded 0). We see this in the NES data when respondents (who voted) were asked whether they voted to re-elect President Obama (nes$obama_vote).

We know whether the NES respondents voted for President Obama in 2012, but we don't know for certain who else did. Given some personal details, we might be willing to guess whether someone supported Obama's re-election. Most of us think in terms of the probability of some event occurring, like the probability that a given person will vote for the Democratic candidate in an election. No doubt, you've heard the term "odds" before, probably in the context of betting. Probabilities and odds are related concepts, but they are not the same thing. Understanding odds is essential to logistic regression, so let's define exactly what we mean by odds:

$$\text{Odds ratio} = \frac{\text{Number of times event expected}}{\text{Number of times event not expected}}$$

So the odds for a given event occurring, like someone voting to re-elect Obama, can be expressed as a ratio of the number of times the event is expected to happen compared to the number of times the event is not excepted to happen. So odds of 3:1 suggest that the event will occur three times for every one time it doesn't occur. Odds of 1:3 mean the event will occur one time for every three times it doesn't occur. Odds of 1:1 suggest that the event of interest is equally likely to occur and not occur, like the probability of observing a heads when you flip a coin.

Figure 10.1   Relationship between Probabilities and Odds

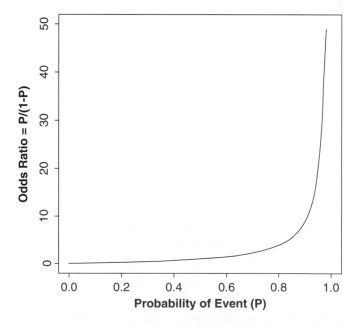

We can also define an odds ratio in terms of probability of an event occurring. If P is equal to the probability of an event occurring, its inverse, $1 - P$, equals the probability of the event not occurring. The odds ratio is equal to $P/(1 - P)$.

The odds ratio of low probability events approaches 0; the odds ratio of very high probability events approaches infinity. What about the middle ground of events just as likely to occur as not occur? The midpoint odds ratio is 1. Because odds ratios have this unbalanced property, we transform odds ratios into logged odds. Logged odds is the natural logarithm of the odds ratio: the power to which you would raise base *e* to obtain the odds ratio. The relationship between logged odds and the probability of the event occurring has a nice, symmetrical pattern, as you can see in Figure 10.1.

Logged odds are a mathematical transformation of odds ratios. We can define logged odds as log(odds ratio) or log(P/(1 – P)). The R function log computes the logarithm of any number greater than 0. The log of a 1:1 odds ratio is 0, which corresponds to a .5 probability of the event occurring. Although the relationship between probabilities and odds ratios is asymmetrical, the relationship between probabilities and logged odds has a nice symmetry, as seen in Figure 10.2.

Figure 10.2 Relationship between Probabilities and Logged Odds

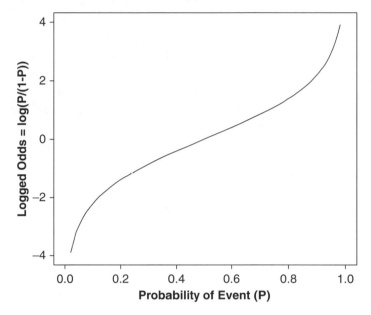

For statistical and substantive reasons, we cannot assume that the relationship between education and voting is linear. Garden-variety regression, often called ordinary least squares or OLS regression, assumes a linear relationship between the independent and dependent variables.[3] Thus, we cannot use lm or svyglm (with its defaults setting) to analyze binary dependent variables.

So if we're interested in analyzing whether someone is likely to vote to re-elect the president, it turns out that the statistical approach we take is based on the *logged odds* of someone voting to re-elect the president. Rather than directly estimate either the odds ratio or the probability of an event occurring with regression analysis, we use logistic regression analysis to estimate how independent variables affect the logged odds of the event, or log(P/(1 – P)). After we estimate the coefficients of a logistic regression model, we can use the mathematical relationship between logged odds, odds ratios, and probabilities to say how a change in an independent variable affects the probability of an event occurring.

ESTIMATING LOGISTIC REGRESSION MODELS

The logistic regression model is quite OLS-like in appearance. Just as in OLS regression, the constant or intercept, "a", estimates the dependent variable (the logged odds of an event occurring) when the independent

---

[3] In arriving at the estimated effect of the independent variable on the dependent variable, linear regression finds the line that minimizes the square of the distance between the observed values of the dependent variable and the predicted values of the dependent variable—predicted, that is, on the basis of the independent variable. The regression line is often referred to as the "least squares" line or "ordinary least squares" line.

variable is equal to 0. And the logistic regression coefficient, "b", will estimate the change in the logged odds of voting for each one-unit increase in the independent variable. Let's put the relationship into logistic regression form:

$$\text{Logged odds(Outcome)} = a + b*(\text{Independent Variable})$$

What's more, the analysis will produce a standard error for b, permitting us to test the null hypothesis that the independent variable has no effect on the outcome of interest. Finally, we can obtain R-square-type measures, giving us an idea of the strength of the relationship between the independent variable and the outcome. In all of these ways, logistic regression is comfortably akin to linear regression.

Let's apply this general discussion of logistic regression with one independent variable to whether people voted to re-elect President Obama. The nes dataset contains the variable obama_vote, coded 1 if the respondent voted to re-elect the president and 0 if he or she voted against Obama. This is the dependent variable. Whether people supported Obama in the 2012 election was probably influenced by their sentiment about the Democratic Party. Respondents' sentiment toward the Democratic Party was measured using a feeling thermometer, ft_dem, an interval-level variable that ranges from 0 (extremely negative) to 100 (extremely positive). We would expect a positive relationship between the independent and dependent variables. As sentiment toward Democrats improves, the probability of voting to re-elect Obama increases as well.

In using svyglm to run logistic regression, type the binary dependent variable on the left-hand side of the tilde and add the argument, "family=quasibinomial". Later, we'll estimate a logistic regression model using the glm function, but for this analysis, we want to use the svyglm function and the weighted design dataset nesD.

$$\text{svyglm}(depvar \sim indepvar, \text{design}=design.dataset, \text{family=quasibinomial})$$

The element, *depvar*, can be a numeric indicator variable (coded 0 or 1) or a two-level factor. The following R code estimates a logistic regression model and saves the results in an object named "obama.logit" and then displays a summary of this object as follows[4]:

```
# logistic regression model with one independent variable
obama.logit = svyglm(obama_vote ~ ft_dem, design=nesD,
                     family="quasibinomial")
summary(obama.logit)
```

```
Coefficients:
              Estimate  Std. Error   t value   Pr(>|t|)
(Intercept)  -4.665066   0.290913    -16.04    <2e-16    ***
ft_dem        0.093648   0.005256     17.82    <2e-16    ***
---
Signif. codes:  0 '***' 0.001 '**' 0.01 '*' 0.05 '.' 0.1 ' ' 1

(Dispersion parameter for quasibinomial family taken to be 1.553351)

Number of Fisher Scoring iterations: 6
```

Write out the model and consider the coefficients:

$$\text{Logged odds(Obama Vote)} = -4.67 + 0.09*(\text{Democratic Therm.})$$

What do these coefficients tell us? The constant indicates that the expected logged odds of someone who gives Democrats a 0 on a feeling thermometer voting to re-elect President Obama is equal to –4.67. And the logistic regression coefficient on ft_dem indicates that the logged odds of voting for Obama increase by 0.09 for each one-unit increase in sentiment toward the Democrats. So, as expected, as the independent variable increases, the likelihood of voting for Obama increases, too.

---

[4] When R sees a two-level factor, it will automatically set the first-named level to 0 and the second-named level to 1.

Does sentiment toward Democrats have a statistically significant effect on the likelihood of voting for Obama? Just as in OLS regression, we would answer this question by consulting the t-statistic ("t value") and the accompanying P-value. Interpretation of this P-value is directly analogous to ordinary regression. If the P-value is greater than .05, do not reject the null hypothesis and conclude that the independent variable does not have a significant effect on the dependent variable. If, instead, the P-value is less than or equal to .05, reject the null hypothesis and infer that the independent variable has a significant relationship with the dependent variable. In our output, the P-value for ft_dem is effectively equal to zero ("<2e-16"), so we can conclude that, yes, sentiment toward Democrats has a significant effect on the probability of voting to re-elect President Obama.

The act of voting might seem simple, but we know that it isn't. Certainly, sentiment toward the president's party is not the only factor that shapes the individual's decision whether to support the president's re-election. Variables such as race and gender may influence who a voter supports in a presidential election. What's more, sentiment toward the president's party might itself be related to gender and race. Thus, you might reasonably want to know the partial effect of Democratic sentiment on the probability of voting for Obama, controlling for the effects of these other independent variables. Logistic regression, like OLS regression, can accommodate multiple predictors of a binary dependent variable. Consider this logistic regression model:

$$\text{Logged odds(Obama Vote)} = a + b_1*(\text{Dem. Therm.}) + b_2*(\text{White}) + b_3*(\text{Gun Owner})$$

Again we are in an OLS-like environment. As before, sentiment toward the Democratic Party is measured on a feeling thermometer that ranges from 0 to 100. From a substantive standpoint, we would again expect b_1, the coefficient on the Democratic thermometer, to be positive: As this value increases, so too should the logged odds of voting for Obama. We might also expect non-whites to offer more support for Obama than whites. Thus, we should find a negative sign on b_2, a variable identifying whether the survey respondent was white. Perhaps it is also the case that gun owners were less likely to support Obama's re-election than non–gun owners were. Just as in OLS, b_1 will estimate the partial effect of Democratic sentiment on voting for Obama, controlling for race and gun ownership; b_2 will estimate the partial effect of race on the dependent variable, controlling for Democratic sentiment and gun ownership; and b_3 will estimate the partial effect of gun ownership, controlling for Democratic sentiment and race.

Let's specify a multi-variate model, named "obama.logit2", that includes multiple predictors on the right-hand side. Notice that we're incorporating the logical statement (owngun_owngun=="1. Yes") into the svyglm function call. After estimating this model, we'll summarize it.

```
# logistic regression model with multiple independent variables
obama.logit2 = svyglm(obama_vote ~ ft_dem + white
                      + (owngun_owngun=="1. Yes"), design=nesD,
                  family="quasibinomial")
summary(obama.logit2)
```

```
Coefficients:
                             Estimate  Std. Error  t value  Pr(>|t|)
(Intercept)                  -3.226702   0.362200   -8.909   < 2e-16  ***
ft_dem                        0.089366   0.005289   16.896   < 2e-16  ***
whiteYes                     -1.229075   0.194125   -6.331   2.69e-10 ***
owngun_owngun == "1. Yes"TRUE -0.569815  0.130670   -4.361   1.33e-05 ***
---
Signif. codes:  0 '***' 0.001 '**' 0.01 '*' 0.05 '.' 0.1 ' ' 1

(Dispersion parameter for quasibinomial family taken to be 1.334891)

Number of Fisher Scoring iterations: 6
```

Let's plug these partial logistic regression coefficients into our model:

$$\text{Logged odds(Obama Vote)} = a + 0.09*(\text{Dem. Therm.}) - 1.23*(\text{White}) - 0.57*(\text{Gun Owner})$$

Interpretation of these coefficients follows a straightforward multiple regression protocol. The coefficient on ft_dem, 0.09, tells us that, controlling for race and gun ownership, each additional degree on the Democratic thermometer increased the logged odds of voting for Obama by 0.09. The logged odds of a white respondent voting for Obama's re-election, controlling for Democratic sentiment and gun ownership, were 1.23 lower than that of a non-white respondent. Gun owners were also less likely to vote for Obama, controlling for other factors; their logged odds of an Obama voter were 0.57 lower than non–gun owners. According to the t-statistics and accompanying P-values, each independent variable is significantly related to the dependent variable.

Logistic regression output is more difficult to interpret than are OLS results. In ordinary regression, the coefficients of interest, the constant (a) and the slope (b), are expressed in actual units of the dependent variable. If we were to use OLS to investigate the relationship between years of education (x) and income in dollars (y), the regression coefficient on education would communicate the dollar-change in income for each 1-year increase in education. With OLS, what you see is what you get. With logistic regression, by contrast, the coefficients of interest are expressed in terms of the logged odds of the dependent variable. The constant (a) will tell us the logged odds of voting when education is 0, and the regression coefficient (b) will estimate the change in the logged odds for each unit change in education. Logged odds, truth be told, have limited intuitive appeal. Thus, we almost always translate logistic regression results into two forms that make better intuitive sense: odds ratios and predicted probabilities.

INTERPRETING LOGISTIC REGRESSION RESULTS WITH ODDS RATIOS

An odds ratio tells us by how much the odds of the outcome of interest occurring change for each unit change in the independent variable. An odds ratio of less than 1 says that the odds decrease as the independent variable increases (a negative relationship). An odds ratio equal to 1 says that the odds do not change as the independent variable increases (no relationship). And an odds ratio of greater than 1 says that the odds of the dependent variable increase as the independent variable increases (a positive relationship).

The workspace function, orci, will convert the model's coefficients to odds ratios. The orci function operates on the result of our svyglm(family=quasibinominal) call. Let's look at the odds ratios for our logistic regression model with one independent variable, obama.logit.

```
# odds ratio for logistic regression with one independent variable
obama.logit = svyglm(obama_vote ~ ft_dem, design=nesD,
                     family="quasibinomial")
orci(obama.logit)
```

```
            OddsRatio 2.5 % 97.5 %
(Intercept) 0.009     0.005 0.017
ft_dem      1.098     1.087 1.110
```

For each parameter, orci gives us the odds ratio ("OddsRatio") and its 95 percent confidence interval. Focus on the odds ratio for the independent variable, 1.098. Where did this number originate? The orci function obtained this number by raising the natural log base e (approximately equal to 2.72) to the power of the logistic regression coefficient, 0.089. This procedure translates the logged odds regression coefficient into an *odds ratio*. An odds ratio of 1.098 means that a one-unit increase in the Democratic thermometer increases the *odds* of a respondent voting to re-elect Obama by 1.098. So a 10-point increase in the sentiment toward Democrats increases the odds of someone voting for Obama by 10.98.

The odds ratio can be used to obtain an even more understandable estimate, the *percentage change in the odds* for each unit change in the independent variable. Mercifully, simple arithmetic accomplishes this task. Subtract 1 from the odds ratio and multiply by 100. In our current example: (1.098 – 1) * 100 = 9.8. We can now say that each one-degree increment in the Democratic thermometer increases the odds of voting for Obama by 9.8 percent. As you can see, when the relationship is positive (that is, when the logistic regression coefficient is greater than 0 and the odds ratio is greater than 1), figuring out the percentage change in the odds requires almost no thought. Just subtract 1 from the odds ratio and move the decimal point two places to the right. But be alert for negative relationships, when the odds ratio is less than 1. Suppose, for example, that the odds ratio was equal to .28, communicating a negative relationship between the independent variable and the probability of the dependent variable. The percentage change in the odds would be equal to (.28 − 1) * 100 = −72.0, indicating that a one-unit change in the independent variable decreases the odds of the dependent variable by 72 percent.[5]

Now let's take a look at the odds ratios for our logistic regression model with multiple independent variables.

```
# odds ratio for logistic regression with multiple independent variables
obama.logit2 = svyglm(obama_vote ~ ft_dem + white
                      + (owngun_owngun=="1. Yes"), design=nesD,
                      family="quasibinomial")
orci(obama.logit2)
```

	OddsRatio	2.5 %	97.5 %
(Intercept)	0.040	0.020	0.081
ft_dem	1.093	1.082	1.105
whiteYes	0.293	0.200	0.428
owngun_owngun == "1. Yes"TRUE	0.566	0.438	0.731

The odds ratio for the Democratic thermometer score is similar to what we saw in the logistic regression with one variable, but we have two additional independent variables to consider: race and gun ownership. Recall that odds ratios less than 1 mean that an independent variable is negatively correlated to the outcome of interest. So a respondent's being white or a gun owner reduced the probability that he or she voted to re-elect President Obama in 2012. By how much? To assess the difference in odds of an Obama vote between white and non-white respondents, we take 0.29, subtract 1, and multiple by 100, which yields −71. The *odds* of a white respondent voting for Obama were 71% lower than that of a non-white respondent, controlling for Democratic sentiment and gun ownership. The same calculation yields the conclusion that the odds of a gun owner voting for Obama were 43% lower than those of a non–gun owner.

VISUALIZING RESULTS WITH PREDICTED PROBABILITIES CURVES

You now know how to perform basic logistic regression analysis, and you know how to interpret the logistic regression coefficient in terms of an odds ratio and in terms of a percentage change in the odds. No doubt, odds ratios are easier to comprehend than are logged odds. And percentage change in the odds seems more understandable still. Not surprisingly, most researchers prefer to think in terms of probabilities. One might reasonably ask, "What is the effect of a one-unit change in an independent variable on the probability of voting for Obama?" Inconveniently, with logistic regression the answer is always, "It depends."

In the first analysis we ran, which examined the relationship between Democratic sentiment and voting for President Obama's re-election, logistic regression assumed that a linear relationship exists between Democratic sentiment and the *logged odds* of voting. This linearity assumption permitted us to arrive at an estimated effect that best fits the data. However, the technique also assumed a *non-linear* relationship between Democratic sentiment and the probability of voting for Obama. That is, it assumed that for people who lie near the extremes of the independent variable—respondents with either extreme disdain or fondness for the Democrats—a one-unit increase in their feeling thermometer scores will have a weaker effect on the probability of voting for Obama than will a one-unit increase for respondents in the middle range of the independent variable. In the middle range of the independent variable, sentiment toward Democrats should have its greatest marginal impact, pushing individuals on the fence between liking and disliking Democrats to one side or the other in a presidential election. So the effect of a one-unit change in the independent variable on the probability of voting for Obama is not linear; rather, the effect depends on where respondents "are" on the thermometer.

---

[5] When using interval-level independent variables with many values, you will often obtain logistic regression coefficients and odds ratios that appear to be quite close to null hypothesis territory (coefficients close to 0 and odds ratios close to 1) but that nonetheless trump the null hypothesis. Remember that logistic regression, like OLS, estimates the marginal effect of a one-unit increment on the logged odds of the dependent variable.

How can we summarize these interaction effects? In dealing with logistic regression models, many researchers use the *predicted probability curves* for presenting and interpreting probabilities. This approach permits the researcher to show how variation in an interval-level independent variable affects the probability of observing the outcome of interest. Multiple predicted probability curves can be added to a single plot to show differences among groups.

Let's generate predicted probabilities, beginning with the simple model that used respondents' Democratic thermometer scores alone to predict voting for Obama. Using our logistic regression results, we can calculate the predicted probability of voting for Obama at each increment of the Democratic thermometer. How does this work? Recall the logistic regression equation estimated in obama.logit:

$$\text{Logged odds(Obama Vote)} = -4.67 + 0.093*(\text{Democratic Therm.})$$

We can use this logistic regression model to obtain an estimated logged odds of voting for Obama for each increment of the Democratic thermometer. The expression above looks like a classic line equation. You can think of the right-hand side of the above equation above as the "linear predictor" of the logistic regression model. But the twist is, instead of plotting logged odds on the y-axis, we want to plot the probability of the outcome of interest, in this case, voting to re-elect President Obama, corresponding to our expected logged odds.

Fortunately, we can follow a mathematic equation to convert a logged odds value into a predicted probability. Recall that the odds of an event occurring are equal to $P/(1 - P)$, where P is the probability of the event. Thus, logged odds equal $\log(P/(1 - P))$. With a little algebraic manipulation, we can use the following formula to convert logged odds (equal to the linear predictor) into a predicted probability:

$$\text{Probability} = \exp(\text{logged odds}) / (1 + \exp(\text{logged odds}))$$

According to this formula, we retrieve the probability of voting by first raising the natural log base *e* to the power of the logged odds of voting. We then divide this number by the quantity one plus *e* raised to the power of the logged odds of voting.

We'll use a function called inverse.logit to calculate predicted probabilities, but let's work through a quick example to clarify the concept. Consider respondents who rate Democrats a neutral 50 on a feeling thermometer. Using the logistic regression equation obtained in obama.logit, we find the logged odds of voting for this group to be $-4.67 + 0.093*50 = -4.67 + 4.65 = -.02$. What is the *predicted probability* of voting for Obama for people who give the Democrats a 50 on the feeling thermometer? It would be $\exp(-.02)/(1 + \exp(-.02)) = 0.980/1.980 = 0.495$. These respondents' votes were really a coin flip.

Now, let's get R to do (most of) the work for us. We want to estimate the probability that someone voted for Obama for each increment of the Democratic feeling thermometer, so we'll generate a sequence of numbers from 0 to 100 by 1. This is the range of independent variable values for which we want to predict probabilities. Next, we'll use the intercept and regression coefficient from our logistic model to calculate the logged odds over the range of possible independent variable values and convert logged odds into predicted probabilities using the inverse logit function. Finally, we'll create predicted probability plot to visualize our logistic regression analysis.

```
# predicted probabilities for Obama vote model
obama.logit = svyglm(obama_vote ~ ft_dem, design=nesD,
                  family="quasibinomial")
# intercept: -4.66507      ft_dem coefficient: 0.09365

ft_dem.values = seq(0,100,by=1)
predicted.logged.odds = -4.66507 + 0.09365*ft_dem.values
predicted.probabilities = inverse.logit(predicted.logged.odds)

# basic predicted probability plot
plot(x="", y="", xlim=range(ft_dem.values), ylim=c(0,1),
    xlab="Feeling Thermometer: Democrats",
    ylab="Probability pf Voting for Obama")
lines(x=ft_dem.values, y=predicted.probabilities)
```

What happens to the predicted probability of voting for Obama as sentiments toward Democrats get warmer? The probability of voting for Obama increases, but notice that the increase is not linear (Figure 10.3). The lower range of the independent variable, say from 0 to 20, has a relatively modest effect of the probability of voting for Obama. The same can be said of the upper range of the independent variable: There's not much difference between 80 and 100 degrees in terms of the voting to re-elect President Obama. However, in the middle range of possible thermometer values, from roughly 30 to 70, variation in respondents' sentiment toward the Democratic Party has a large effect on the probability of voting for Obama and the graphic curve shows its steepest slope within this range.

Figure 10.3 Predicted Probabilities Curve with an Interval-Level Independent Variable

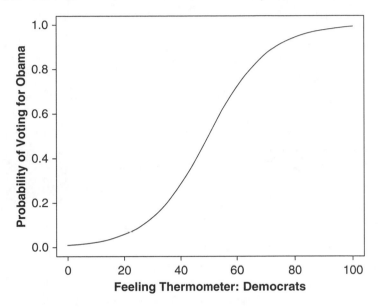

In logistic regression models having more than one independent variable, such as our model of voting to re-elect Obama that considers sentiment toward Democrats, race, and gun ownership, working with predicted probabilities is a bit more challenging, but a basic understanding of odds, logged odds, and probabilities will serve you well. Recall that when we estimated this logistic regression model with multiple independent variables, we obtained the following equation for the expected logged odds of an Obama vote:

Logged odds(Obama Vote) = a + 0.09*(Dem. Therm.) – 1.23*(White) – 0.57*(Gun Owner)

This equation assumes that the independent variables have additive effects on the *logged odds* of the dependent variable. Thus, for any combination of values of the independent variables, we arrive at an estimated value of the logged odds of the dependent variable by adding up the partial effects the predictor variables. However, as we've seen, the effect of a unit change in an independent variable on the *probability* of the outcome of interest is not linear. So the effect of each independent variable on the probability of the dependent variable will depend on the values of the other predictors in the model. Thus, the effect of, say, Democratic Party sentiment on the probability of voting for Obama will be different for whites than non-whites, and different for gun owners compared to non–gun owners.

We can also use predicted probabilities to visually compare the effects of one independent variable at two (or more) values of another independent variable. Such comparisons can provide a clearer picture of the interaction relationships between the independent variables and the probability of the dependent variable.

To illustrate, we'll incorporate race and gun ownership into our analysis of the relationship between Democratic Party support and the probability someone voted to re-elect President Obama. Based on our logistic regression model, we can identify four subpopulations: white gun owners, white non–gun owners, non-white gun owners, and non-white non–gun owners. According to our model, the effect of Democratic sentiment on the logged odds of an Obama vote are the same for each group, but the logged odds for white and gun owners are lower. To show these differences on a predicted probabilities plot, we'll calculate the logged odds of an Obama vote for each group across the range of possible Democratic thermometer values and then plot the corresponding probabilities. For compactness, in the sample code below, we're computing probabilities from logged odds when we call the lines function to plot predicted probability lines for each of the four cases. Adding a legend to this kind of plot is essential (Figure 10.4).[6]

```
# predicted probabilities for Obama votes, multiple indep. variables
obama.logit2 = svyglm(obama_vote ~ ft_dem + white
                      + (owngun_owngun=="1. Yes"), design=nesD,
                      family="quasibinomial")
# intercept: -3.22670      ft_dem coefficient: 0.08937
# white coef: -1.22907     gun owner coef: -0.56981


ft_dem.values = seq(0,100,by=1)

# case one: white gun owners
log.odds.white.gunown = -3.22670 + 0.08937*ft_dem.values -1.22907 -0.56981
# case two: white non-gun owners
log.odds.white.nongun = -3.22670 + 0.08937*ft_dem.values -1.22907
# case three: non-white gun owners
log.odds.nonwhite.gunown = -3.22670 + 0.08937*ft_dem.values        -0.56981
# case four: non-white non-gun owners
log.odds.nonwhite.nongun = -3.22670 + 0.08937*ft_dem.values

# basic predicted probability plot
plot(x="", y="", xlim=range(ft_dem.values), ylim=c(0,1),
     xlab="Feeling Thermometer: Democrats",
     ylab="Probability pf Voting for Obama")
lines(x=ft_dem.values, y=inverse.logit(log.odds.white.gunown), lty=1)
lines(x=ft_dem.values, y=inverse.logit(log.odds.white.nongun), lty=2)
lines(x=ft_dem.values, y=inverse.logit(log.odds.nonwhite.gunown), lty=3)
lines(x=ft_dem.values, y=inverse.logit(log.odds.nonwhite.nongun), lty=4)

legend("topleft", lty=c(1,2,3,4), bty="n", cex=.8,
       legend=c("White Gun Owners","White Non-Gun Owners",
       "Non-White Gun Owners","white Non-Gun Owners"))
```

PROBABILITY PROFILES FOR DISCRETE CASES

It isn't always possible to use predicted probability curves to visualize logistic regression results because you may not have an independent variable measured at the interval level to define the x-axis, or you may wish to focus on the effects of nominal- or ordinal-level independent variables only.

The sample averages method is a convenient way of summarizing the effect of an independent variable on the probability of a dependent variable. In the sample averages approach, the analyst examines the effect of each independent variable while holding the other independent variables constant at their sample means. This is particularly useful when your logistic regression includes an interval-level variable that's merely intended to control for rival explanations. In this way, we can get an idea of the effect of select variables in otherwise average cases.

To illustrate this method, we'll stick with our example of the likelihood of voting to re-elect President Obama, focusing on the effect of the nominal independent variables, race and gun ownership, for individuals with average sentiment toward the Democratic Party. For each subpopulation of interest, white gun owners, white non–gun owners, non-white gun owners, and non-white non–gun owners, let's estimate the probability of voting to re-elect Obama and show the standard error of each prediction. Our approach is similar to the method we demonstrated in Chapter 9 for visualizing the results of a multiple regression with only nominal or

---

[6] We're setting to the lty argument of the lines function to draw different line types. To see the different line types available in R, run the command lineType().

Figure 10.4 Predicted Probabilities Curve with Nominal- and Interval-Level Independent Variables

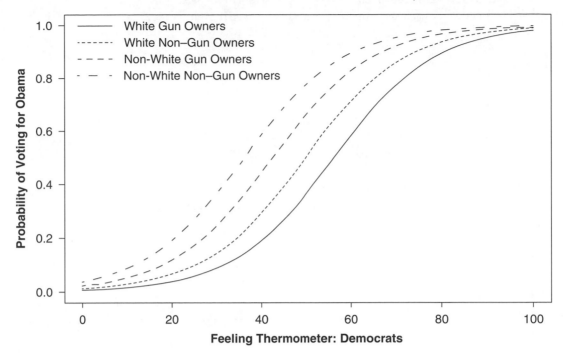

ordinal independent variables. We'll define a prediction frame that enumerates the different cases, use our logistic regression model results to generate predicted probabilities for each case, and then plot these predictions. For demonstration purposes, we're going to generate and examine our prediction frame first.

```
# probability profiles for discrete cases
obama.logit2 = svyglm(obama_vote ~ ft_dem + white
                  + (owngun_owngun=="1. Yes"), design=nesD,
                  family="quasibinomial")


ft_dem.mean = wtd.mean(nes$ft_dem, nes$wt)


# create, then display prediction frame
prediction.frame = expand.grid(ft_dem=ft_dem.mean,
                        white=levels(nes$white),
                        owngun_owngun=levels(nes$owngun_owngun))
prediction.frame       # view object for demo purposes
```

```
> prediction.frame

    ft_dem  white  owngun_owngun
1  51.69163    No        1. Yes
2  51.69163   Yes        1. Yes
3  51.69163    No        2. No
4  51.69163   Yes        2. No
```

A nice feature of the predict.glm function is that it allows us to set the prediction type to the probability of the response (outcome) of interest. We don't have to use translate logged odds into probability; the predict .glm function can do it for us. In the sample plot in Figure 10.5, the vertical line segments represent the 95% confidence intervals of our predicted probabilities, which is 1.96 standard errors above and below the point estimate, but one can widen or narrow the confidence interval as needed.

```
# generate and plot predicted probabilities for discrete cases
predictions = predict.glm(obama.logit2, newdata = prediction.frame,
                          type="response", se.fit=T)


# plot the results
plot(x=1:4, y=predictions$fit, ylim=c(0, 1), axes=F,
     xlab="Voter Types (with Mean Democratic Party Sentiment)",
     ylab="Probability of Obama Vote", pch=16)
segments(x0=1:4, y0=predictions$fit - 1.96*predictions$se.fit,
         x1=1:4, y1=predictions$fit + 1.96*predictions$se.fit)
axis(side=1, at=1:4,
     labels=c("Non-White Gun Owner", "White Gun Owner",
     "Non-White Non-Gun Owner","White Non-Gun Owner"), cex.axis=.7)
axis(side=2, las=2)
box()
```

Figure 10.5 Predicted Probabilities for Discrete Cases

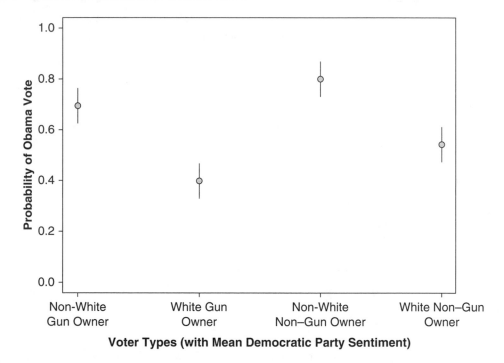

Voter Types (with Mean Democratic Party Sentiment)

Box 10.1 Marginal Effects and Expected Changes in Probability

Although most political researchers like to get a handle on predicted probabilities, as we have just done, there is no agreed-upon format for succinctly summarizing logistic regression results in terms of probabilities. One commonly used approach is to report the so-called full effect of the independent variable on the probability of the dependent variable. The full effect is calculated by subtracting the probability associated with the lowest value of the independent variable from the probability associated with the highest value of the independent variable.

Another way of summarizing a relationship in terms of probabilities is to report the interval of the independent variable that has the biggest impact on the probability of the dependent variable. The largest marginal effect of the independent variable on the probability of the dependent variable is sometimes called the *instantaneous effect*. The effect of a one-unit change in the independent variable on the probability of the dependent variable is always greatest for the interval containing a probability equal to .5. The instantaneous effect is approximately b/4, in which b is the value of the partial logistic regression coefficient.[7]

MODEL FIT STATISTICS FOR LOGISTIC REGRESSIONS

How strong is the relationship between feelings for the Democratic Party and the likelihood of voting to re-elect President Obama? OLS researchers are quite fond of R-square, the overall measure of strength that gauges the amount of variation in the dependent variable that is explained by the independent variable(s). For statistical reasons, however, the notion of "explained variation" has no direct analog in logistic regression. Even so, methodologists have proposed various "pseudo R-square" measures that gauge the strength of association between the dependent and independent variables, from 0 (no relationship) to 1 (perfect relationship). The function, logregR2, reports several model fit statistics:

```
# model fit statistics for logistic regression, one independent variable
logregR2(obama.logit)
```

```
Chi2                    2698.382
Df                             1
Sig.                      <.001
Cox and Snell Index      0.476
Nagelkerke Index         0.645
McFadden's R2            0.483
```

The Cox-Snell and Nagelkerke indexes, featured in SPSS output (a proprietary data analysis package), are popular pseudo R-square measures. Cox-Snell is the more conservative measure—that is, its maximum achievable value is less than 1. The Nagelkerke index adjusts for this, and so it generally reports a higher pseudo R-square than does Cox-Snell. McFadden's R-square (familiar to Stata aficionados) is the most conservative of the three, returning values closer to Cox-Snell than Nagelkerke. Differences aside, the three measures are never wildly divergent, and they do give the researcher a ballpark feel for the strength of the relationship. With values in the range of 0.476 to 0.646, you could conclude that Democratic Party sentiment by itself provides a powerful explanation of Obama's re-election.[8]

One other measure is reported by logregR2, "Chi2", equal to 2698.382. This is a chi-square statistic, and it tests the null hypothesis that the independent variable provides no leverage in predicting the dependent variable. In figuring out the most accurate estimates for the model's coefficients, logistic regression uses a technique called maximum likelihood estimation (MLE). When it begins the analysis, MLE finds out how well it can predict the observed values of the dependent variable without using the independent variable as a predictive tool. So MLE first determined how accurately it could predict whether individuals voted for Obama without knowing their Democratic Party sentiment. MLE then brings the independent variable into its calculations, running the analysis again—and again and again—to find the best possible predictive fit. According to the output from the summary of our logistic regression model with one independent variable, svyglm ran through six iterations (labeled "Number of Fisher Scoring iterations"), finally deciding that it had maximized its ability to predict voting for Obama by using Democratic thermometer scores as a predictive instrument. The amount of explanatory leverage gained

---

[7] For a discussion of the instantaneous effect, see Pampel, F. C. (2000). *Logistic regression: A primer*, SAGE University Papers Series on Quantitative Applications in the Social Sciences, series no. 07-132. Thousand Oaks, CA: SAGE, 24–26.

[8] Cox-Snell's maximum achievable value depends on the analysis at hand, but it can never exactly equal 1. For a binary dependent variable in which the probabilities of 0 and 1 are equal (probability of 0 = .5 and probability of 1 = .5), Cox-Snell reaches a maximum of only .75 for a model in which all cases are predicted perfectly. Nagelkerke's adjustment divides the calculated value of Cox-Snell by the maximum achievable value of Cox-Snell, returning a coefficient that varies between 0 and 1. See Cox, D. R., and Snell, E. J. (1989). *The analysis of binary data*. London, England: Chapman and Hall; and Nagelkerke, N. J. D. (1991). A note on a general definition of the coefficient of determination. *Biometrika, 78*, 691–692.

by including Democratic thermometer scores as a predictor is determined by subtracting the residual deviance from the null deviance.[9]

We can illustrate this model fit calculation using our logistic regression model of voting for Obama with one independent variable. The null deviance and residual deviance values were calculated when we estimated the model. These numbers also form the basis for McFadden's R-square, which is the proportionate reduction of the model with predictors compared to the null model.

```
# model fit statistics for logistic regression
obama.logit$null
obama.logit$deviance
obama.logit$null - obama.logit$deviance  # reported as Chi2

# McFadden's R-Squared statistic
(obama.logit$null - obama.logit$deviance) / obama.logit$null
```

```
> obama.logit$null
[1] 5581.473
> obama.logit$deviance
[1] 2883.091
> obama.logit$null - obama.logit$deviance
[1] 2698.382
> (obama.logit$null - obama.logit$deviance) / obama.logit$null
[1] 0.4834533
```

The "Sig." number, equal to 0, is the P-value for the chi-square statistic. Thus, we can conclude the following: Compared with how well we can predict voting without knowing respondents' feelings about the Democrats, including Democratic thermometer scores as a predictor significantly enhances the performance of the model.

Now let's look at the model fit statistics for our logistic regression model of voting to re-elect Obama that takes race and gun ownership in account.

```
# model fit stats for logistic regression, multiple indep. variables
logregR2(obama.logit2)
```

```
Chi2                    2731.403
Df                      3
Sig.                    <.001
Cox and Snell Index     0.490
Nagelkerke Index        0.665
McFadden's R2           0.505
```

According to McFadden (.505), Cox-Snell (.490), and Nagelkerke (.665), adding race and gun ownership to the model increased its explanatory power, at least when compared with the simple analysis using Democratic sentiment as the sole predictor. The chi-square statistic (2731.403.089) and P-value (<.001) tell us that, compared with the know-nothing model, both independent variables significantly improve our ability to predict the likelihood of voting. Clearly, both models outperform the know-nothing model, in which no independent variables are used to predict the likelihood of voting for Obama.

You may be wondering whether the obama.logit2 model is significantly better than the original obama .logit model. Yes, it is. For any logistic regression model, as we have seen, this question is answered by a chi-square test statistic that compares the model's residual deviance with its null deviance. You can take a similar

---

[9] Other computer programs use different labels for null deviance and residual deviance. Ordinarily, null deviance is labeled "initial −2 log likelihood," and residual deviance is labeled "final −2 log likelihood." Terminology aside, the concepts are identical.

approach to compare two models, one of which (the "full" model) uses more independent variables than does a more austere counterpart (the "reduced" model). The pchisqC function, which applies a chi-square test to the difference between two models, will help you make these model-to-model comparisons. The syntax:

$$\text{pchisqC}(reduced, \quad full)$$

Substitute the model names for "reduced" and "full". In our running example, obama.logit is the reduced model and obama.logit2 is the full model.

```
# comparing logistic regression models
pchisqC(obama.logit, obama.logit2)
```

```
Warning: These models have different numbers of observations.
[1] "<.001"
```

The pchisqC function returns a P-value that tests that null hypothesis that the full model offers no improvement over the reduced model. With a P-value of less than .001, we can conclude that, compared with using Democratic sentiment alone, adding race and gun ownership as independent variables significantly improves the predictive power of the model.[10]

AN ADDITIONAL EXAMPLE OF MULTIVARIABLE LOGISTIC REGRESSION

Let's work through one more example—this time using the glm function to analyze one of the unweighted datasets, states. If you're analyzing unweighted data, this workhorse function is an alternative to the svyglm function, which is tailored to analyzing weighted survey data.

As you know, presidential elections in the United States take place within an unusual institutional context. Naturally, candidates seek as many votes as they can get, but the real electoral prizes come in winner-take-all, state-sized chunks: The plurality-vote winner in each state receives all the electoral college votes from that state. Cast in logistic regression terms, each state represents a binary outcome—it goes either Democratic or Republican. What variables shape this outcome?

As a candidate for the Democratic nomination in 2008, Barack Obama pointed toward several plausible variables. During a campaign appearance, Obama suggested that many voters, frustrated by the disappearance of economic opportunities, "cling to guns or religion or antipathy to people who aren't like them or anti-immigrant sentiment or anti-trade sentiment as a way to explain their frustrations." Obama said that these factors helped explain why his electoral support was weaker in certain geographical areas of the country. These remarks were controversial, to be sure. But they also suggested two empirical relationships, one positive and one negative. (i) States with more secularized populations—fewer churchgoers, for example—will be more likely to award their electoral votes to the Democrat. (ii) States with fewer restrictions on gun ownership will be less likely to award their electoral votes to the Democrat. Let's test both ideas using the glm function, optioned for logistic regression.[11]

The states dataset contains the variable obama_win12, an indicator coded 1 if the state's electoral vote went to the president in 2012, and coded 0 if the state went to his challenger Gov. Mitt Romney. This is the dependent variable. The dataset also has secularism, an index that combines several measures of religiosity into an index that ranges from 4 (least secular) to 180 (most secular). Finally, states has gunlaw_rank, the Brady Campaign's ranking of states' gun laws. Higher scores on gunlaw_rank denote fewer restrictions on firearms ownership. From a substantive standpoint, we would expect that as secularism increases, the likelihood of an Obama win would increase (a positive relationship). As gunlaw_rank increases, the likelihood of an Obama win should decrease (a negative relationship). Of course, the two independent

---

[10] In this example, the pchisqC function alerts us to the fact that the number of observations in our reduced model is greater than the number of observations in our full model because of some missing data in the race and gun ownership variables. For a more conservative test, one could estimate the reduced model on the subset of observations without missing data and compare that model to the full model.

[11] Obama reportedly made this remark at a fundraising event in San Francisco on April 6, 2008.

variables are themselves fairly strongly related, so a multivariate model will allow us to isolate the partial effect of each on the likelihood that Obama carried the state in 2012.

Here is the glm syntax, tailored for logistic regression[12]:

glm(*depvar* ~ *indepvar1* + *indepvar2* +...*indepvarn*, data=*dataset*, family=binomial)

Let's create an object, states.obama, by applying the glm expression to the problem at hand and apply some familiar functions to summarize the model (summary), generate odds ratios for the independent variables (orci), and obtain the model fit statistics (logregR2).

```
# estimating logistic regression model with glm function
states.obama = glm(obama_win12 ~ secularism + gunlaw_rank, data=states,
                family=binomial)

summary(states.obama)
orci(states.obama)
logregR2(states.obama)
```

```
Deviance Residuals:
Min              1Q     Median        3Q         Max
-1.50562   -0.20026    0.03132   0.21780     2.42177


Coefficients:
             Estimate  Std. Error  z value   Pr(>|z|)
(Intercept)   1.21467     1.80898    0.671    0.50192
secularism    0.04126     0.01513    2.728    0.00638   **
gunlaw_rank  -0.20996     0.06853   -3.064    0.00219   **
---
Signif. codes:  0 '***' 0.001 '**' 0.01 '*' 0.05 '.' 0.1 ' ' 1

(Dispersion parameter for binomial family taken to be 1)

    Null deviance: 69.235  on 49   degrees of freedom
Residual deviance: 20.210  on 47   degrees of freedom
AIC: 26.21

Number of Fisher Scoring iterations: 7


             OddsRatio        2.5 %        97.5 %
(Intercept)  3.3691973   0.09147249   158.9557693
secularism   1.0421266   1.01692457     1.0826866
gunlaw_rank  0.8106166   0.68298173     0.9046248


Chi2                       49.02446
Df                                2
Sig.                 2.261902e-11
Cox and Snell Index       0.6248725
Nagelkerke Index          0.8336083
McFadden's R2             0.7080909
```

These commands provide us a lot of information about the relationship between secularism, gun rights, and how states voted in the 2012 election. To help digest these results, let's write out the estimates:

Logged odds(Obama win) = 1.215 + 0.041*(secularism) − 0.210*(gunlaw_rank)

---

[12] To find out how strongly correlated these variables are, run "wtd.cor (states$gunlaw_rank, states$secularism)".

As hypothesized, as secularism increases, so does the likelihood of an Obama win. Translating orci's odds ratio (1.042) into a percentage change in the odds, each one-point increase in secularism increases the odds of an Obama victory by over 4 percent: 100 * (1.042 − 1) = 4.2. Also, as states' gun laws become less restrictive (higher scores on gunlaw_rank), the logged odds of an Obama win decline. Each one-unit increase in gunlaw_rank decreases the odds of an Obama win by 18.9 percent: 100 * (.811 − 1) = −18.9. According to the P-values, both gunlaw_rank (P = .002) and secularism (P = .006) trump the null hypothesis. With pseudo-R squares in the .60 to .80 neighborhood, together the two independent variables provide a powerful tool for predicting the outcome of the electoral vote.

How can we capture these relationships in graphic form? In this instance, we are estimating a logistic regression model with two interval-level independent variables. You'll recall from Chapter 9 that when you estimate a regression model with two interval-level variables, R has some nice options for plotting relationships in three dimensions. We can follow this approach here as well, but we need to keep in mind that we really want to see predicted probabilities rather than logged odds. Translating our logistic regression results from logged odds to probabilities requires a bit of setup, but the work pays off in a nice-looking plot. For this visualization of results, we'll create a three-dimensional figure that looks like a contoured wireframe covering all the possible values of secularism and gun rights. As we've done with other predicted probability plots, we'll first generate a prediction frame that covers all the independent variable values we want to visualize, estimate the probability of an Obama vote in each case, and then plot the results. In this case, the prediction frame has many rows because both secularism and gunlaw_rank are interval-level variables (we've actually thinned the prediction frame to simplify the plot rendering).

```
# 3-d plot of predicted probabilities, two interval indep. Variables
states.obama = glm(obama_win12 ~ secularism + gunlaw_rank,
                data=states, family=binomial)


# create prediction frame of indep. values to be plotted
secularism_values  = seq(0,180,by=5)
gunlaw_rank_values = seq(1, 50,by=1)
prediction.frame = expand.grid(secularism=secularism_values,
                          gunlaw_rank=gunlaw_rank_values)


# predict probabilities
predictions = predict.glm(states.obama, newdata=prediction.frame,
                     type="response")


# plot the results
persp(x=secularism_values, y=gunlaw_rank_values,
      z=matrix(predictions, nrow=37, ncol=50), ticktype="detailed",
      theta=-70, phi=25, col="gray90", border="gray30",
      xlab="Secularism", ylab="Gun Rights Rank",
      zlab="Probability Obama Win")
```

We've used a number of the optional arguments of the persp function to fine-tune the graphic in Figure 10.6. For example, we've adjusted the angle from which one views the figure using the theta and phi arguments as well as the colors of the surface and border facets. The possibilities are wide open. When you create a figure like this, we recommend starting with the most basic possible version and then refining the figure through trial and error until you are happy with your final product.

Figure 10.6 Predicted Probabilities in Three Dimensions

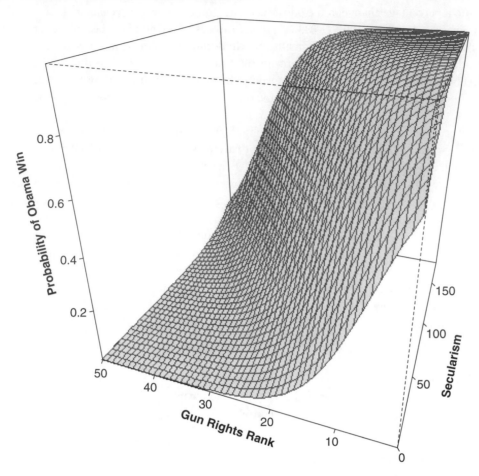

EXERCISES

1. (Dataset: nesD. Variables: voted2012, dem_edugroup, dem_age_group_r.) In this exercise, you will use the nesD dataset to examine the effect of education and age on the likelihood of voting in 2012. The nesD set contains voted2012 (coded 1 for voters and 0 for nonvoters). Education is included in the nesD dataset as the dem_edugroup variable but it's in the form of an ordered factor, so it becomes unwieldy when it is incorporated in a multiple regression model. Similarly, dem_age_group_r is an ordered factor. Therefore, transform dem_edugroup and dem_age_group_r into numeric class variables by using the as.numeric function. Or you can simply enter as.numeric(dem_edugroup) and as.numeric(dem_age_group_r) directly into your svyglm function call. The education variable is coded 1–5; the age variable is coded 1–13.

    A. Run an svyglm analysis on nesD to estimate a new model, "modelA". Obtain a full complement of statistics for modelA. Write the correct values for modelA next to the question marks in the following table:

Model Estimates	Coefficient	P-Value	Odds Ratio
Constant	?		
Education	?	?	?
Age	?	?	?
logregR2 Statistics	Statistic	Significance	
Chi-square	?	?	
Cox-Snell index	?		

Nagelkerke index	?		
McFadden's R2	?		

B. Consider this statement: Education significantly increases the likelihood of voting. This statement is (Circle one.)

correct.   incorrect.

Explain how you know.

_____

_____

C. Consider this statement: Controlling for education, each one-unit increase in age increases the odds of voting by .176. This statement is (Circle one.)

correct.   incorrect.

Explain how you know.

_____

_____

2. (Dataset: nes. Variables: dhsinvolv_message, polknow_combined.) Online political activism is a relatively new phenomenon. In recent years, online social networks like Facebook and Twitter have become part of our everyday experiences and, for many people, a forum for political news and debate. From your own personal experiences, you may have some impressions about who is likely to post political messages online, but our personal perspectives are bound to be limited and incomplete. Let's use the nes dataset to gain a better understanding of who uses social media to promote political ideas. Survey participants were asked whether they had posted a political message on Facebook or Twitter in the last 4 years and the dhsinvolv_message variable recorded their responses.

A. According to the nes dataset, roughly 20% of respondents indicated that they had posted a social media message about politics in the past 4 years. If the probability of an event occurring is 0.20, what are the odds of the event occurring? What is the log of the odds of the event occurring?

odds: _____

logged odds: _____

B. Are politically knowledgeable people more or less likely to post political messages on social media? In order to analyze this question with logistic regression, you need to transform the dependent variables, dhsinvolv_message, into a binary variable, with 1 corresponding to the event of interest (posting a social media message) and 0 corresponding to its non-occurrence. You might use the following command: nes$dhsinvolv_message.y = as.numeric (nes$dhsinvolv_message == "1. Have done this in past 4 years"). To make sure you've recoded the dependent variable correctly, apply the freq function to the binary variable you created.

_____

C. Estimate a logistic regression model that uses the variable polknow_combined to explain the likelihood that someone posted a political message on social media. The polknow_combined variable measures the number of questions about politics the respondent answered correctly, with higher numbers indicating more political knowledge. Include a summary of the results in your answer.

D. Based on the results you obtained for part C, are politically knowledgeable people more likely to post social media messages about politics than those who know less about politics? Use the inferential statistics reported by R to assess the possibility that whatever differences you observe in this sample could be the results of random error, rather than a real effect of political knowledge.

E. Make the results of your logistic regression analysis clearer by creating a figure that shows the predicted probability of posting a social message about politics at varying levels of political knowledge. The y-axis of your plot should range from 0 to 1 and correspond to the predicted probability of posting a message. The x-axis of your plot should range from 0 to 8, which is the range of the political knowledge scale in the nes dataset.

3. (Dataset: world. Variables: democ_regime, frac_eth, gdp_10_thou.) In Chapter 5, you tested the following hypothesis: In a comparison of countries, those having lower levels of ethnic heterogeneity will be more likely to be democracies than will those having higher levels of ethnic heterogeneity. This hypothesis says that, as heterogeneity goes up, the probability of democracy goes down. You then re-ran the analysis, controlling for a measure of countries' economic development, per-capita gross domestic product (GDP). For this independent variable, the relationship is thought to be positive: As economic development increases, so does the likelihood that a country will be democratic. In the current exercise, you will re-examine this set of relationships, using interval-level independent variables and a more powerful method of analysis, logistic regression.

The world dataset contains these three variables: democ_regime, frac_eth, and gdp_10_thou. The democ_regime is coded "Yes" if a country is a democracy and "No" if it is not. We'll transform these into 1's and 0's to create our dependent variable. The frac_eth variable varies between 0 (denoting low fractionalization) and 1 (high fractionalization). The other independent variable, gdp_10_thou, measures per-capita GDP in units of $10,000.

A. Estimate a logistic regression model that explains the existence of democratic regimes as a function of GDP and ethnic fractionalization. The democ_regime variable has "Yes" and "No" values. So if you're estimating the logistic regression model with the svyglm function and the world design dataset, you can use as.numeric($democ_regime=="Yes") as your binary response variable, or you can create a new variable and update the world design dataset as described in Chapter 8. For ease of reference, save the results of your estimation with an object name like model.democracy. Apply the summary function to your model and fill in the correct value next to each question mark.

Model Estimates	Coefficient	T-Statistic	P-Value
Intercept	0.648	?	?
gdp_10_thou	0.120	?	?
frac_eth	−0.265	?	?

B. Now apply the orci function to model.democracy (or whatever you named the object that stores your estimation results). Fill in the correct value next to each question mark below.

Model Estimates	Odds Ratio
Intercept	?
gdp_10_thou	?
frac_eth	?

C. Apply the logregR2 function to your model.democracy. Fill in the correct values next to the question marks below to get an idea of how well your logistic regression model explains the occurrence of democracy in the world.

logregR2 statistics	Statistic
Chi-square	?
Cox-Snell index	?
Nagelkerke index	?
McFadden's R2	?

D. Use each odds ratio to calculate a percentage change in the odds. Controlling for gdp_10_thou, a one-unit change in frac_eth, from low heterogeneity to high heterogeneity (Check one.)

❑ increases the odds of democracy by about 25 percent.

❑ decreases the odds of democracy by about 25 percent.

❑ decreases the odds of democracy by about 80 percent.

Controlling for frac_eth, each $10,000 increase in per-capita GDP (Check one.)

❑ increases the odds of democracy by about 10 percent.

❑ increases the odds of democracy by about 100 percent.

❑ decreases the odds of democracy by about 50 percent.

E. As an empirical matter, the least fractionalized country in the world dataset has a value of 0 on frac_eth, and the most fractionalized country has a value of .93 on frac_eth. According to your model.democracy, the predicted probability of democracy for a country with low fractionalization (frac_eth = 0) at the mean value of gdp_10_thou is equal to (Fill in the blank.) _____. The predicted probability of democracy for a highly fractionalized country (frac_eth = .93) at the mean value of gdp_10_thou is equal to (Fill in the blank.) _____.

F. Consider this statement: At all levels of fractionalization, richer countries are more likely to be democracies than are poorer countries. Do your findings support this statement? Answer yes or no and explain.

_____

_____

G. Consider this statement: At the median value of fractionalization, all countries—low-GDP, middle-GDP, and high-GDP—are probably democracies. Do your findings support this statement? Answer yes or no and explain.

_____

_____

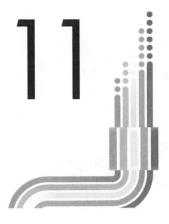

11

Doing Your Own Political Analysis

Objective	Functions Introduced	Author or Source
Importing data into R	spss.get {Hmisc} stata.get {Hmisc} csv.get {Hmisc}	Frank E. Harrell, Jr.[1]

In working through the guided examples in this book, and in performing the exercises, you have developed some solid analytic skills. In our examples and chapter exercises, we have analyzed a number of interesting political phenomena. We've only scratched the surface with respect to the research possibilities of the four datasets supplied with this book. To get you thinking about doing your own research, we begin by laying out the stages of the research process and by offering some manageable ideas for original analysis you could conduct using the datasets supplied with this book.

We would not be disappointed, however, if you were to look elsewhere for data for your own political science research. High-quality social science data on a wide variety of phenomena and units of analysis—individuals, census tracts, states, countries—are widely accessible via the Internet and might serve as the centerpiece for your own research. Your school, for example, may be a member of the Inter-university Consortium for Political and Social Research (ICPSR), the premier organizational clearinghouse for datasets of all kinds.[2] In this chapter, we will take a look at various sources of available data and provide practical guidance for inputting them into R. In the process, we will also cover situations in which you are confronted with raw, uncoded data—perhaps from an original questionnaire you developed and administered—that you need to code and analyze.

We conclude this chapter by describing a serviceable format for an organized and presentable research paper.

SEVEN DOABLE IDEAS

Let's begin by describing an ideal research procedure and then discuss some practical considerations and constraints. In an ideal world, you would

1. Observe an interesting behavior or relationship and frame a research question about it;

2. Develop a causal explanation for what you have observed and construct a hypothesis;

3. Read and learn from the work of other researchers who have tackled similar questions;

---

[1] Harrell, F. E., Jr. (2012). *Hmisc: Harrell miscellaneous* (R package version 3.9-3). Contributions from many other users. Available at http://CRAN.R-project.org/package=Hmisc

[2] You can browse ICPSR's holdings at http://www.icpsr.umich.edu

4. Collect and analyze the data that will address the hypothesis; and

5. Write a research paper or article in which you present and interpret your findings.

In this scenario, the phenomenon that you observe in stage 1 drives the whole process. First, think up a question, then research it and obtain the data that will address it. As a practical matter, the process is almost never this clear-cut. Often someone else's idea or assertion may pique your interest. For example, you might read articles or attend lectures on a variety of topics—democratization in developing countries, global environmental issues, ideological change in the Democratic or Republican Party, the effect of election laws on turnout and party competition, and so on—that suggest hypotheses you would like to examine. So you may begin the process at stage 3, then return to stage 1 and refine your own ideas. Furthermore, the availability of relevant data, considered in stage 4, almost always plays a role in the sorts of questions we address.

Suppose, for example, that you want to assess the organizational efforts to mobilize African Americans in your state in the last presidential election. You want precinct-level registration data, and you need to compare these numbers with the figures from previous elections. You would soon become an expert in the bureaucratic hassles and expense involved in dealing with county governments, and you might have to revise your research agenda. Indeed, for professional researchers and academics, data collection in itself can be a full-time job. For students who wish to produce a competent and manageable project, the so-called law of available data can be a source of frustration and discouragement.

A doable project often requires a compromise between stage 1 and stage 4. What interesting questions can you ask, given the datasets available with this book? To help you get started doing your own political analysis, we'll discuss seven possible lines of research.

Political Knowledge and Interest

As you may have learned in other political science courses, scholars continue to debate the levels of knowledge and political awareness among ordinary citizens. Do citizens know the length of a U.S. senator's term of office? Do they know what constitutional protections are guaranteed by the First Amendment? Do people tend to know more about some things, such as Internet privacy or abortion policy, and less about other things, such as foreign policy or international politics? Political knowledge is a promising variable because the researcher is likely to find some people who know a lot about politics, some who know a fair amount, and others who know very little.[3] One could ask, "What causes this variation?"

The nes dataset contains a number of variables that measure respondents' political knowledge. Some variables measure respondents' knowledge of particular topics, like the terms of senators and presidents, whereas other variables are constructed to differentiate respondents' political knowledge at the ordinal or interval level. See Appendix Table A.2 for an alphabetical list of all variables in the nes dataset.

If you want to know why some people are more interested in political issues than others are, the gss dataset includes a number of measures of political interest. Refer to Appendix Table A.1, which lists all the variables in the gss dataset in alphabetical order; there is a set of variables that begin with "int" that measure respondents' interest in specific issues as well as at a general level.

Self-Interest and Policy Preferences

It is widely thought that people support policies to advance their personal interests. This view is consistent with the economist's view that people generally act in a way that maximizes their personal happiness. There's often no conflict between self-interest and public interest. For example, if you think the federal government should do more to curb global warming, you probably think limiting greenhouses gasses is in everybody's interest, not just yours. Sometimes, however, our general views on public policy conflict with our self-interest. For example, one might generally favor protecting the environment, but if a proposal to do so decreases the value of one's personal property, self-interest may prevail over public interest.

There is a good body of political science research on the role of self-interest in the formulation of policy preferences. The empirical research is mixed.[4] The nes and gss datasets offer students a number of opportunities

---

[3] For excellent guidance on the meaning and measurement of political knowledge, see Delli Carpini, M. X., and Keeter, S. (1993). Measuring political knowledge: Putting first things first. *American Journal of Political Science*, 37(4), 1179–1206.

[4] See Wolpert, R., and Gimpel, J. (1998). Self-interest, symbolic politics, and public attitudes toward gun control. *Political Behavior*, 20(3), 241–262.

to explore how self-interest affects the formulation of individual policy preferences. To pursue this line of research, consider the variables that record personal information about the gss and nes survey respondents, such as their age, occupation, parental status, and so forth. There are many such variables. Then consider how different personal characteristics would alter policy preferences if the respondent was motivated by self-interest and look for a variable that measures individual preferences on these policies. For example, do gun owners have significantly different preferences with respect to gun control than do non–gun owners? Do parents express fundamentally different preferences on public school education policies than non-parents? The datasets provided with this book offer numerous opportunities to test the theory that people act in a politically self-interested manner.

When you conduct this research, we suggest you consider and try to control for the possibility that respondents' policy preferences reflect their own conception of public interest, which may coincide with their own self-interest at times. You might, for example, incorporate some measure of political ideology or party identification to help isolate the extent to which selfishness compels people to disregard their general political views.

Economic Performance and Election Outcomes

Here is one of the most widely discussed ideas in political science: how the state of the economy before an election affects election results. If the economy is strong, the candidate of the incumbent party does well, probably winning the election. If the economy is performing poorly, the incumbent party's nominee pays the price, probably losing. There are a couple of intriguing aspects to this idea. For one thing, it works well—but not perfectly. Moreover, the economy-election relationship has several researchable layers.

Focusing on state-by-state results in presidential elections, you can imagine a simple two-category measure of the dependent variable—the incumbent party wins or the incumbent party loses—or an interval-level measure of the percentage of state residents who vote for the incumbent president's party. Now consider some potential independent variables that measure the strength of the economy in the states, such as the state unemployment rate. Or you could modify and refine the basic idea, as many scholars have done, by adding additional noneconomic variables you believe to be important. To what extent do demographic factors or varying opinions on social issues challenge the view that elections are a referendum on the president's handling of the economy? You'll find the variables you need to get started with this research in the states dataset.

Electoral Turnout in Comparative Perspective

The record of voter turnout in American presidential elections is relatively low. The situation in other democratic countries is strikingly different. Turnouts in some Western European countries average well above 70 percent. Why? More generally, what causes turnout to vary between countries? Some scholars have focused on institutional differences in electoral systems. Many countries, for example, have systems of proportional representation in which narrowly focused parties with relatively few supporters nonetheless can gain representation in the legislature. The variable world$pr_sys identifies countries with proportional representation systems. Are citizens more likely to be mobilized to vote under such institutional arrangements? You could see if other variables are associated with differences in turnout around the world.

This area of research might also open the door for some informed speculation on your part. What sort of electoral reforms, if instituted in the United States, might enhance electoral turnout? What other (perhaps unintended) consequences might such reforms have?

Interviewer Effects on Public Opinion Surveys

The GSS and NES surveys ask participants some sensitive and controversial questions. These surveys, for example, ask people questions about racism, sexism, and homosexuality. These are important topics, but one of the challenges that researchers face when they attempt to discern public opinions on sensitive topics is the human tendency to give socially acceptable answers on certain topics. What's acceptable or expected behavior depends on social context. Behavior that's normal at a football game is not acceptable during a church service.

Public opinion researchers do their best to avoid influencing how people respond to surveys, but surveys are inevitably administered in some context that may affect how people respond to questions, particularly sensitive and controversial topics. For example, a survey can be administered in person, over the phone, or over the Internet. Do people give significantly different responses to a live person than they do to an Internet survey? Identify an NES variable you think would be affected by context and compare responses obtained face-to-face with those obtained over the Internet (using the nes$mode variable).

The gss dataset includes a number of variables about the person conducting the interview, such as the interviewer's age, race, ethnicity, and gender. How might the interviewer's race, ethnicity, and/or gender define the parameters of social acceptability in the interview? Identify a question in the gss dataset you think could be affected by who conducted the interview and see if who asked the question affected the answers given.

Religion and Politics

All four datasets include variables related to religion and religious practices, facilitating research into the relationship between religion and politics. Most political science research on religion and politics will treat religion as the independent variable and analyze how religious beliefs influence political outcomes. The gss and nes datasets include variables related to respondents' religious beliefs, or lack thereof, and one can analyze how individuals' beliefs affect their political attitudes and opinions. Similarly, the states and world datasets include aggregate-level measures of religious beliefs and practices, allowing researchers to examine how varying religious practices affect state or national politics.

A couple words of caution are in order for those interested in researching how religion affects politics. First, it's important for the researcher to control for other variables, such as political ideology, that offer alternative explanations for the observed political outcomes. In some cases, conservative political ideology may offer a better explanation of variation in a dependent variable than do religious beliefs. Second, if one analyzes aggregate-level data from the states or world dataset, it is important to make inferences about individuals from aggregate-level results. For example, if one finds that states with more frequent church attendance have significantly more gun violence than states with fewer attenders, one should not infer that people who go to church frequently are more violent than others are. This mistake is known as the ecological fallacy.

There are also some opportunities to examine attitudes and opinions related to religion as the dependent variable. For example, the gss dataset asks respondents whether someone with an anti-religion message should be permitted to teach in college (gss$colath), speak in the respondent's community (gss$spkath), or have a book in the library (gss$libath). These are interesting questions because they raise First Amendment issues about the proper role of religion in public affairs. We would discourage political science students from analyzing religious affiliations and beliefs as a dependent variable to determine what causes someone to believe in God or go to church. The nature and origins of religious beliefs are certainly important topics, but these topics are largely outside the scope of political science.

Race and Politics

Race is one of the most enduring and difficult issues in politics. There are many ways to analyze the relationship between race and politics using the datasets that accompany this book. To help students identify potential research topics, we'll first discuss research designs that use race (or ethnicity) as an independent variable and then discuss designs where race-related variables are the outcome of interest.

How does race affect political beliefs and outcomes? Do individuals who identify as racial or ethnic minorities express significantly different political views than others do? Both the gss and nes datasets include variables identifying respondents' race and ethnicity. Do states or countries with greater proportions of racial or ethnic minorities have different political outcomes than those with lesser proportions of minorities? You can find data to conduct this inquiry in both the states and world datasets. Because race is such an enduring and important issue, the results of this kind of analysis are usually interesting whether one finds that race makes or does not make a significant difference. At the same time, we encourage students interested in the effect of race on politics to read the words of caution above (about studying the effect of religion on politics), which are equally applicable here.

One can also examine race-related political beliefs, attitudes, or outcomes as the dependent variable in political science research. In the gss dataset, one can find variables measuring respondents' support for affirmative action and government relief, belief in racial stereotypes, and sense of shared fate. The nes dataset also contains a number of variables measuring respondents' opinions and attitudes about racial discrimination and minority communities in the United States. Some predictors, like respondents' race and party identification, should seem obvious and you should include these explanations in your analysis. Can you identify other significant predictors of race-related political beliefs and attitudes? Consider examining the influence of factors such as age, employment status, and education.

IMPORTING DATA

Although ready-to-analyze R-formatted datasets are not widely available on the Internet,[5] several common data types, such as SPSS and Stata datasets, are easy to import into R. Other familiar formats, including Excel spreadsheets, require more effort. This section reviews different data sources, data preparation, and import procedures. Depending on your computer's settings, you may be able to read external data files into R from the Internet using URLs in place of the name of files in your working directory, but this is not always possible and someone may delete or remove the remote data file.

SPSS and Stata Formatted Datasets

The least labor-intensive sources provide SPSS or Stata datasets that are ready to download, import, and analyze. One such source, the ICPSR's data clearinghouse at the University of Michigan, was mentioned at the beginning of this chapter (http://www.icpsr.umich.edu). Many other sites exist, often maintained by scholars, academic departments, and private foundations. For example, if you are interested in comparative politics or international relations topics, visit Pippa Norris's website at Harvard's John F. Kennedy School of Government (http://www.pippanorris.com/). For links to a number of SPSS and Stata datasets having a particular emphasis on Latino politics, see Prof. Matt A. Barreto's site (http://mattbarreto.com/data/index.html). More generally, the University of California at Berkeley's Survey Documentation and Analysis (SDA) website—a clearinghouse for the General Social Surveys, the American National Election Studies, and Census Microdata—allows you to download customized datasets and codebooks in a variety of formats, including SPSS and Stata (http://sda.berkeley.edu/archive.htm).

When you have found an interesting SPSS or Stata dataset on the Internet, use spss.get or stata.get (from the Hmisc package) to import it.[6] To illustrate, consider Figure 11.1, a detail from a screenshot of Pippa Norris's dataset page:

Figure 11.1 Pippa Norris's Data Page

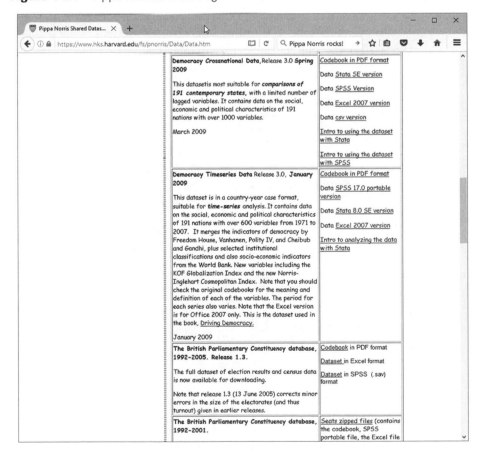

---

[5] This situation is changing. For example, in March 2013, ICPSR announced the release of new datasets in R format. See http://www.icpsr.umich.edu/icpsrweb/ICPSR/support/announcements/2013/03/icpsr-releases-new-datasets-in-r-format
[6] The foreign package is another option for reading datasets written for other formats.

Both datasets of interest, the Stata set and the SPSS set, contain Prof. Norris's Democracy Crossnational Data, Release 3.0 (Spring 2009). To download an SPSS dataset, follow these steps. (Procedures are virtually identical for Stata datasets. Differences are discussed below.)

1. Right-click on the dataset link. Click "Save link as".
2. Navigate to R's working directory. If you do not know the working directory, type 'getwd ()' at the R prompt.
3. Save the dataset in the working directory. It might make things simpler to abbreviate long dataset names.
4. At the R prompt, or in a script file, use the spss.get function to create a new object containing the dataset:

```
# Read dataset in SPSS format
this.dataset = spss.get("name_of_dataset.sav")
```

To import a Stata dataset, follow the same steps, except enlist the stata.get function and the ".dta" file extension:

```
# Read dataset in Stata format
this.dataset = stata.get("name_of_dataset.dta")
```

Microsoft Excel Datasets

Many Internet data are available in spreadsheet form, predominately in Microsoft Excel format. The good news is that Excel spreadsheets can be saved as .csv files, which can in turn be imported into R using the csv.get function. The bad news is that many of the Excel files you will find on the Internet contain a lot of non-importable text and graphics junk. A fair amount of editing and cleaning may be required.

Consider Figure 11.2, which shows an Excel file downloaded from a U.S. Census site (http://www2.census.gov/library/publications/2011/compendia/statab/131ed/tables/12s0337.xls). This particular dataset

Figure 11.2 R-Unfriendly Excel Dataset

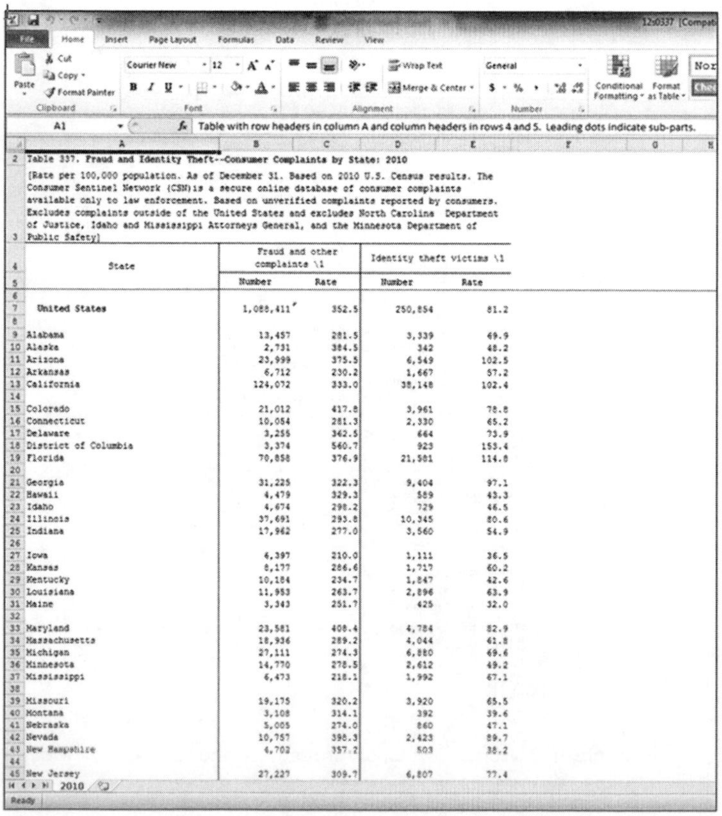

Table with row headers in column A and column headers in rows 4 and 5. Leading dots indicate sub-parts.

Table 337. Fraud and Identity Theft--Consumer Complaints by State: 2010

[Rate per 100,000 population. As of December 31. Based on 2010 U.S. Census results. The Consumer Sentinel Network (CSN) is a secure online database of consumer complaints available only to law enforcement. Based on unverified complaints reported by consumers. Excludes complaints outside of the United States and excludes North Carolina Department of Justice, Idaho and Mississippi Attorneys General, and the Minnesota Department of Public Safety]

State	Fraud and other complaints \1		Identity theft victims \1	
	Number	Rate	Number	Rate
United States	1,088,411	352.5	250,854	81.2
Alabama	13,457	281.5	3,339	69.9
Alaska	2,731	384.5	342	48.2
Arizona	23,999	375.5	6,549	102.5
Arkansas	6,712	230.2	1,667	57.2
California	124,072	333.0	38,148	102.4
Colorado	21,012	417.8	3,961	78.8
Connecticut	10,054	281.3	2,330	65.2
Delaware	3,255	362.5	664	73.9
District of Columbia	3,374	560.7	923	153.4
Florida	70,858	376.9	21,581	114.8
Georgia	31,225	322.3	9,404	97.1
Hawaii	4,479	329.3	589	43.3
Idaho	4,674	298.2	729	46.5
Illinois	37,691	293.8	10,345	80.6
Indiana	17,962	277.0	3,560	54.9
Iowa	6,397	210.0	1,111	36.5
Kansas	8,177	286.6	1,717	60.2
Kentucky	10,184	234.7	1,847	42.6
Louisiana	11,953	263.7	2,896	63.9
Maine	3,343	251.7	425	32.0
Maryland	23,581	408.4	4,784	82.9
Massachusetts	18,936	289.2	4,044	61.8
Michigan	27,111	274.3	6,880	69.6
Minnesota	14,770	278.5	2,612	49.2
Mississippi	6,473	218.1	1,992	67.1
Missouri	19,175	320.2	3,920	65.5
Montana	3,108	314.1	392	39.6
Nebraska	5,005	274.0	860	47.1
Nevada	10,757	398.3	2,423	89.7
New Hampshire	4,702	357.2	503	38.2
New Jersey	27,227	309.7	6,807	77.4

records consumer complaints of fraud and identity theft, by state. This set could be saved as a .csv file, but R would not import it correctly. The large text header, the long column labels, the eye-pleasing blank rows, even the commas in the values in the "Number" columns—are all features designed to make the file easy for humans to peruse and interpret. Unfortunately, these features are not R-friendly. Now consider Figure 11.3, an R-friendly version of the same data. This dataset is symmetrical. Each column has a brief label, the blank rows are gone, and the large number values no longer contain commas. (In R imports, numerics with decimal points are fine, but numerics with commas are not.) Once it is saved as a .csv file, R would happily import this dataset. Figure 11.4 demonstrates how to transform an Excel file from an R-unfriendly spreadsheet to an R-friendly spreadsheet.

Figure 11.3   R-Friendly Excel Dataset

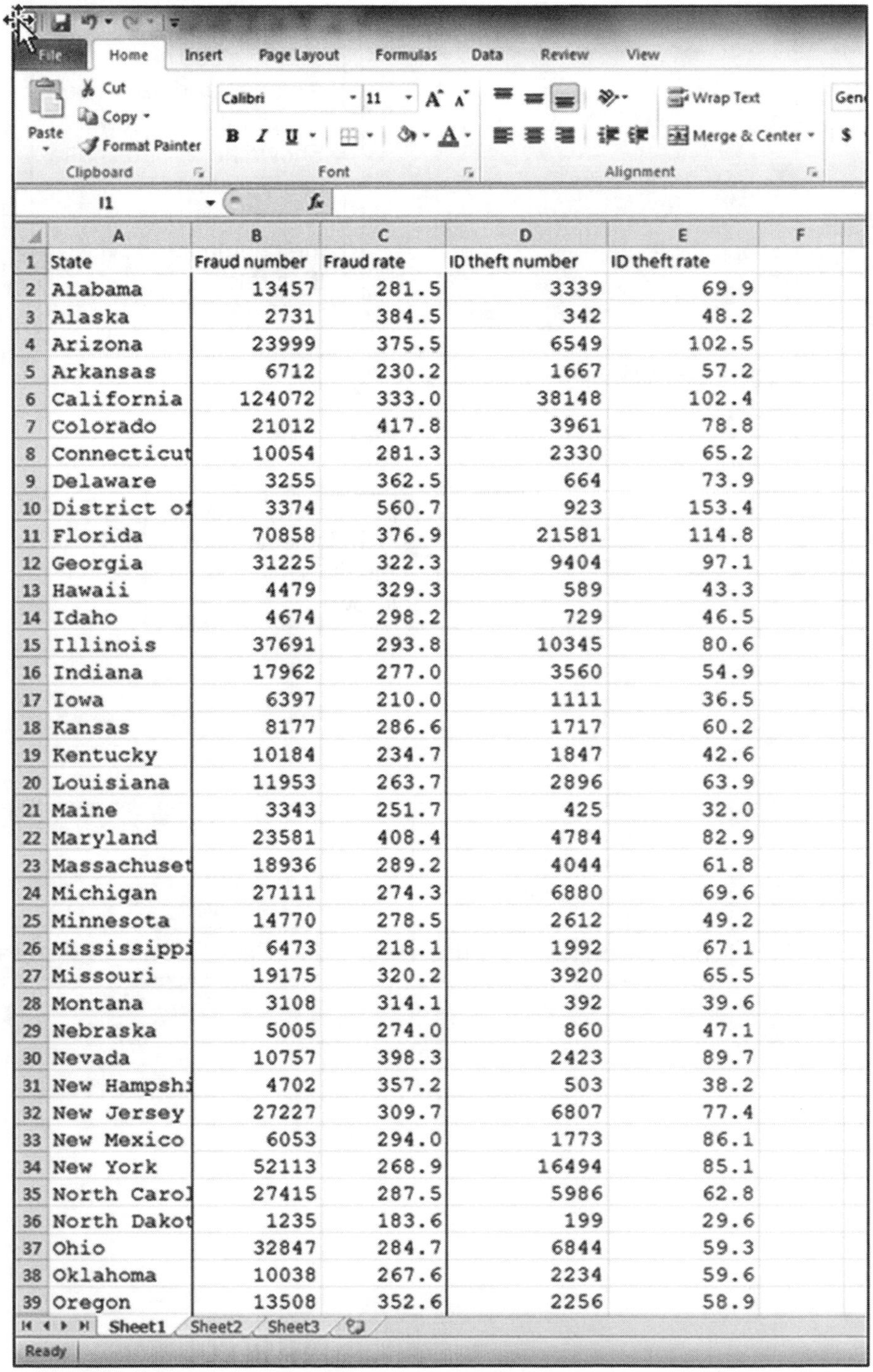

	A	B	C	D	E	F
1	State	Fraud number	Fraud rate	ID theft number	ID theft rate	
2	Alabama	13457	281.5	3339	69.9	
3	Alaska	2731	384.5	342	48.2	
4	Arizona	23999	375.5	6549	102.5	
5	Arkansas	6712	230.2	1667	57.2	
6	California	124072	333.0	38148	102.4	
7	Colorado	21012	417.8	3961	78.8	
8	Connecticut	10054	281.3	2330	65.2	
9	Delaware	3255	362.5	664	73.9	
10	District of	3374	560.7	923	153.4	
11	Florida	70858	376.9	21581	114.8	
12	Georgia	31225	322.3	9404	97.1	
13	Hawaii	4479	329.3	589	43.3	
14	Idaho	4674	298.2	729	46.5	
15	Illinois	37691	293.8	10345	80.6	
16	Indiana	17962	277.0	3560	54.9	
17	Iowa	6397	210.0	1111	36.5	
18	Kansas	8177	286.6	1717	60.2	
19	Kentucky	10184	234.7	1847	42.6	
20	Louisiana	11953	263.7	2896	63.9	
21	Maine	3343	251.7	425	32.0	
22	Maryland	23581	408.4	4784	82.9	
23	Massachuset	18936	289.2	4044	61.8	
24	Michigan	27111	274.3	6880	69.6	
25	Minnesota	14770	278.5	2612	49.2	
26	Mississippi	6473	218.1	1992	67.1	
27	Missouri	19175	320.2	3920	65.5	
28	Montana	3108	314.1	392	39.6	
29	Nebraska	5005	274.0	860	47.1	
30	Nevada	10757	398.3	2423	89.7	
31	New Hampshi	4702	357.2	503	38.2	
32	New Jersey	27227	309.7	6807	77.4	
33	New Mexico	6053	294.0	1773	86.1	
34	New York	52113	268.9	16494	85.1	
35	North Carol	27415	287.5	5986	62.8	
36	North Dakot	1235	183.6	199	29.6	
37	Ohio	32847	284.7	6844	59.3	
38	Oklahoma	10038	267.6	2234	59.6	
39	Oregon	13508	352.6	2256	58.9	

Figure 11.4   Creating an R-Friendly Excel Spreadsheet

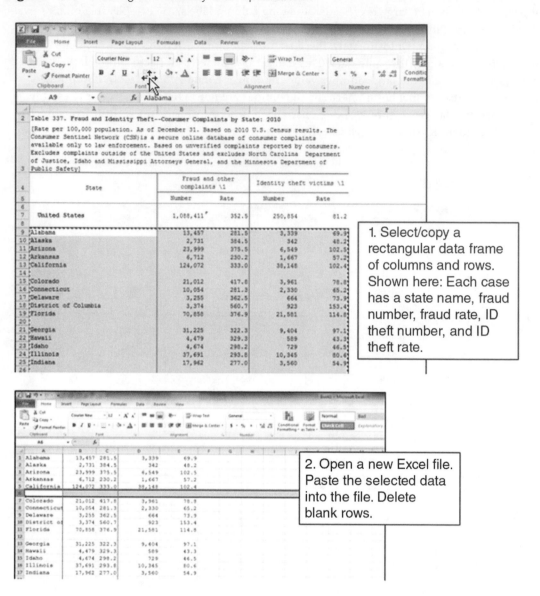

1. Select/copy a rectangular data frame of columns and rows. Shown here: Each case has a state name, fraud number, fraud rate, ID theft number, and ID theft rate.

2. Open a new Excel file. Paste the selected data into the file. Delete blank rows.

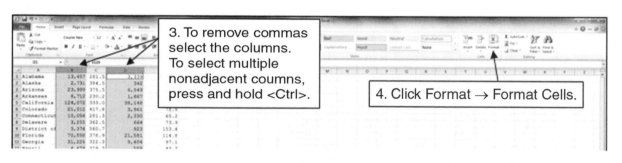

3. To remove commas select the columns. To select multiple nonadjacent coumns, press and hold <Ctrl>.

4. Click Format → Format Cells.

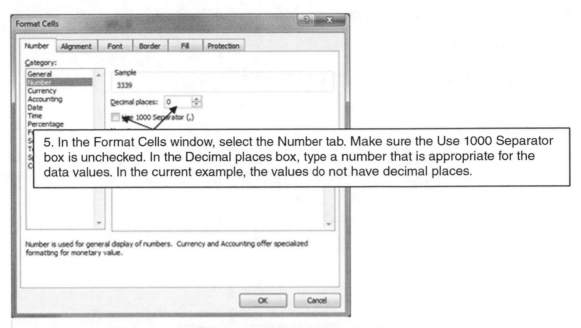

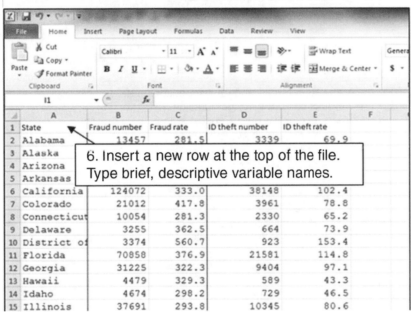

1. Select the desired data columns and rows. Make sure that the data selection is rectangular—that each row contains the same number of columns.

2. Open a blank Excel worksheet. Paste the selected data into the new file. To delete blank rows, select the row, right-click, and click on Delete.

3. To remove commas from data values, select the columns. To select multiple nonadjacent columns, press and hold <Ctrl>.

4. Click Format→Format Cells.

5. In the Format Cells window, click on the Number tab. Make sure that the Use 1000 Separator box is unchecked. (Excel may already have unchecked the box.) In Decimal places, type an appropriate value. In the example, the numbers we are re-formatting do not have decimal places, so a value of 0 is appropriate.

6. Insert a new row at the top of the data file. To accomplish this, select the current top row (the data line for Alabama), right-click, and click on Insert. Type descriptive variable names at the top of each column.

To import an R-friendly Excel file, follow these steps, as illustrated in Figure 11.5.

Figure 11.5 Converting and Importing an Excel File

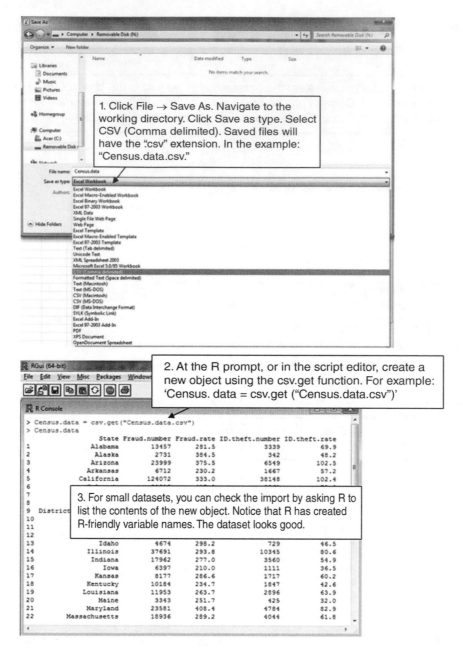

1. Click File→Save As. Navigate to the working directory. Click the "Save as type" drop-down and select CSV (Comma delimited). Comma delimited files use the ".csv" extension.

2. At the R prompt, or in the script editor, create a new object using the csv.get function:

```
# Read dataset in Stata format
this.dataset = csv.get("name_of_dataset.csv")


# applied to example
census.data = csv.get("Census.data.csv")
```

3. Check the import by typing the new object's name. The import worked as planned.

HTML Datasets

As we have just seen, once you get data into Excel format and make them R-friendly, you can convert the data to .csv and import them into R. If the data are in html format, it is usually a relatively simple matter to copy/paste into Excel. Note, however, that the HTML-to-Excel procedure works best with Internet Explorer, but it may not work consistently with Mozilla Firefox or Google Chrome. By way of illustration, consider the Freedom House's Freedom on the Net 2016 Scores for 65 countries around the world. This table offers an interval-level measurement of Internet freedom based on obstacles to access, limits on content, and violation of user rights. It would make an interesting variable for political science research.

Figure 11.6 Importing Data in HTML Format

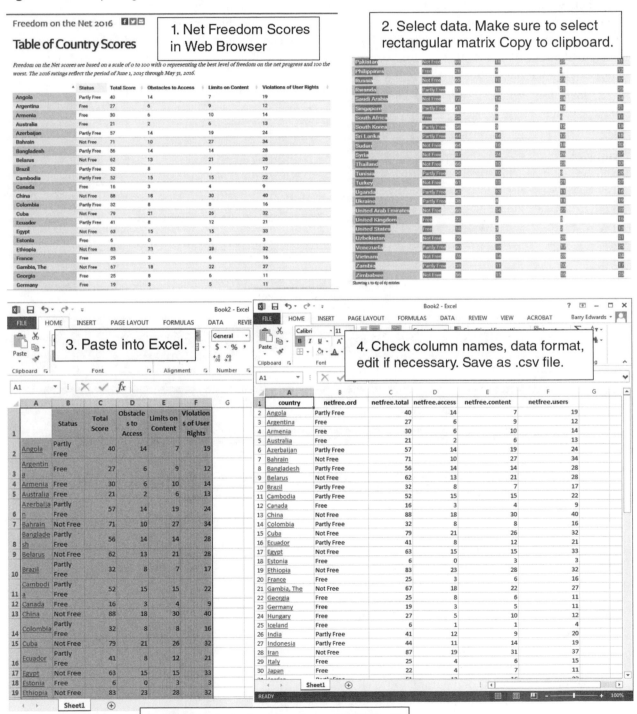

As shown in Figure 11.6, to convert this table to an R-friendly format, we would select the data, copy it to the clipboard, and paste it into Excel. Once in Excel, check the first row which should contain the variable names. Verify that the variable names are properly aligned and have acceptable variable names. You may want to shorten variable names and eliminate white spaces. Also, make sure numbers in your spreadsheet are rendered as numeric values, rather than text; if large numbers have separating commas, you'll want to remove the separating commas at this stage. Finally, save the dataset as a .csv file in the working directory and use csv.get to import it into R.

PDF Format or Hand-Coded Data

By now it is clear that, unless you luck into SPSS or Stata data, an Excel-to-.csv conversion is your best bet. So, when your data are in paper-and-pencil form (a stack of completed questionnaires, for example), you would code the data into Excel, convert to .csv, and then import into R. Similarly, if you find interesting data in hard copy or PDF format, you can code the data into Excel and follow the steps described above. We close this section with a few pointers for direct-coding data, using an especially unfriendly PDF file to illustrate.

Figure 11.7 displays a partial web page from the Americans for Democratic Action (ADA) website, which reports ratings of the 2011 Senate.

Figure 11.7 Sample Data in PDF Format

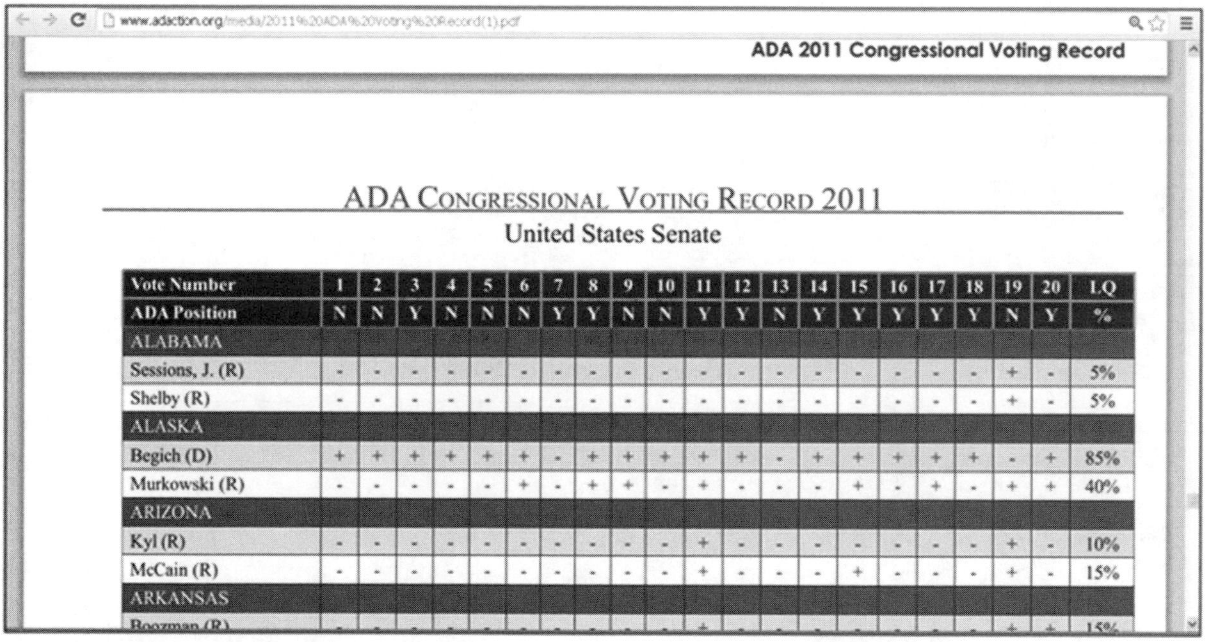

ADA CONGRESSIONAL VOTING RECORD 2011

United States Senate

Vote Number	1	2	3	4	5	6	7	8	9	10	11	12	13	14	15	16	17	18	19	20	LQ
ADA Position	N	N	Y	N	N	N	Y	Y	N	N	Y	Y	N	Y	Y	Y	Y	Y	N	Y	%
ALABAMA																					
Sessions, J. (R)	-	-	-	-	-	-	-	-	-	-	-	-	-	-	-	-	-	-	+	-	5%
Shelby (R)	-	-	-	-	-	-	-	-	-	-	-	-	-	-	-	-	-	-	+	-	5%
ALASKA																					
Begich (D)	+	+	+	+	+	+	-	+	+	+	+	+	-	+	+	+	+	+	-	+	85%
Murkowski (R)	-	-	-	-	-	+	-	+	+	-	+	-	-	-	+	-	+	-	+	+	40%
ARIZONA																					
Kyl (R)	-	-	-	-	-	-	-	-	-	-	+	-	-	-	-	-	-	-	+	-	10%
McCain (R)	-	-	-	-	-	-	-	-	-	-	+	-	-	-	+	-	-	-	+	-	15%
ARKANSAS																					
Boozman (R)	-	-	-	-	-	-	-	-	-	-	+	-	-	-	-	-	-	-	+	+	15%

The ADA is a liberal group that uses a series of key votes to rate members of congress, awarding a plus sign (+) for a liberal vote and a minus sign (–) for a conservative vote. In 2011, the ADA monitored 20 key votes, denoted by the numbers 1 through 20 on the web page. Elsewhere on the ADA site, we find that the first key vote involved repeal of an important health care provision. Because the ADA opposed repeal, any senator who voted for the legislation is coded as "–", and those opposed are coded "+". To the right of the page, we find ADA's overall liberalism score for 2011, under the heading "LQ," which stands for "Liberal Quotient." ADA arrives at the Liberal Quotient by determining the percentage of votes on which the senator supported ADA's position. Scores can range from 0% (most conservative) to 100% (most liberal). How would you take the information from this site and put it into Excel?

Here, in raw form, is the fourth data line, for Senator Murkowski of Alaska:

Murkowski (R) - - - - - + - + + - + - - - + - + - + + 40%

Figure 11.8 Editing PDF Data to R-Friendly Format

Sessions, J. (R) - - - - - - - - - - - - - - - - - - + - 5%
Shelby (R) - - - - - - - - - - - - - - - - - - + - 5%

Begich (D) + + + + + + - + + + + + - + + + + + - + 85%
Murkowski (R) - - - - - + - + + - + - - - + - + - + + 40%

Kyl (R) - - - - - - - - - - + - - - - - - - + - 10%
McCain (R) - - - - - - - - - - + - - - + - - - + - 15%

Boozman (R) - - - - - - - - - - + - - - - - - - + + 15%
Pryor (D) + ? + + - + + + + - + + - + + - + + + + 75%

> 1. Copy/paste from the Web page.

> 2. Use Find/Replace to clean up the data and convert symbols to numerics. For missing data, use "NA," as in Senator Pryor's data line.

Sessions R 0 0 0 0 0 0 0 0 0 0 0 0 0 0 0 0 0 1 0 5
Shelby R 0 0 0 0 0 0 0 0 0 0 0 0 0 0 0 0 0 1 0 5
Begich D 1 1 1 1 1 1 0 1 1 1 1 1 0 1 1 1 1 1 0 1 85
Murkowski R 0 0 0 0 0 1 0 1 1 0 1 0 0 0 1 0 1 0 1 1 40
Kyl R 0 0 0 0 0 0 0 0 0 1 0 0 0 0 0 0 0 1 0 10
McCain R 0 0 0 0 0 0 0 0 0 1 0 0 0 1 0 0 0 1 0 15
Boozman R 0 0 0 0 0 0 0 0 0 1 0 0 0 0 0 0 0 1 1 15
Pryor D 1 NA 1 1 0 1 1 1 1 0 1 1 0 1 1 0 1 1 1 1 75

Sessions R 0 0 0 0 0 0 0 0 0 0 0 0 0 0 0 0 0 1 0 5
Shelby R 0 0 0 0 0 0 0 0 0 0 0 0 0 0 0 0 0 1 0 5
Begich D 1 1 1 1 1 1 0 1 1 1 1 1 0 1 1 1 1 1 0 1 85
Murkowski R 0 0 0 0 0 1 0 1 1 0 1 0 0 0 1 0 1 0 1 1 40
Kyl R 0 0 0 0 0 0 0 0 0 1 0 0 0 0 0 0 0 1 0 10
McCain R 0 0 0 0 0 0 0 0 0 1 0 0 0 1 0 0 0 1 0 15
Boozman R 0 0 0 0 0 0 0 0 0 1 0 0 0 0 0 0 0 1 1 15
Pryor D 1 NA 1 1 0 1 1 1 1 0 1 1 0 1 1 0 1 1 1 1 75

> 3. Select the clean text. Click Insert → Table → Convert Text to Table. In the bottom panel, click Other and type a blank space in the box. Click OK.

Sessions	R	0	0	0	0	0	0	0	0	0	0	0	0	0	0	0	0	0	1	0	5
Shelby	R	0	0	0	0	0	0	0	0	0	0	0	0	0	0	0	0	0	1	0	5
Begich	D	1	1	1	1	1	1	0	1	1	1	1	1	0	1	1	1	1	1	0	1	85
Murkowski	R	0	0	0	0	0	1	0	1	1	0	1	0	0	0	1	0	1	0	1	1	40
Kyl	R	0	0	0	0	0	0	0	0	0	1	0	0	0	0	0	0	0	1	0	10
McCain	R	0	0	0	0	0	0	0	0	0	1	0	0	0	1	0	0	0	1	0	15
Boozman	R	0	0	0	0	0	0	0	0	0	1	0	0	0	0	0	0	0	1	1	15
Pryor	D	1	NA	1	1	0	1	1	1	1	0	1	1	0	1	1	0	1	1	1	1	75

> 4. Copy/paste the table's cells directly into Excel.

Virtually every data value in this line of code is unreadable by R. If you were coding this data into Excel, you would first want to convert all the values, except the senators' names and their party affiliations, to numbers. An intuitive scheme might be to code minus signs as 0's and plus signs as 1's, and to remove the symbol "%" from the LQ scores. Here is Senator Murkowski's information, converted to numbers:

Murkowski R 0 0 0 0 0 1 0 1 1 0 1 0 0 0 1 0 1 0 1 1 40

Once the coding protocol is established, you could type the data directly into Excel. However, a more efficient approach is to enlist Word's substantial editing power to clean up the text data and convert the text to a table, as demonstrated in Figure 11.8.

1. Copy/paste from the web page to a Word document.

2. Use Find/Replace to delete unwanted characters, such as the parentheses around party affiliation. Find unreadable symbols, such as "+", and replace with numeric, such as "1". Make sure every column entry has a value. For missing data, type "NA".

3. Select the cleaned up text. Click Insert→Table→Convert Text to Table. In the bottom panel, click Other and type a blank space in the box. Word puts the text data into table format.

4. Copy/paste from the Word table directly into Excel.

Once you are in Excel, you are on familiar terrain.

WRITING IT UP

Several of the datasets described thus far would provide great raw material for analysis. After inputting your data, you can let the creative juices flow—describing the variables, performing cross-tabulation and mean comparison analyses, running linear regression and logistic regression models. Rewarding findings are guaranteed. Yet at some point the analysis ends, and the writing must begin. It is at this point, as well, that two contradictory considerations often collide. On one hand, you have an embarrassment of riches. You have worked on your research for several weeks, and you know the topic well—better, perhaps, than does anyone who will read the paper. There may be a large amount of material that you want to include in your paper. On the other hand, you want to get it written, and you do not want to write a book. Viewed from an instructor's perspective, the two questions most frequently asked by students are "How should my paper be organized?" and "How long should it be?" (The questions are not necessarily asked in this order.)

Of course, different projects and instructors might call for different requirements. But the following is a rough outline for a well-organized paper of 16–24 double-spaced pages (in 12-point font).

    I. The research question (3–4 pages)

        A. Introduction to the problem (1 page)

        B. Theory and process (1–2 pages)

        C. Propositions (1 page)

   II. Previous research (2–4 pages)

        A. Descriptive review (1–2 pages)

        B. Critical review (1–2 pages)

  III. Data and hypotheses (3–4 pages)

        A. Data and variables (1–2 pages)

        B. Measurement (1 page)

        C. Hypotheses (1 page)

  IV. Analysis (5–8 pages, including tables)

        A. Descriptive statistics (1–2 pages)

        B. Bivariate comparisons (2–3 pages)

        C. Controlled comparisons (2–3 pages)

   V. Conclusions and implications (3–4 pages)

       A. Summary of findings (1 page)

       B. Implications for theory (1–2 pages)

       C. New issues or questions (1 page)

The Research Question

Because of its rhetorical challenges, the opening section of a paper is often the most difficult to write. In this section, the writer must both engage the reader's interest and describe the purpose of the research. Here is a heuristic device that may be useful: In the first page of the write-up, place the specific research problem in the context of larger, clearly important issues or questions. For example, suppose your research is centered on the landmark healthcare legislation passed by Congress in 2010. A narrowly focused topic? Yes. A dry topic? Not at all. The opening page of this paper could frame larger questions about the sometimes conflicting roles of congressional party leadership and constituency interests in shaping the behavior of representatives and senators. Thus your analysis will advance our knowledge by illuminating one facet of a larger, more complex question.

Following the introduction, begin to zero in on the problem at hand. The "theory and process" section describes the logic of the relationships you are studying. Many political phenomena, as you have learned, have competing or alternative explanations. You should describe these alternatives, and the tension between them, in this section. Although a complete description of previous research does not appear in this section, you should give appropriate attribution to the most prominent work. These references tie your work to the scholarly community, and they raise the points you will cover in a more detailed review.

You should round out the introductory section of your paper with a brief statement of purpose or intent. Think about it from the reader's perspective. Thus far, you have made the reader aware of the larger context of the analysis, and you have described the process that may explain the relationships of interest. If this process has merit, then it should submit to an empirical test of some kind. What test do you propose? The "Propositions" page serves this role. Here you set the parameters of the research—informing the reader about the units of analysis, the concepts to be measured, and the type of analysis to be performed.

Previous Research

Here you provide an intellectual history of the research problem, a description and critique of the published research on which the analysis is based. You first would describe these previous analyses in some detail. What data and variables were used? What were the main findings? Did different researchers arrive at different conclusions? Political scientists who share a research interest often agree on many things. Yet knowledge is nourished through criticism, and in reviewing previous work you will notice key points of disagreement—about how concepts should be measured, what are the best data to use, or which variables need to be controlled. In the latter part of this section of the paper, you would review these points and perhaps contribute to the debate. A practical point: The frequently asked question "How many articles and books should be reviewed?" has no set answer. It depends on the project. However, here is an estimate: A well-grounded yet manageable review should discuss at least four references.

Data, Hypotheses, and Analysis

Together, the sections "Data and Hypotheses" and "Analysis" form the heart of the project, and they have been the primary concerns of this book. By now you are well versed in how to describe your data and variables and how to frame hypotheses. You also know how to set up a cross-tabulation or mean comparison table, and you can make controlled comparisons and interpret your findings.

In writing these sections, however, you should bear in mind a few reader-centered considerations. First, assume that the reader might want to replicate your study—collect the data you gathered, define and measure the concepts as you have defined and measured them, manipulate the variables just as you have computed and recoded them, and produce the tables you have reported. By explaining precisely what you did, your write-up should provide a clear guide for such a replication. Second, devote some space to a statistical description of the variables. Often you can add depth and interest to your analysis by briefly presenting the frequency distributions of the variables, particularly the dependent variable. Finally, exercise care in constructing readable tables. You can select, copy, and paste the tables generated by SPSS directly into a word processor, but they always require further editing for readability.

Conclusions and Implications

No section of a research paper can write itself. But the final section comes closest to realizing this optimistic hope. Here you discuss the analysis on three levels. First, you provide a condensed recapitulation. What are the main findings? Are the hypotheses borne out? Were there any unexpected findings? Second, you describe where the results fit in the larger fabric of scholarly research on the topic. In what ways are the findings consistent with the work of previous researchers? Does your analysis lend support to one scholarly perspective as opposed to another? Third, research papers often include obligatory "suggestions for further research." Indeed, you might have encountered some methodological problems that still must be worked out, or you might have unearthed a noteworthy substantive relationship that could bear future scrutiny. You should describe these new issues or questions. Here, too, you are allowed some room to speculate—to venture beyond the edge of the data and engage in a little "What if?" thinking. After all, the truth is still out there.

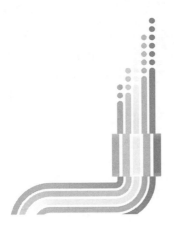

Appendix

Table A.1 Alphabetical List of Variables in the GSS Dataset

Variable Name	Description
abany	Abortion Permissible: Woman Wants For Any Reason
abdefect	Abortion Permissible: Strong Chance of Serious Defect
abhlth	Abortion Permissible: Woman's Health Seriously Endangered
abnomore	Abortion Permissible: Woman Married–Wants No More Children
abortion	Under How Many Conditions Abortion Permissible?
abortion_3	Under How Many Conditions Abortion Permissible? 3 Categories
abpoor	Abortion Permissible: Low Income–Can't Afford More Children
abrape	Abortion Permissible: Pregnant as Result of Rape
absingle	Abortion Permissible: Not Married
affrmact	Favor Preference in Hiring Blacks
affrmact2	Support Affirmative Action?
age	Respondent's Age
age.f	Respondent's Age (as Ordered Factor)
age2	Respondent's Age: 2 Categories
age_3	Age Group: 3 Categories
age_5	Age Group: 5 Categories
attend	How Often Respondent Attends Religious Services
attend2	Attendance at Religious Services: Low or High
attend3	Attendance at Religious Services: 3 Categories
attend7	Attendance at Religious Services: 7 Categories

(Continued)

Table A.1   (Continued)

Variable Name	Description
authoritarianism	Authoritarianism Scale
bible	Feelings about the Bible
black	Is Respondent African American?
black_traits	Black stereotypes, numeric scale. Positive values indicate positive stereotypes (hardworking and intelligent).
born	Was Respondent Born in This Country
cappun	Favor or Oppose Death Penalty for Murder
childs	Number of Children
closeblk	How Close Do You Feel to Blacks?
closeblk2	How Close Do You Feel to Blacks? 2 Categories
closewht	How Close Do You Feel to Whites?
closewht2	How Close Do You Feel to Whites? 2 Categories
cohort	Year of Birth
colath	College Teaching: Allow Anti-Religionist to Teach
colcom	College Teaching: Should Communist Teacher Be Fired
colhomo	College Teaching: Allow Homosexual to Teach
colmil	College Teaching: Allow Militarist to Teach
colmslm	College Teaching: Allow Anti-American Muslim Clergymen to Teach
colrac	College Teaching: Allow Racist to Teach
con_govt	Confidence in Government Institutions
conarmy	Confidence in Military
conbus	Confidence in Major Companies
conclerg	Confidence in Organized Religion
coneduc	Confidence in Education
confed	Confidence in Exec Branch of Fed Government
confinan	Confidence in Banks & Financial Institutions
conjudge	Confidence in United States Supreme Court
conlabor	Confidence in Organized Labor
conlegis	Confidence in Congress
conmedic	Confidence in Medicine
conpress	Confidence in Press
consci	Confidence in Scientific Community
contv	Confidence in Television
courts	Courts Dealing with Criminals

Variable Name	Description
dateintv	Date of Interview
degree	Respondent's Highest Degree
dem	Is Respondent a Democrat?
divlaw	Divorce Laws
divlaw2	Should Divorce Laws Make It More Difficult?
educ	Highest Year of School
educ_2	Education: 2 Categories
educ_4	Education: 4 Categories
egalit_scale	Egalitarianism Scale
egalit_scale3	Egalitarianism: 3 Categories
egalit_scale4	Egalitarianism: 4 Categories
eqwlth	Should Government Reduce Income Differences?
ethnic	Country of Family Origin
evangelical	Evangelical Scale
fechld	Female Roles: Mother Working Doesn't Hurt Children
feelevel	Amount of Fees Paid (to Respondent for Interview)
feeused	Fee Given to Get Case (for the Interview)
fefam	Female Roles: Better for Man to Work, Woman Tend Home
femrole	Female Role (Scale of Values)
femrole2	Female Role: 2 Categories
fepresch	Female Roles: Preschool Kids Suffer If Mother Works
fucitzn	Is Respondent Planning/Applying for US Citizenship?
fund	How Fundamentalist Is Respondent Currently?
fund2	Is Respondent Fundamentalist?
getahead	Opinion of How People Get Ahead
god_r	Know God Exists?
grass	Should Marijuana Be Made Legal?
grass.legal	Should Marijuana Be Made Legal? (numeric)
gunlaw	Favor or Oppose Gun Permits?
happy	General Happiness
helpblk	Should Government Aid Blacks?
helpnot	Should Government Do More or Less?
helpoth	To Help Others
helppoor	Should Government Improve Standard of Living?

(Continued)

Table A.1 (Continued)

Variable Name	Description
helpsick	Should Government Help Pay for Medical Care?
hhtype1	Household Type (Condensed)
hispanic	Hispanic Specified
hispanic_2	Is Respondent Hispanic?
homosex	Homosexual Sex Relations
homosex2	Homosexuality Always Wrong?
id	Respondent Id Number
income06	Total Family Income
int_info_scale	Interest in Current Issues? (Additive Index)
intage	Interviewer: Age of Interviewer
intecon	Interested in Economic Issues?
inteduc	Interested in Local School Issues?
intenvir	Interested in Environmental Issues?
intethn	Interviewer: Race of Interviewer
intethn_2	Interviewer: Interviewer's Race
intfarm	Interested in Farm Issues?
inthisp	Interviewer: Is Interviewer Spanish, Hispanic, or Latino
intintl	Interested in International Issues?
intmed	Interested in Medical Discoveries?
intmil	Interested in Military Policy?
intrace1	Interviewer: Interviewer's Race1
intrace2	Interviewer: Interviewer's Race2
intrace3	Interviewer: Interviewer's Race3
intsci	Interested in New Scientific Discoveries?
intsex	Interviewer: Sex of Interviewer
intspace	Interested in Space Exploration?
inttech	Interested in Technologies?
intyrs	Interviewer: Years of Service as an Interviewer at NORC
kids	Does Respondent Have Kids?
libath	Allow Anti-Religious Book in Library?
libcom	Allow Communist's Book in Library?
libhomo	Allow Homosexual's Book in Library?
libmil	Allow Militarist's Book in Library?
libmslm	Allow Anti-American Muslim Clergymen's Book in Library?

Variable Name	Description
librac	Allow Racist's Book in Library?
lngthinv	How Long Was Interview
marital	Marital Status
militarist_tol	Tolerance toward Militarists
mobile16	Geographic Mobility since Age 16
mode	Interview Done in Person or over the Phone
mslm_col	Muslims: Teach in College?
mslm_lib	Muslims: Book in Library?
mslm_spk	Muslims: Preach?
mslm_spk.yes	Muslims: Preach? (as numeric)
mslm_spk.high	Muslims: Preach? (as numeric)
nataid	Federal Spending: Foreign Aid
natarms	Federal Spending: Military, Armaments, and Defense
natchld	Federal Spending: Assistance for Childcare
natcity	Federal Spending: Solving Problems of Big Cities
natcrime	Federal Spending: Halting Rising Crime Rate
natdrug	Federal Spending: Dealing with Drug Addiction
nateduc	Federal Spending: Improving Nation's Education System
natenrgy	Federal Spending: Developing Alternative Energy Sources
natenvir	Federal Spending: Improving & Protecting Environment
natfare	Federal Spending: Welfare
natheal	Federal Spending: Improving & Protecting Nation's Health
natmass	Federal Spending: Mass Transportation
natpark	Federal Spending: Parks and Recreation
natrace	Federal Spending: Improving the Conditions of Blacks
natroad	Federal Spending: Highways and Bridges
natsci	Federal Spending: Supporting Scientific Research
natsoc	Federal Spending: Social Security
natspac	Federal Spending: Space Exploration Program
news	How Often Does Respondent Read Newspaper
obey	To Obey
obey2	Obedience Important in Children?
owngun	Have Gun in Home
partyid	Political Party Affiliation

(Continued)

Table A.1 (Continued)

Variable Name	Description
partyid_3	Party Id: 3 Categories
polviews	Ideological Self-Placement
popular	Important for Child: To Be Well Liked or Popular
pornlaw	Feelings about Pornography Laws
pornlaw2	Pornography Opinion
postlife	Belief in Life after Death
pray	How Often Does Respondent Pray
premarsx	Sex before Marriage
pres08	Vote Obama or McCain
racdif1	Differences Due to Discrimination
racdif2	Differences Due to Inborn Disability
racdif3	Differences Due to Lack of Education
racdif4	Differences Due to Lack of Will
race	Race of Respondent
race_2	Race: Black/White
racial_liberal3	Racial Liberalism
reborn_r	Born Again?
region	Region of Interview
relig	Respondent's Religious Preference
reliten	Strength of Affiliation
reliten2	Strong Religious Affiliation
rincom06	Respondent Income
rincom06_5	Respondent Income: 5 Categories
savesoul_r	Tried to Convince Others of Jesus?
science_quiz	Number Correct on Science Quiz
sex	Respondent's Sex
sibs	Number of Brothers and Sisters
size	Size of Place in 1000s
social_connect	Social Connectedness
social_cons3	Social Conservatism
social_trust	Social Trust (Numeric Scale)
south	Respondent from South?
spanking	Favor Spanking to Discipline Child?
spanking2	Approve of Spanking

Variable Name	Description
spend3	Econ Liberalism
spkath	Allow Speaker in Your Community: Anti-Religionist
spkcom	Allow Speaker in Your Community: Communist
spkhomo	Allow Speaker in Your Community: Homosexual
spkmil	Allow Speaker in Your Community: Militarist
spkmslm	Allow Speaker in Your Community: Muslim Clergymen Preaching Hatred
spkrac	Allow Speaker in Your Community: Allow Racist to Speak
teensex	Sex before Marriage–Teens 14–16
thnkself	Important for Child: To Think For Oneself
tolerance	Tolerance Scale
tolerance4	Tolerance Scale (Binned)
tvhours	Hours per Day Watching TV
tvhours5	Hours per Day Watching TV, 5 Categories
union	Does Respondent or Spouse Belong to Union
uscitzn	Is Respondent US Citizen
vetyears	Years in Armed Forces
vote08_coded	Did Respondent Vote in 2008 Election
voted08	Did Respondent Vote in 2008
white_traits	White Stereotypes, numeric scale. Positive values indicate positive stereotypes (hardworking and intelligent).
wordsum	Number Words Correct in Vocabulary Test
workhard	To Work Hard
wrkgvt	Respondent Work for Government or Private Employee
wrkslf	Respondent Self-Employed or Work For Somebody
wrkstat	Labor Force Status
wrkwayup	Irish, Italian, Jewish, and Other Should Overcome Prejudice without Favors
wtss	Weight Variable
wtssall	Weight Variable (Same as wtss)
xmarsex	Sex With Person Other than Spouse
year	GSS Year for This Respondent
zodiac	Respondent's Astrological Sign

Notes: The GSS dataset used in this *R Companion to Political Analysis* comes from the 2012 General Social Survey. To find question wording for any GSS survey item, go to the University of California Berkeley's Survey Documentation and Analysis (SDA) website (http://sda.berkeley.edu/archive.htm) and follow the link for General Social Survey (GSS) Cumulative Datafile 1972–2012. For additional information on the General Social Survey, including further documentation, see http://gss.norc.org.

Table A.2 Alphabetical List of Variables in the NES Dataset

Variable Name	Description
abort_scale	Anti-abortion Scale
abort4	Abortion opinion: self-placement, 4 categories
abortpre_4point	Abortion opinion: self-placsement, 4 categories
aidblack_self	Support for government assistance to blacks scale, 7-point scale
auth_consid	Child trait more important: considerate or well-behaved
auth_cur	Child trait more important: curiosity or good manners
auth_ind	Child trait more important: independence or respect
auth_obed	Child trait more important: obedience or self-reliance
authoritarianism	Authoritarianism (4-point scale based on child trait questions)
black	Is respondent black?
budget_deficit_x	Favor reducing the federal budget deficit, 7-point scale
caseid	Case ID
casistart_iwrset4	Does respondent have a dog (Interview set-up test)
casistartpo_iwrset4	Does respondent have a dog (Interview set-up test)
cog_opin_x	Number of opinions respondent has compared to average person
congapp_job_x	Approval of Congress
congapp_jobst	Strength of approve/disapprove Congress handling its job
conservatism	Feeling thermometer conservatives minus feeling thermometer liberals
cses_closepty	Close to any political party?
cses_contct	Campaign mobilization: institutional contact
cses_email	Campaign mobilization: institutional contact—email
cses_ftf	Campaign mobilization: institutional contact—in person
cses_gotv	Respondent contacted by party/candidate?
cses_govtact	Support for government action income inequality (5-point scale)
cses_govtact_3	Government action on income inequality (3-point scale)
cses_mail	Campaign mobilization: institutional contact—by mail
cses_mobph	Campaign mobilization: sign up online information or alerts
cses_perseml	Campaign mobilization: personal contact—email
cses_persftf	Campaign mobilization: personal contact—in person
cses_persmail	Campaign mobilization: personal contact—by mail
cses_persph	Campaign mobilization: personal contact—by phone
cses_perstxt	Campaign mobilization: personal contact—text message
cses_persuade	Campaign mobilization: personal contact
cses_persweb	Campaign mobilization: personal contact—social network

Variable Name	Description
cses_phone	Campaign mobilization: institutional contact—by phone
cses_poliinffour	Political information—Secretary of the U.N.
cses_poliinfone	Political information—Secretary of the Treasury
cses_poliinfthree	Political information—party 2nd in House seats won
cses_polinf_x	Pol info scale
cses_polinftwo	Political information—unemployment rate
cses_polinftwo_date	Political information—date used for date of unemployment rate
cses_polinftwo_rate	Political information—number used for unemployment rate
cses_spending	Econ conservatism (numeric scale)
deathpen	Death penalty opinion
defsppr_self	Support for defense spending, 7-point scale
dem_age_group_r	Demographic: Age groups
dem_age3	Demographic: Age group
dem_age6	Demographic: Six age groups
dem_agegrp_iwdate	Demographic: Respondent age on interview date (age group)
dem_educ3	Demographic: Education
dem_edugroup	Demographic: Respondent level of highest education
dem_hisp	Demographic: Is respondent Spanish, Hispanic, or Latino
dem_marital	Demographic: Marital status
dem_parents	Demographic: Native status of parents
dem_racecps_black	Demographic: Race self-identification: mention Black
dem_racecps_racedkrf	Demographic: Race self-identification with don't know or refused to say
dem_racecps_white	Demographic: Race self-identification: mention White
dem_raceeth	Demographic: Respondent race and ethnicity group
dem_raceeth2	Demographic: White/Black
dem_raceeth4	Demographic: Respondent race and ethnicity group
dem_unionhh	Demographic: Anyone in household belong to labor union
dem_veteran	Demographic: Respondent ever served on active duty in armed forces
dem2_numchild	Demographic: Total number of children in household
dem3_ownhome	Demographic: Does respondent family own/rent home
dem3_yearscomm	Demographic: How many years has respondent lived in this community?
dhs_appterr_x	Homeland security: Approve/disapprove of efforts to reduce terrorism
dhs_attack	Homeland security: Likely terrorist attack kill 100/more in next year?
dhs_threat_x	Homeland security: Is fed. gov't a threat to rights and freedoms? (numeric scale)

(Continued)

Table A.2 (Continued)

Variable Name	Description
dhs_threat3	Homeland security: Is fed. gov't a threat to rights and freedoms?
dhs_torture_x	Homeland security: Favor/oppose torture for suspected terrorists
dhsinvolv_board	Civic engagement: Has respondent in past 4 years: attended city/school board meeting
dhsinvolv_call	Civic engagement: Has respondent in past 4 years: called radio/TV about political issue
dhsinvolv_contact1	Civic engagement: Contact U.S. representative or senator
dhsinvolv_letter	Civic engagement: written a letter to newspaper/magazine about political issue
dhsinvolv_march	Civic engagement: Has respondent joined a protest march
dhsinvolv_message	Civic engagement: sent Facebook/Twitter message about political issue
dhsinvolv_netpetition	Civic engagement: Has respondent in past 4 years: sign internet petition
dhsinvolv_org	Civic engagement: Has respondent in past 4 years: gave money to social/political organization
dhsinvolv_petition	Civic engagement: Has respondent signed paper petition
dhsinvolv_relig	Civic engagement: Has respondent in past 4 years: given money to religious organization
discrim_blacks	Discrimination: Amount against Blacks
discrim_blacks_r	Discrimination: Against Blacks? (yes/no)
discrim_gays	Discrimination: Amount against gays and lesbians?
discrim_gays_r	Discrimination: Against gays? (yes/no)
discrim_hispanics	Discrimination: Amount against Hispanics
discrim_hispanics_r	Discrimination: Against Hispanics? (yes/no)
discrim_scale	Discrimination: How much discrimination against Blacks, gays, Hispanics, women? (Sum of yes answers)
discrim_self	Discrimination: How much discrimination faced personally?
discrim_whites	Discrimination: Amount against Whites
discrim_women	Discrimination: Amount against Women
discrim_women_r	Discrimination: Against women? (yes/no)
discuss_disc	Ever discuss politics with family or friends
discuss_discpstwk	Days in past week discussed politics
ecblame_fmpr	Economy: How much is former president to blame for poor economy?
ecblame_pres	Economy: How much is president to blame for poor economy?
econ_ecnext_x	Economy: U.S. economy better or worse 1 year from now
econ_ecnextamt	Economy: How much better/worse next 12 months
econ_ecnow	Economy: Currently good or bad
econ_ecpast	Economy: Better/worse in last year

Variable Name	Description
econ_ecpast_x	Economy: Better or worse than 1 year ago
econ_ecpastamt	Economy: How much better/worse in last year
econ_unlast	Economy: How much unemployment better/worse in last year
econ_unnext	Economy: More/less unemployment in next year
econ_unpast	Economy: Unemployment better/worse in last year
econ_unpast_x	Economy: Unemployment better/worse than 1 year ago
econcand_dwin	Economy: Better/worse if Democratic presidential candidate wins
econcand_rwin	Economy: Better/worse if Republican presidential candidate wins
ecperil_home	How do you pay for your home?
effic_carerev	Political efficacy: Public officials don't care what people think
effic_carestd	Political efficacy: Public officials don't care what people think
effic_complicrev	Political efficacy: Politics/government too complicated to understand
effic_complicstd	Political efficacy: Politics/government too complicated to understand
effic_external	Political efficacy: External political efficacy (numeric scale)
effic_external3	Political efficacy: External political efficacy (3 categories)
effic_internal	Political efficacy: Internal political efficacy (numeric scale)
effic_internal3	Political efficacy: Internal political efficacy (3 categories)
effic_sayrev	Political efficacy: Have no say about what government does
effic_saystd	Political efficacy: Have no say about what government does
effic_undrev	Political efficacy: Good understanding of political issues
effic_undstd	Political efficacy: Good understanding of political issues
efficpo_bothside	Political efficacy: How often see both disagreeing parties as right
egal_bigprob	Equality: It's a big problem that we don't give equal chance to succeed
egal_equal	Equality: Society should make sure everyone has equal opportunity
egal_fewerprobs	Equality: If people were treated more fairly would be fewer problems
egal_notbigprob	Equality: Not a big problem if some have more chance in life
egal_scale	Equality: Egalitarianism (numeric scale)
egal_scale_3	Equality: Egalitarianism: 3 categories
egal_toofar	Equality: We have gone too far pushing equal rights
egal_worryless	Equality: We'd be better off if worried less about equality
envir_drill	Environment: Favor/oppose increased U.S. offshore drilling
envir_gwarm	Environment: Is global warming happening or not
envir_gwgood	Environment: Rising temperatures good or bad
envir_gwhow	Environment: Anthropogenic climate change

(Continued)

Table A.2 (Continued)

Variable Name	Description
envir_nuke	Environment: Should U.S. have more/fewer nuclear power plants
envjob_3	Environment: Environment or jobs more important?
envjob_self	Environment: 7-point scale environment-jobs tradeoff
fairjob_opin_x	Opinion about government ensuring fair jobs for blacks
fedspend_child	Federal budget increase/decrease: child care
fedspend_childr	Federal budget increase/decrease: child care (rev. scale)
fedspend_crime	Federal budget increase/decrease: crime control
fedspend_crimer	Federal budget increase/decrease: crime control (rev. scale)
fedspend_enviro	Federal budget increase/decrease: protecting environment
fedspend_enviror	Federal budget increase/decrease: protecting environment (rev. scale)
fedspend_poor	Federal budget increase/decrease: aid to the poor
fedspend_poorr	Federal budget increase/decrease: aid to the poor (rev. scale)
fedspend_scale	Federal spending scale (numeric scale, sum of increase responses)
fedspend_schools	Federal budget increase/decrease: public schools
fedspend_schoolsr	Federal budget increase/decrease: public schools (rev. scale)
fedspend_scitech	Federal budget increase/decrease: science and technology
fedspend_scitechr	Federal budget increase/decrease: science and technology (rev. scale)
fedspend_ss	Federal budget increase/decrease: Social Security
fedspend_ssr	Federal budget increase/decrease: Social Security (rev. scale)
fedspend_welfare	Federal budget increase/decrease: welfare programs
fedspend_welfarer	Federal budget increase/decrease: welfare programs (rev. scale)
fem3	Feeling about feminists (recode of ftgr_feminists into 3 categories)
finance_finfam	Financial situation: Respondent living with how many family members
finance_finnext_x	Financial situation: Better or worse off 1 year from now
finance_finpast_x	Financial situation: Better or worse off than 1 year ago
ft_dem	Feeling thermometer: Democratic Party
ft_dpc	Feeling thermometer: Democratic presidential candidate
ft_dvpc	Feeling thermometer: Democratic vice presidential candidate
ft_gwb	Feeling thermometer: G.W. Bush
ft_hclinton	Feeling thermometer: Hillary Clinton
ft_rep	Feeling thermometer: Republican Party
ft_rpc	Feeling thermometer: Republican presidential candidate
ft_rvpc	Feeling thermometer: Republican vice presidential candidate
ftcasi_asian	Feeling thermometer: Asian-Americans

Variable Name	Description
ftcasi_black	Feeling thermometer: Blacks
ftcasi_hisp	Feeling thermometer: Hispanics
ftcasi_illegal	Feeling thermometer: Illegal Immigrants
ftcasi_white	Feeling thermometer: Whites
ftf_oversample	Was respondent a 2012 time series oversample case?
ftgr_atheists	Feeling thermometer: Atheists
ftgr_bigbus	Feeling thermometer: Big business
ftgr_catholics	Feeling thermometer: Catholics
ftgr_congress	Feeling thermometer: Congress
ftgr_cons	Feeling thermometer: Conservatives
ftgr_fedgov	Feeling thermometer: Federal government
ftgr_fem3	Feeling thermometer: Feminists (3 categories)
ftgr_feminists	Feeling thermometer: Feminists
ftgr_gay	Feeling thermometer: Gay men and lesbians
ftgr_liberals	Feeling thermometer: Liberals
ftgr_middle	Feeling thermometer: Middle-class people
ftgr_military	Feeling thermometer: The military
ftgr_mormons	Feeling thermometer: Mormons
ftgr_muslims	Feeling thermometer: Muslims
ftgr_poor	Feeling thermometer: Poor people
ftgr_rich	Feeling thermometer: Rich people
ftgr_tea	Feeling thermometer: Tea Party
ftgr_unions	Feeling thermometer: Labor unions
ftgr_ussc	Feeling thermometer: The U.S. Supreme Court
ftgr_welfare	Feeling thermometer: People on welfare
ftgr_working	Feeling thermometer: Working-class people
ftgr_xfund	Feeling thermometer: Christian fundamentalists
ftgr_xian	Feeling thermometer: Christians
ftpo_dpcsp	Feeling thermometer: Spouse of Democratic presidential candidate
ftpo_dvpc	Feeling thermometer: Democratic vice presidential candidate
ftpo_hdc	Feeling thermometer: House Democratic candidate
ftpo_hoth	Feeling thermometer: House independent/3rd-party candidate
ftpo_hrc	Feeling thermometer: House Republican candidate
ftpo_pres	Feeling thermometer: Democratic presidential candidate

(Continued)

Table A.2 (Continued)

Variable Name	Description
ftpo_roberts	Feeling thermometer: John Roberts
ftpo_rpc	Feeling thermometer: Republican presidential candidate
ftpo_rpcsp	Feeling thermometer: Spouse of Republican presidential candidate
ftpo_rvpc	Feeling thermometer: Republican vice presidential candidate
ftpo_sdc	Feeling thermometer: Senate Democratic candidate
ftpo_senjr	Feeling thermometer: Jr. senator in state without race
ftpo_sennot	Feeling thermometer: Non-running senator in state w/race
ftpo_sensr	Feeling thermometer: Sr. senator in state without race
ftpo_soth	Feeling thermometer: Senate independent/3rd-party candidate
ftpo_src	Feeling thermometer: Senate Republican candidate
gay_adopt	Gay rights: gayrt_adopt==1. Yes
gay_disc	Gay rights: gayrt_discstd_x==1. Approve strongly
gay_marry	Gay rights: Approve same-sex marriage?
gay_mil	Gay rights: gayrt_milstd_x==1. Feel strongly that homosexuals should be allowed to serve
gay_rights3	Gay rights: Gay rights support (3 categories)
gayrt_adopt	Gay rights: Should gay and lesbian couples be allowed to adopt?
gayrt_discrev_x	Gay rights: favor laws against gays/lesbians job discrimination (rev.)
gayrt_discstd_x	Gay rights: favor laws against gays/lesbians job discrimination
gayrt_marry	Gay rights: Respondent position on gay marriage
gayrt_milrev_x	Gay rights: allow gays/lesbians serve in U.S. armed forces (reversed)
gayrt_milstd_x	Gay rights: allow gays/lesbians serve in U.S. armed forces
gender	Respondent's gender
govrole_scale	Pro-government scale (numeric scale)
guarpr_self	Should gov't guarantee a job and standard of living? (7-point scale)
gun_control	Gun control: Should federal gov't make it more difficult to buy a gun?
gun_control2	Gun control: Make it more difficult to buy a gun?
gun_importance	Gun control: Importance of gun access issue to R
gun_importance3	Gun control: How important is gun issue?
happ_lifesatisf	How satisfied is respondent with life?
health_2010hcr_x	Health care: Support 2010 health care law
health_insured	Health care: Does respondent have health insurance
health_self	Health care: Health of respondent
health_smoke	Health care: Smoked cigarettes

Variable Name	Description
health_smokeamt	Health care: If smoked, how many now
hispanic	Is respondent Hispanic?
hlthlaw_num	Health care: Health care law effect on number insured
hlthlaw_qual	Health care: Health care law effect on health care services
hseinc_approval	Congress: Approve or disapprove of House incumbent
hseinc_approval_x	Congress: House incumbent approval
hseinc_appstr	Congress: How much approve House incumbent
hseinc_disstr	Congress: How much disapprove House incumbent
hseinc_hinctouch	Congress: How good a job does House incumbent do in district
immig_checks	Immigration: Opinion on immigration status checks on suspects
immig_citizen	Immigration: Opinion on allowing citizenship to some illegal aliens
immig_policy	Immigration: U.S. government policy toward unauthorized immigrants
immigpo_jobs	Immigration: How likely immigration will take away jobs
immigpo_level	Immigration: What should immigration levels be
imports_limit	Favor or oppose limits on foreign imports
inc_incgroup_pre	Respondent's family income
incgroup_prepost	Respondent's family income
income5	Respondent's income quintile
indifference	Indifference scale
ineq_incgap_x	Income gap size compared to 20 years ago
ineqinc_ineqgb	Is increased income inequality in U.S. good?
ineqinc_ineqreduc	Does respondent favor/oppose government reducing income inequality?
inspre_self	Health care: Should care be insured by government or by private medical insurance? (7-point scale)
involv_contact	Involvement in politics: Contact congress?
involv_message	Involvement in politics: post political message?
involv_numorgs_4	Involvement in politics: Number of group memberships
involv_org	Involvement in politics: Give money to political organization?
involv_petition	Involvement in politics: Sign net petition?
involv_voltr	Involvement in politics: Has respondent done any volunteer work in past 12 months?
israel_support	Is U.S. too supportive of Israel or not supportive enough
knowl_housemaj	Political knowledge: Know party with most members in House?
knowl_senmaj	Political knowledge: Know party with most members in Senate?
libcon3	Respondent's political ideology (3 categories)

(Continued)

Table A.2 (Continued)

Variable Name	Description
libcpo_self	Respondent's political ideology (7-point scale)
libcpre_ptyd	Ideological placement of Democrats (7-point scale)
libcpre_ptyr	Ideological placement of Republicans (7-point scale)
libcpre_rpc	Ideological placement of Republican pres. candidate (7-point scale)
libcpre_self	Respondent's political ideology (7-point scale)
libcpre_self_x	Respondent's political ideology (7-point scale)
link_black_scale	Linked fate: blacks
link_hisp_scale	Linked fate: Hispanics
link_oth_scale	Linked fate: other people
link_white_scale	Linked fate: whites
link_wom_scale	Linked fate: women
mobilpo_x	Campaign mobilization: Respondent contacted by party, candidates, GOTV (numeric scale)
mode	Mode of interview (face-to-face or internet)
modsex_disc	Sex discrimination: How much job discrimination against women
modsex_discamt	Sex discrimination: Discrimination against women
modsex_media_x	Sex discrimination: How much attention media should pay to discrimination against women
modsex_oppor_x	Sex discrimination: Opportunities compared for women and men
modsex_prob	Sex discrimination: Do women complaining about discrimination cause more problems
modsex_scale	Sex discrimination: Modern sexism
modsex_special	Sex discrimination: Do women demanding equality seek special favors
modsex_wommore	Sex discrimination: How much more opportunities do women have
mormon_xn	Mormon a Christian religion?
nesw	Sampling weights: Weight variable
nesw_rnd	Sampling weights: Weight variable (rounded)
obama_therm	Obama rating
obama_vote	Respondent vote for Obama?
orientn_knowgay	Sexual orientation of family and friends
orientn_rgay	Respondent's sexual orientation
own_dog	Does respondent own a dog?
owngun_owngun	Does respondent own a gun
patriot_amident	Patriotism: Important being American
patriot_flag	Patriotism: Emotion seeing flag fly

Variable Name	Description
patriot_love	Patriotism: Love of country
patriotism	Patriotism scale
penalty_dpenstr	Strength respondent favors/opposes death penalty
penalty_favdpen	Respondent favor/oppose death penalty
penalty_favopp_x	Favor death penalty?
pid_3	Party identification, 3 categories
pid_x	Party identification, 7 categories
polknow_combined	Political knowledge: Number political facts correct
polknow3	Political knowledge, 3 categories
postvote_presvt	Did respondent vote for president
postvote_presvtwho	For whom did respondent vote for president
postvote_rvote	Did respondent vote in the November general election
postvote_votehs	Did respondent vote for U.S. House of Representatives
pot_legal	Should marijuana be legal?
pot_legal3	Legalize marijuana?
preknow_leastsp	Political knowledge: Program that federal gov't spends the least on
preknow_medicare	Political knowledge: What is Medicare
preknow_prestimes	Political knowledge: Number of times president can be elected
preknow_senterm	Political knowledge: Years senator elected
preknow_sizedef	Political knowledge: Size of federal deficit
preknow3	Political knowledge, 3 categories
pres_econ	Presidential approval: Handling of economy (Recode of presapp_econ)
pres_vote12	Respondent's vote in 2012 presidential election
presapp_econ_x	Presidential approval: Handling of economy
presapp_foreign	Presidential approval: Handling of foreign relations
presapp_foreign_x	Presidential approval: Handling of foreign relations
presapp_health_x	Presidential approval: Handling of health care
presapp_job_x	Presidential approval: Handling of job
presapp_scale	Presidential approval scale
presapp_war_x	Presidential approval: Handling of war in Afghanistan
presvote2012_2	Respondent's vote in 2012 presidential election
presvote2012_x	Respondent's vote in 2012 presidential election
preswin_care	Care who wins presidential election
preswin_dutychoice_x	Does respondent consider voting as duty/choice

(Continued)

Table A.2 (Continued)

Variable Name	Description
prevote_primv	Did respondent vote in the presidential primary or caucus
prevote_primvwho	Which candidate did respondent vote for in pres. primary or caucus
prochoice_scale	Abortion: Pro-choice scale
relig_4cat	Religion: Catholic, other Christian, other, or not religious?
relig_attend	Religion: Attend services
relig_attend3	Religion: Attend services
relig_bornagn	Religion: Does Christian respondent consider self born-again?
relig_guide	Religion: Provides guidance in day-to-day living
relig_imp	Religion: Important to respondent?
relig_imp2	Religion: Important to respondent?
relig_import	Religion: Important part of respondent's life
relig_pray	Religion: How often does respondent pray
relig_wordgod	Religion: Is Bible word of God or men
resent_deserve	Black community: Agree/disagree blacks have gotten less than deserve
resent_racial_scale	Black community: Racial conservatism scale
resent_slavery	Black community: Agree/disagree past slavery make life more difficult
resent_try	Black community: Agree/disagree blacks must try harder to get ahead
resent_workway	Black community: Agree/disagree that blacks should work way up without special favors
rvote2012_x	Did respondent vote in November general election?
sample_district	Respondent's congressional district (in 113th U.S. Congress)
sample_ftfpsu	Sample strata: Primary sampling unit for face-to-face cases
sample_state	State of respondent address
science_use	How often should gov't use scientific methods to solve problems?
scourt_elim_x	Should the Supreme Court be done away with?
scourt_remove_x	Should it be possible to remove Supreme Court justices?
south	Respondent from South?
spsrvpr_ssself	Support for government services/spending (7-point scale)
strata_ftf	Sample strata for face-to-face sample component
strata_full	Sample strata for full sample
tarp_favopp_x	Favor the TARP program?
tea_supp_x	Tea Party support
trad_adjust	Traditional values: Agree/disagree world is changing we should adjust
trad_famval	Traditional values: Agree/disagree that more emphasis needed on traditional family values

Variable Name	Description
trad_lifestyle	Traditional values: Agree/disagree are newer lifestyles are breaking down society
trad_tolerant	Traditional values: Agree/disagree that one should be more tolerant of other moral standards
trad_values_scale	Traditional values: Moral traditionalism scale
trust_social	Trust: How often can people be trusted?
trustgov_bigintrst	Trust: Is government run by a few big interests or for benefit of all?
trustgov_corrpt	Trust: How many in government are corrupt?
trustgov_trustgrev	Trust: How often trust gov't in Wash to do what is right? (reversed)
trustgov_trustgstd	Trust: How often trust government in Wash to do what is right?
trustgov_waste	Trust: Does government waste much tax money?
trustgvpo_crook	Trust: How many in government are crooked?
usworld_stay	International relations: Country better off if we just stayed home
usworld_stronger	International relations: During last year, U.S. position in world is weaker/stronger/same?
version	ANES 2012 time series release version
voted2008	Did respondent vote for president in 2008? (Recode of interest_voted2008)
voted2012	Did respondent vote in 2012?
voter_type	Voter type (non, new, voter)
weight_ftf	Post-stratified weight for face-to-face cases, preliminary
weight_full	Post-stratified weight for full sample, preliminary release
weight_web	Post-stratified weight for web cases, preliminary release
white	Is respondent white?
wiretap_warrant	Wiretaps: Favor or oppose authority to wiretap terrorism suspects?
wiretappo_toofar	Wiretaps: Has government power gone too far?
women_bond_x	Working women: Harder to establish bond with child?
women_role	Working women: Women's role (numeric scale)
women_role_2	Working women: Women's role at home or work?
women_works_x	Working women: Better if man works and woman takes care of home and family?
wpres_gdbd_x	How good/bad to have woman president in next 20 years?
wt	Sampling weight
year	ANES year

Notes: The NES dataset used in this *R Companion to Political Analysis* comes from the 2012 American National Election Study 2012 Time Series. To find question wording for any NES survey item, go to the University of California Berkeley's Survey Documentation and Analysis (SDA) website http://sda.berkeley.edu/archive.htm/ and follow the link for American National Election Study 2012. For additional information on the study, including further documentation, see http://www.electionstudies.org/studypages/anes_timeseries_2012/anes_timeseries_2012.htm.

Table A.3 Alphabetical List of Variables in the States Dataset

Variable Name	Description
abort_rank3	Abortion restrictions (3-category ranking)
abort_rate05	Abortions per 1000 women (2005)
abort_rate08	Number of abortions per 1000 women aged 15–44 (2008)
abortion_rank12	2012 abortion rank (Americans United for Life)
abortlaw10	Number of restrictions on abortion (2010)
abortlaw3	Abortion restrictions (three tiers of number of restrictions)
adv_or_more	Percent of population with advanced degree or higher
alcohol	Alcohol consumption in gallons per capita (2007)
attend_pct	Percent frequently attend religious serviced (Pew)
ba_or_more	Percent of population with college degree or higher
battle04	Battleground state in 2004?
blkleg	Percent of state legislators who are black
blkpct04	Percent black (2004)
blkpct08	Percent black (2008)
blkpct10	Percent black (2010)
bush00	Percent voting for Bush in 2000
bush04	Percent voting for Bush in 2004
carfatal	Motor vehicle fatalities (per 100,000 pop)
carfatal07	Motor vehicle fatalities per 100,000 pop (2007)
cig_tax	Cigarette tax per pack (2007)
cig_tax_3	Cigarette tax per pack: 3 categories (2007)
cig_tax12	Cigarette tax per pack (2012)
cig_tax12_3	Cigarette tax per pack: 3 categories (2012)
cigarettes	Packs smoked bimonthly per adult (2003)
college	Percent of population with college or higher
conpct_m	Percent mass public conservative
cons_hr06	Conservatism score, U.S. House delegation (2006)
cons_hr09	Conservatism score, U.S. House delegation (2009)
conserv_advantage	Conservative advantage, mass public (2012)
conserv_public	Percent mass public conservative (2013)
cook_index	Cook Index: Higher scores mean more Democratic
cook_index3	3 quantiles of cook_index
defexpen	Federal defense expenditures per capita

Variable Name	Description
dem_advantage	Democratic advantage, mass public (2012)
dem_hr09	Percent U.S. House delegation Democratic (2009)
demhr11	Percent HR delegation Democratic (2011)
demnat06	Percent U.S. House and Senate Democratic (2006)
dempct_m	Percent mass public Democratic
demstate06	Percent of state legislators who are Democrats (2006)
demstate09	Percent of state legislators who are Democrats (2009)
demstate13	Percent state legislature Democrats (2013)
density	Population density (2010)
division	Census division (9 different regions of country)
earmarks_pcap	Earmarks per capita (in dollars)
evm	State electoral vote: McCain (2008)
evo	State electoral vote: Obama (2008)
evo2012	Obama's Electoral College vote
evr2012	Romney's Electoral College vote
gay_policy	Billman's policy scale (4 ordinal categories)
gay_policy_con	Does state have "most conservative" gay policies?
gay_policy2	RECODE of gay_policy (Billman's policy scale)
gay_support	Lax-Phillips opinion index
gay_support3	Gay rights: public support (3 categories)
gb_win00	Did Bush win electoral vote, 2000?
gb_win04	Did Bush win electoral vote, 2004?
gore00	Percent voting for Gore 2000
govt_worker	Percentage workforce government workers (2012)
gun_check	Background checks for gun purchases per 100,000 pop (2012)
gun_dealer	Gun dealers per 100,000 pop
gun_murder10	Gun murder rate (2010)
gun_rank_rev	Recode of gun_rank11 so higher number ranks = more gun restrictions
gun_rank11	Brady gun rank (2011)
gun_rank3	Recode of gun_rank11 (3 ordinal categories)
gun_scale11	Brady gun law scale (2011)
gunlaw_rank	Brady campaign rank (2008)
gunlaw_rank3_rev	Number of restrictions (2008)

(Continued)

Table A.3 (Continued)

Variable Name	Description
gunlaw_scale	Brady campaign score (2008)
hispanic04	Percent Hispanic (2004)
hispanic08	Percent Hispanic (2008)
hispanic10	Percent Hispanic (2010)
hr_cons_rank11	Conservativism ranking of House of Representatives delegation (2011, American Conservative Union)
hr_conserv11	Conservativism rating of House of Representatives delegation (2011, American Conservative Union)
hr_lib_rank11	Liberalism ranking of House of Representatives delegation (2011, Americans for Democratic Action)
hr_liberal11	Liberalism rating of House of Representatives delegation (2011, Americans for Democratic Action)
hs_or_more	Percent population high school education or higher
indpct_m	Percent mass public Independent
kerry04	Percent voting for Kerry 2004
libpct_m	Percent mass public Liberal
mccain08	Percent voting for McCain 2008
modpct_m	Percent mass public moderate
nader00	Percent voting for Nader 2000
obama_win08	Did Obama win electoral vote, 2008?
obama_win12	Did Obama win the state in 2012?
obama08	Percent voting for Obama 2008
obama2012	Obama vote share in 2012
over64	Percent population over age 64
permit	Percent public that would always permit abortion (2004 NES)
pop_18_24	Percent population aged 18–24 (2004)
pop_18_24_10	Percent population aged 18–24 (2010)
pop2000	State population, 2000
pop2010	State population, 2010
pop2010_hun_thou	State population, 2010 (in 100k)
popchng0010	State population, 2000–2012
popchngpct	State population percentage, 2000–2010
pot_policy	Marijuana laws
prcapinc	Per capita income
prochoice	Percent public pro-choice
prolife	Percent public pro-life
region	Census region (4 categories)

Variable Name	Description
relig_cath	Percentage Catholic (2012)
relig_high	Percentage high religiosity (2012)
relig_import	Percent religion "A great deal of guidance"
relig_low	Percentage low religiosity (2012)
relig_prot	Percentage Protestant (2012)
religiosity	Religious observance-belief scale (Pew)
religiosity3	Religiosity (3 categories)
reppct_m	Percent mass public Republican
romney2012	Romney vote share in 2012
rtw	Right to work state?
secularism	Secularism scale (Pew)
secularism3	3 quantiles of secularism
seniority_sen2	Does state have influential U.S. senator?
smokers12	Percentage of population who smoke
south	Southern state?
state	State name
stateid	Two letter postal abbreviation for state name
to_0004	Percentage point change in turnout from 2000 to 2004
to_0408	Percentage point change in turnout from 2004 to 2008
to_0812	Percentage point change in turnout from 2008 to 2012
trnout00	Turnout in 2000 presidential election
trnout04	Turnout in 2004 presidential election
unemploy	Unemployment rate (2004)
uninsured_pct	Percentage without health insurance (2012)
union04	Percent workers who are union members (2004)
union07	Percent workers who are union members (2007)
union10	Percent workforce unionized (2010)
urban	Percent urban population (2000)
vep00_turnout	Percent turnout of voting eligible population in 2000
vep04_turnout	Percent turnout of voting eligible population in 2004
vep08_turnout	Percent turnout of voting eligible population in 2008
vep12_turnout	Percent turnout of voting eligible population in 2012
womleg_2007	Percent of state legislators who are women (2007)
womleg_2010	Percent of state legislators who are women (2010)
womleg_2011	Percent of state legislators who are women (2011)
womleg_2015	Percent of state legislators who are women (2015)

Table A.4 Alphabetical List of Variables in the World Dataset

Variable Name	Description
arda	Country numerical code
colony	Colony of what country? (CIA)
confidence	Confidence in institutions scale (World Values Survey)
country	Country/territory name (title case)
debt	Public debt as a percentage of GDP (CIA)
decent08	Democratic decentralization, 2008 (UN)
dem_economist	Full or part democracy (Economist, 2014)
dem_level4	Regime type (Economist 2014)
dem_other	Percentage of other democracies in region
dem_other5	Percentage of other democracies in region: 5 categories
dem_rank14	Democracy rank, lower scores more democratic (Economist 2014)
dem_score14	Democracy score, higher scores more democratic (Economist 2014)
democ	Is government a democracy? (Based on regime_type3)
democ_regime	Is regime a democracy? (1990)
democ_regime08	Is government a democracy? (may be redundant)
democ11	Democracy score, 2011 (UN)
district_size3	Average # of members per district (World Values Survey)
dnpp_3	Effective number of parliamentary parties
durable	Number of years since the last regime transition (Polity)
effectiveness	Government effectiveness scale (Kaufmann, 2002)
enpp3_democ	Effective number of parliamentary parties: 3 categories
enpp3_democ08	Effective number of parliamentary parties (World Values Survey)
eu	EU member state (yes/no)
fertility	Total fertility rate: Number children born per woman (CIA)
fhrate04_rev	Freedom House rating of democracy (reversed)
fhrate08_rev	Freedom House 1–7 scale reversed, rescaled 0–12
frac_eth	Ethnic factionalization (combined linguistic and racial) (Alesina et al., 2003)
frac_eth2	Ethnic factionalization (combined linguistic and racial) (binned)
frac_eth3	Level of ethnic fractionalization: 3 categories
free_business	Heritage Foundation rating: bus. freedom (2010)
free_corrupt	Heritage Foundation rating: corruption (2010)
free_finance	Heritage Foundation rating: financial freedom (2010)
free_fiscal	Heritage Foundation rating: fiscal freedom (2010)

Variable Name	Description
free_govspend	Heritage Foundation rating: government spending (2010)
free_invest	Heritage Foundation rating: invest freedom (2010)
free_labor	Heritage Foundation rating: labor freedom (2010)
free_monetary	Heritage Foundation rating: monetary freedom (2010)
free_overall	Heritage Foundation rating: overall economic freedom (2010)
free_overall_4	4 quantiles of free_overall
free_property	Heritage Foundation rating: property rights (2010)
free_trade	Heritage Foundation rating: free trade (2010)
gdp_10_thou	GDP per capita in 10K US$ (2002)
gdp_cap2	GDP per capita (US$): 2 categories (2002)
gdp_cap3	GDP per capita (US$): 3 categories (2002)
gdp08	GDP in billions in 2008 (World Bank)
gdpcap08_2	GDP per capita (US$) in 2008, 2 categories
gdpcap2_08	GDP per capita (US$) in 2008, 2 categories (may be redundant)
gdpcap3_08	GDP per capita (US$) in 2008 (Binned)
gdppcap08	GDP per capita in 2008 (World Bank)
gdppcap08_3	3 quantiles of gdppcap08 (as numeric)
gender_equal3	Gender empowerment measure, 3 categories (World Values Survey)
gender_unequal	Gender Inequality Index value, 2008 (UN)
gender_unequal_rank	Gender Inequality Index rank, 2008 (UN)
gini04	Gini coefficient (UN 2004)
gini08	Gini coeff (UN 2008)
gini10	Income Gini coefficient, 2000-2010 (UN)
govregrel	Government regulation of religion index, 2008 (CIA)
hdi	Human Development Index (HDI) value, 2010 (UN)
hi_gdp	High GDP dummy
indy	Year of independence (CIA)
ipu_wom13_all	Percent women in lower house of legislature, all countries, 2013 (Inter-Parliamentary Union)
lifeex_f	Life expectancy at birth among females (CIA)
lifeex_m	Life expectancy at birth among males (CIA)
lifeex_total	Life expectancy at birth, total population (CIA)
literacy	Literacy rate (CIA)
muslim	Is Muslim predominate religious group?

(Continued)

Table A.4 (Continued)

Variable Name	Description
natcode	Name of country (lower case)
oecd	OECD member state (yes/no)
oil	Oil production, in barrels per day (CIA)
pmat12_3	Post-materialism, 3 categories (World Values Survey)
polity	Higher scores more democratic (Polity)
pop_0_14	Percentage of population age 0–14 (CIA)
pop_15_64	Percentage of population age 15–64 (CIA)
pop_65_older	Percent of population age 65 and older (CIA)
pop_age	Median age in years, 2010
pop_total	Total population in millions, 2010 (UN)
pop_urban	Percentage of the total population living in urban areas, 2010 (UN)
pr_sys	Proportional representation system? (Institute for Democracy and Electoral Assistance)
protact3	Protest activity (World Values Survey)
regime_type3	Regime type (Cheibub's Democracy Dictatorship dataset)
regionun	United Nations region
religoin	Largest religion by proportion (UN)
rich_democ	Rich democracy, interaction of Hi_gdp*democ_regime
sexratio	Sex ratio at birth (male births per 100 female births), 2010
spendeduc	Public expenditure on education as a percentage of GDP (UN)
spendhealth	Public expenditure on health as a percentage of GDP (UN)
spendmil	Public expenditure on the military as a percentage of GDP, 2008 (UN)
unions	Union density (www.ilo.org)
unnetgro	Percent growth in the number of Internet users, population based, 2000–2008 (UN)
unnetuse	Internet users per 100 people, 2008 (UN)
unpovnpl	Percentage of population below national poverty line, 2000–2008 (UN)
unremitp	Per capita remittance inflows in US dollars, 2008
unremitt	Remittance inflows as a percentage of GDP, 2008
vi_rel3	Percent saying religion very important, 3 categories
votevap00s	Turnout: most recent election in 2000s (Institute for Democracy and Electoral Assistance)

Variable Name	Description
votevap90s	Turnout: elections in 1990s (Institute for Democracy and Electoral Assistance)
women05	Percent women in lower house of legislature, democracies only, 2005 (Inter-Parliamentary Union)
women09	Percent women in lower house of legislature, democracies only, 2009 (Inter-Parliamentary Union)
women13	Percent Women in lower house of legislature, democracies only, 2013 (Inter-Parliamentary Union)
womyear	Year women first enfranchised (Inter-Parliamentary Union)
womyear2	Women's suffrage (Inter-Parliamentary Union)

About the Authors

Philip H. Pollock III is a professor of political science at the University of Central Florida. He has taught courses in research methods at the undergraduate and graduate levels for more than 30 years. His main research interests are American public opinion, voting behavior, techniques of quantitative analysis, and the scholarship of teaching and learning. His recent research has been of the effectiveness of Internet-based instruction. He has served as co-editor of the *Journal of Political Science Education*. Pollock's research has appeared in the *American Journal of Political Science*, *Social Science Quarterly*, and the *British Journal of Political Science*. Recent scholarly publications include articles in *Political Research Quarterly*, the *Journal of Political Science Education*, and *PS: Political Science and Politics*.

Barry C. Edwards is a lecturer in the Department of Political Science at the University of Central Florida, where he also serves as the department's undergraduate coordinator. He received his BA from Stanford University, a JD from New York University, and a PhD from the University of Georgia. His teaching and research interests include American politics, public law, dispute resolution, and research methods. His research has been published in the *Journal of Politics*, *Political Research Quarterly*, the *Election Law Journal*, the *Harvard Negotiation Law Review*, the *Georgia Bar Journal*, *American Politics Research*, *Presidential Studies Quarterly*, and *State Politics and Policy Quarterly*.